THE GOD OF DREAMS

UNDERSTANDING *the*
Meaning *and* Significance
of DREAMING

ARCHIE W.N. ROY PhD

Published by Deep River Books
Sisters, Oregon
www.deepriverbooks.com

ISBN 13: 9781632694393
Library of Congress: 2017932162
For Worldwide Distribution, Printed in the USA
Cover Design by Joe Bailen

DEDICATION

For Victor, Mirjam, Satu, Domenica, Sofia, and Mia

ACKNOWLEDGMENTS

The writing of a book is not a solo effort, and I very much want to thank the readers who gave me so much feedback when they read the early and entire manuscript of *The God of Dreams*. I'd also like to thank the Reverend Alex Gillies in particular, as well as Ronnie McKeitch and my colleagues Stephen Shilton, Jim Campbell, and Ann Duff.

I want to thank Andy Carmichael, Kit Tosello, Tamara Barnet, Crystal Vogt, and Bev Tucker at Deep River Books for their input, responsiveness, and encouragement. I am also very grateful to Angela Rickabaugh Shears and Rachel Starr Thomson, who edited early versions of *The God of Dreams*.

Thanks to Debbie Broom who saw this book ahead of time. Also, and for many reasons, I want to thank my mother Frances H. Roy.

PRAISE FOR *THE GOD OF DREAMS*

Archie Roy has given us a well-researched and well-balanced book on the meaning and significance of dreams. His coverage of the various approaches to interpretation of dreams and dream symbolism is solidly grounded and in line with good biblical teaching. In addition to dreams recorded in Scripture, he also helpfully includes dreams and visions experienced by well-known Christians past and present. A great and inspiring resource on an important and fascinating subject!

RANDALL STALEY

Transformation in Christ
London, England

This is a very well-written book. I can say I have never seen a more thorough or readable book on dreams anywhere by anyone. The biblical dreams scattered throughout are especially important for the new believer or anyone unfamiliar with the Bible. The book is a succinct and well-presented explanation of the brain dynamics of dreams. I especially like the way Archie Roy moves from technical to biblical to experiential, keeping the flow of the text while now and then continuing to give adequate warning to guard against New Age, occult, sensationalistic, and soulish fancy.

The testimonies of real-life examples, along with the basic how-to-do-it teaching, drawing from a wide variety of trusted sources, makes for a text that is comprehensive in its scope and readable without being simplistic.

This book is truly needed. I have not seen any works like it. Archie Roy has brought together many sources that need to be identified together, as most books on dreams sit rather on their own without this scholarly network offered. And the psychoanalytical as well as the brain research is *so* important and sadly ignored by most Christians.

CLAY MCLEAN

McLean Ministries

Hickory, North Carolina, USA

The God of Dreams leaves the reader in absolutely no doubt that God really does use dreams and continues to use them today. Archie Roy's exposition is detailed and easy to read. The book puts real, tangible flesh onto biblical concepts and encourages readers to seek the practical application for themselves. I found myself writing down far more dreams than I had before reading the book.

I also found the work extremely informative. I had read a few other books about dreaming in the past but was always left with more questions than I had answers. This book really has an excellent timbre of multilayered answers that I really enjoyed. Archie has come at the topic from various angles, which really enrich his argument. People who are wired differently will feel the power of his argument because of the variety of perspectives. I think this is one of the major strengths of the book.

I absolutely loved Archie Roy's dismissal of postmodernity—in an area that is especially susceptible to multiple truths and meanings. I found his emphasis on dreams leading to a real message very encouraging. I also enjoyed watching him critique Carl Jung, because there is a huge and unhealthy influence of Jung's theories within the charismatic movement. I actually found this quite eye-opening.

The book is very applicable to the Christian life. I enjoyed where he wrote about the symbolic nature of color, for example. I'm sure anyone who reads this will be able to study his or her dreams in more depth because of this. I had also never thought about 90 percent of our dreams being about ourselves. This has really changed the way I think about my own dreams.

CALUM PATON, BRANCH PASTOR

Elim Christian Fellowship

Ralston, Paisley, Scotland

For someone who has a pen at the side of the bed to record dreams or early morning thoughts, *The God of Dreams* was exciting. Having the expectation that there might be a significant dream is good and a preparation for the more perplexing part—fully understanding the dream and its interpretation! This is the subject of Archie Roy's book, and I am glad of that. I am also glad that he comments that the interpretation of a given dream might be less important than its effect of drawing us closer to God.

Dreams are one of the multifarious ways God can speak to us even today, and we would do well to benefit from this well-researched book on the subject. I am all for hearing from God in ways that I can least pollute or taint. The symbolic nature of dreams is key in my opinion. How thrilling to find an author who wades through various deceptions in our "modern age" only to glean the truth of the Bible. Perhaps this book will single-handedly propel us out of the spiritual gutter Archie Roy alludes to. What joy to think that we Christians can become more discerning through reading his book.

MRS. GWEN PURDIE

Founder of Dove Christian Counselling, Scotland

CONTENTS

"High King of Heaven, after victory won,
May I reach Heaven's joys, O bright Heaven's Sun!
Heart of my own heart, whatever befall,
Still be my Vision, O ruler of all. Amen."

From the ancient Irish hymn, "Be Thou My Vision,
O Lord of My Heart," translated by Mary Byrne (1905)
and versified by Eleanor Hull (1912)

"He is there and He is not silent."

Francis Schaeffer, 1990

"I will praise the Lord, who counsels me; even at night my
heart instructs me."

Psalm 16:7

"And it shall come to pass in the last days, saith God,
I will pour out of my Spirit upon all flesh: and your sons
and your daughters shall prophesy, and your young men
shall see visions, and your old men shall dream dreams."

Acts 2:17, KJV

INTRODUCTION

Do you keep a pen and notepad or the electronic equivalent of choice at your bedside to record your dreams? If not, may I suggest you do? God speaks through your dreams as well as in many other ways. When He speaks through dreams, He is speaking indirectly, bypassing the dreamer's conscious mind. In this, He uses a language of symbols and pictures, the language of the heart. The Bible reveals that God will also speak directly sometimes, either audibly or inaudibly. Between these ways of speaking are His parables and other types of figurative language. Dreams are similar to parables, to some extent, but are not the same since parables always use language—but in a symbolic way.

Often we think of dreams, if we think of them at all, as spurious and inconsequential. We completely neglect them. But from time to time when I am chatting with folks in the office or with friends in a restaurant, someone mentions a dream. Sometimes it is a dream they often had in childhood, and they still remember its impact. In other cases, it is a disturbing dream they are still having. By definition, these types of recurring dreams are not spurious or inconsequential. They have to mean something! Why are these people's unconscious minds stuck on a repeated series of images and actions night after night? Perhaps the messenger is bringing the same message time after time and saying, "Please understand it; please take action; this is so important to you."

A number of Christian writers and commentators, including Herman Riffel and Sharon Stone, have noted that approximately one third of the Bible consists of dreams and visions. In all these events, God was communicating with men and women. At the time the dream occured, as you will see in this book, some of the dreamers believed in God, some did not. Their beliefs did not determine whether or not God chose to speak; as the Creator, who has made humankind spiritual creatures who dream, God can speak to anyone He chooses anytime He likes.

But whether the dreamer is a Jewish patriarch or king or a pagan ruler such as Abimelek or Pharaoh, on all occasions the dreamers noted the seriousness of the dream. They took action. If they did not understand the dream, they demanded its interpretation. When they heard the correct interpretation, they were relieved and satisfied, even if they disliked the revelation and the situation they were facing. Their own hearts bore witness; it was clear to their understanding that they had the right interpretation.

Although interest in dreams and dreaming has been rising in recent years, a lot of the writing about it is secular and often reductionist, in the sense that pictures and images appearing in dreams are reduced to the level of dream dictionaries. It would be unwise simply to go to a dream dictionary for an explanation of a particular dream, since a symbol's meaning is often found in the context of the dreamer's life and in what the symbol actually means to the person who had the dream. Also, even in Christian literature produced over the past forty years or so in which dreams are touched on, the emphasis is not placed on biblical dreams, even if some treatment is given to them in passing. I believe that needs to be remedied. If we can understand God's dealings with humanity through the dreams and historical narratives recorded in Scripture, we will be better placed to understand something of His dealings with us today through dreams.

In this book I spend some time on dream language and symbols and also on psychoanalytic perspectives. I do believe, as Herman Riffel did, that some insights can be gained from the psychoanalysts, although I also believe that some Christian writers have gone far too far in their wholly uncritical embrace of analytical psychology, the system of thought developed by the Swiss analyst Carl Jung. This problem will be discussed in these pages as well.

The final part of this book examines a number of dream accounts by Christians writing over the past three hundred years. As in the Bible, these dreams were life-changing and have, in some instances, helped to change the world.

Dreams in the Bible are always important. God gave them during critical junctures for humanity, pivotal moments in His dealings with humankind and in the flow of human history. I believe that today, after the cross of Christ, we live in a time very different from the past. We have more revelation, especially regarding God's grace and the way of salvation by means of the new covenant. Praise God! But are we not also living in a time of critical junctures and pivotal moments? We are fast-forwarding now toward the end of all things and to the New Jerusalem. Surely there is a place for listening to God's dreams for us at such a time. What would He say to His spiritual creatures now as the earth wears out like a garment? We should listen to what He says through all the means He uses, including dreams, and take action.

PART I

THE GOD OF DREAMS

CHAPTER 1

The Dream of Imminent Death

The first time dreams come into play in the Bible's records occurs in the book of Genesis and concerns Abimelek, the king of the Philistines. He rules his territory from the stronghold of Gerar, located very near the contemporary border between Gaza and Israel. It is likely that *Abimelek* is the man's royal title rather than his actual name. In the Philistine language,[1] it seems to mean "my father is king" or "father of a king," and given that it is used by a number of the Philistine kings, it may be similar in usage to titles such as Pharaoh or Caesar. An almost identical title, *Padishah* or "father king," was used by the ancient Persian kings.

The following events in Abimelek's life occurred around 1897 BC. For this date and the dates of later dreams recorded in the Bible, I have chosen to go with the traditional dating of this and subsequent events. I have taken dates from the Larry and Marion Pierce chronology *The Annals of the World* (2003). However, other biblical chronologies, such as the Jewish and Septuagint vary; see, for instance, *The Genesis Record* by Henry M. Morris (1976).

The events involving Abimelek also involve Abraham and his wife, Sarah, who journey together into Abimelek's territory. Although reputed to have been born in Ur of the Chaldees, Abraham was initially called by God to journey westward and settle in a land that He would show him. Abraham set out in faith, not knowing his destination. He had been promised that he would be the father of many nations and that all the earth was to be blessed through him.

Today both Jews and the Arab nations acknowledge Abraham as their father and as a major patriarch and prophet; he is honored around the world by Jews, Christians, and Muslims alike. Abraham is also a direct forebearer of Christ through Isaac, his son with Sarah. He fathered seven other sons with Hagar and Keturah, becoming the father of many nations indeed. After his arrival in Canaan, Abraham embarked on at least two additional journeys further south, first into Egypt because of a famine in Canaan, and then to the territory controlled by the Philistines.

The Subterfuge That Never Worked

On each occasion that Abraham traveled south into potential enemy territory, he persuaded Sarah to say that she was not his wife, only his sister. The rationale for this was that Sarah, being very beautiful, would be a very desirable acquisition. If the local ruler or one of the nobility thought she was his wife, they might kill him in order to have her. It was better for them all to think she was his sister. He would be treated well because of her. The sister story was in fact a half-truth, since she was his half-sister.[2]

On the first occasion, this subterfuge was uncovered quickly. Pharaoh thought Sarah was very beautiful and had her brought into his palace, presumably with the intention of marrying her and adding her to his harem. Shortly afterward, a series of serious diseases broke out, one after another, among Pharaoh and all his household. He made the connection at once and demanded to know from Abraham why he had deceived him and caused him and his palace all this suffering. Pharaoh confirmed the truth of the matter, rebuked the couple, and sent them packing.

Before letting them go, Pharaoh would no doubt have been struck by a dilemma. This couple had deceived him. He was the ruler of the most powerful nation on earth, and they had caused him to lose face. The couple should therefore die. But on the other hand, they and their marriage were being protected by their God, who was powerful enough to come against Pharaoh and his court. Who knew why this was so, but their God had shown His power and His will by inflicting Pharaoh's court and Pharaoh himself with plagues.[3] If Pharaoh moved to kill Abraham and Sarah, he would therefore surely suffer the consequences and probably die himself. No doubt, their God possessed the power to do that. There was only one solution—get them out of his kingdom!

For Abraham and Sarah, it would all have been a bit embarrassing and discomfiting. Probably they should not have gone to Egypt in the first place. At the same time, though, the subterfuge had enabled them to survive a famine.

Many years later, the embarrassment must have been forgotten, because the couple tried the same thing again—only this time they headed south to Philistine territory and to Abimelek. Again Abraham feared for his life and failed to hold on to his faith that God was well able to protect him. The same crisis as before triggered the use of the same subterfuge as before.

Abimelek's Dream and Its Timing

This time, we do not know why Abraham and Sarah made a journey into potentially hostile territory, only that they arrived in Philistine land and that they stayed for a while in Gerar, the Philistine royal city in the Negev. By now, Abraham's reputation was enhanced, and he would have been known as a tribal and military leader. The book of Genesis records what occurred at Gerar.

> For a while he stayed in Gerar, and there Abraham said of his wife Sarah, "She is my sister." Then Abimelek king of Gerar sent for Sarah and took her. But *God came to Abimelek in a dream* one night and said to him, "You are as good as dead because of the woman you have taken; she is a married woman."
>
> Now Abimelek had not gone near her, so he said, "Lord, will you destroy an innocent nation? Did he not say to me, 'She is my sister,' and didn't she also say, 'He is my brother'? I have done this with a clear conscience and clean hands."
>
> Then God said to him in the dream, "Yes, I know you did this with a clear conscience, and so I have kept you from sinning against me. That is why I did not let you touch her. Now return the man's wife, for he is a prophet, and he will pray for you and you will live. But if you do not return her, you may be sure that you and all who belong to you will die."

Early the next morning Abimelek summoned all his officials, and when he told them all that had happened, they were
very much afraid. (Genesis 20:1–8, emphasis mine)

To some extent, the dream came to Abimelek out of the blue. But there
were also other things going on for him. Although he did not know it, his
court had been plunged into the same kind of situation as Pharaoh's court
had been. Prior to the dream, but subsequent to his grabbing of Sarah, he
and his family had been inflicted by some sort of disease or disorder. All the
females, even the slave girls, were unable to have children.[4]

For God, the risk to the fulfillment of His plans was even greater
now than it had been at Pharaoh's court. Isaac was due to be conceived
soon, and his lineage was destined to lead to the creation of Israel, the
birth of the Messiah, and the salvation through Him of the world.
Abimelek's desire to continue the expansion of his harem had to be
thwarted. Although the Philistine king was clearly of a more principled
disposition than Pharaoh, his plans were still threatening to cut across
what God sought to do regarding His plan of salvation. If need be, he
had to die.

God did not spell all this out in a dream, of course, but He did emphasize the importance He placed on Abraham. He referred to him as a
prophet, the first time the term is used in Scripture. No doubt something
of the meaning of this term would come through and affect the impact of
Abimelek's dream. The term itself may have been foreign to him, a pagan
king, but its meaning could still have been clear enough. He was being told
that Abraham was a man with whom God directly communicated and that
Abraham shared this gift with the people, interceding with God Himself
for them. This message would combine with the imminent threat of death
to cause great fear in Abimelek's mind. Yet at the same time, this prophet
of God had deceived him. Abimelek got very upset.

The Encounter Between Abraham and Abimelek

Abimelek sent for Abraham and despite his fear, rebuked him publicly for deceiving him, inferring that according to the common laws

of hospitality, such things just were not done. Abraham's deception had caused Abimelek to behave in such a way as to unwittingly bring his palace and his nation under God's judgment. He demanded an explanation from God's prophet!

As best he could, Abraham explained himself before the king. Abraham's reasons were various, just as they were the previous time in Egypt. They included his perspective that Abimelek's people were a godless lot and that if he had not deceived him, they would probably have killed him and taken his wife regardless. The fact that Abimelek did not repudiate this is interesting: it may have been just as the prophet said. After the explanation, Abimelek offered the couple a generous compensation, primarily because of their relationship to the God who protected them. He had already said to this God that he was not to blame.

> Then Abimelek brought sheep and cattle and male and female slaves and gave them to Abraham, and he returned Sarah his wife to him. And Abimelek said, "My land is before you; live wherever you like." To Sarah he said, "I am giving your brother a thousand shekels of silver. This is to cover the offense against you before all who are with you; you are completely vindicated."
>
> Then Abraham prayed to God, and God healed Abimelek, his wife and his female slaves so they could have children again, for the Lord had kept all the women in Abimelek's household from conceiving because of Abraham's wife Sarah. (Genesis 20:14–18)

Abraham received back his wife and accepted the king's gifts. To not accept the gifts would have been a grave insult and would aggravate a very delicate situation further. The monetary sum was lavish and is equivalent to about $6 million or £5 million in today's money.[5] The reparations and the public apology were designed to restore Sarah's reputation and to get their relationship with the king on a better footing. Abimelek was aware that he and all the barren women at his court still needed to be prayed for—by Abraham. This Abraham did. He interceded before God for the king and his court, and all were healed. Ironically, Abraham's wife had also been barren for many years. However, this too was soon to change.

Conclusions

The first recorded dream in Scripture occurs at an extreme moment in history. God's plan of salvation has been put in jeopardy by a prophet lacking in faith and by a pagan king seeking to further extend his harem. It is a strange set of circumstances, though one that almost entirely replicates Abraham and Sarah's experiences in Egypt.

God uses the dream to break into the situation and to confirm His earlier signs to Abimelek that he has strayed across God's line in the sand and into territory that is about to prove fatal. He has already prevented Abimelek from committing adultery with the woman who is about to conceive with Abraham the lineage from which the Messiah will come. This prevention has in all likelihood been by strong-arm tactics, by rendering the king impotent or otherwise disabling him with a potentially fatal disease. But the king needs to be triggered into action. He must backtrack from where he is. He must be spoken to directly, hence the dream.

The dream is an unusual combination of warning and mercy. The king is as good as dead. But he has been prevented by God from sinning further because he acted in ignorance. He is also assured that he, his family, and his court will be spared after the prophet has interceded for them. He is assured that they will live *if* he does what he is being commanded to do. Abimelek then immediately does what is right and prudent. After consulting his nobles, he swings into action.

While the king behaved with generosity, candor, and alacrity, there is no evidence that Abimelek accepted the faith of Abraham. Despite having heard directly from Abraham's God, there is no recorded evidence that he sought to reach out to Him. Like Pharaoh, he was really just concerned with getting healed and then getting this couple off the premises. It is fairly likely that God never spoke to the king again.

CHAPTER 2

What Are Dreams?

Now let's shift gears and consider sleep from a scientific standpoint. We all sleep, and almost all of us dream during sleep. Human beings have been sleeping since the Garden of Eden, with recordings of dreams going at least as far back as the biblical accounts, which date back almost four thousand years. Yet it is only in the past sixty years or so that sleep research has developed as a scientific endeavor.

The university where I work, the University of Glasgow in Scotland, has a sleep research center located within its Department of Psychological Medicine, and for many years it has been conducting research into sleep and disorders of sleep. Research centers have also developed in universities such as Stanford in California, the first center of its kind, as well as Columbia University in New York, Harley Street in London, and many other locations, especially in the Western world. What have these sleep researchers and clinicians to say about sleep as an activity? Research has thrown up some surprising discoveries, with much of it counterintuitive. Sleep is not the passive and quiescent activity that many once thought it was.

Dreams and Sleep Defined

Although there is no absolute agreement as to what dreams are, we can at least say that dreams are experiences occurring during sleep in which the dreamer has thoughts, images, or feelings. Usually these occur in a sequence but sometimes not. A dream can consist of a single image, like a video still. Often, though, there is organization to these thoughts, images, or feelings, at least to the dreamer's mind when he or she recalls the experience. While there can often be an organizing theme or sequence, at other times dreams seem to be chaotic and jumbled.

If we think of the principle characteristics of the sleep state, in what ways is it unique compared to other states such as mere relaxation, pretending to sleep, or a coma state? In normal sleep, a barrier is erected between the conscious mind and the world outside, but it is a barrier that can be overcome through stimulation such as a sudden noise. A sudden or persistent stimulation causes the sleeper to wake up. In mere relaxation, the barrier does not exist. In a coma state or when anesthetized, the stimulation fails to bring the person round. Sleep is also a completely natural, daily process for us. Unlike some of the states just mentioned, it is not caused by any trauma or medical intervention.

The Science of Sleep and Dreaming

Humanity always knew that waking and sleeping were different states, but until the 1950s, it was assumed that the human body's physiology was the same during sleep as during waking hours. We now know, however, that sleep changes the brain's activity—your brain waves (the rhythmic rise and fall in your brain's electrical activity) change in shape and oscillation when you are asleep. Machines called electroencephalographs (EEGs) graphically display these changes in activity, and much of the research conducted in sleep laboratories focuses on this. The research environment allows sleepers to sleep naturally while EEGs monitor and record brainwave activity via electrodes attached to the sleeper's head.

Sleep causes other physiological changes as well. In the sleep clinics around the world, sleepers are also wired up to electroculograms (EOGs). These machines are connected to the outer corners of the sleeper's eyes and measure eye movements during sleep. Measuring eye-movement "waves" has been an important aspect of sleep research since some significant discoveries in the 1950s. And some additional physiological changes brought about by sleep, for instance, the sleeper's muscle tension, are also recorded via electrodes placed around the neck.

Research into the sleep state over the past sixty years has led to a profound change in how we perceive the activity of sleeping. Investigators discovered that the sleep state is not a unified state but combines together at least five different types of sleep, REM being just one of them.

REM Sleep

Phases of rapid-eye movement during sleep occur at regular and reasonably predictable intervals, and since the publication of this discovery in 1953[1] until very recently, it was thought that they correlated closely with dreaming. After observing the existence of these rapid-eye movements for some time by means of quite primitive electrodes, researchers decided to wake sleepers up while the movements were still occurring and question them about what they had just been aware of, if anything. Sleepers would then typically relate long and detailed descriptions of their dreams.

Subsequent research revealed an amazing fact: a sleeper's REM brain waves indicated that the sleeper's brain was acting as if it were awake. The person and the person's body were asleep, but the brain was awake. And this was a normal sleep stage! Yet because the body's muscles of movement are paralyzed in REM sleep, the active brain's activity does not usually trigger physical activity.

The original sleep research team then developed a theory based on their observations. The theory held that everyone experienced the same ninety-minute sleep cycle and that this shifted through five stages: stage 1, stage 2, stage 3, stage 4, and REM sleep. As the cycle repeated itself during the night, the REM period tended to increase in duration.

The names of these stages have held over the subsequent and much more intensive period of sleep research, which now exists as a scientific field in its own right. Researchers have investigated these stages across the age span, including newborn infants, as well as cross-culturally with many different people groups and even with individuals who were born congenitally blind. Blind people experience REM sleep as much as sighted people do and have reported their dreams during this stage to investigators. Their dreams are detailed in terms of experiences and emotions but contain no visual images. If one does the math based on the clinical observation that about one quarter of an eight-hour sleep cycle is REM sleep, one finds that a person will have dreamed for about fifty-one thousand hours by the time he or she is seventy years of age. The person has dreamed for six years—*if* most dreaming occurs during this phase, as REM sleep researchers insisted.

REM sleep is not confined to human beings. Experiments from the 1960s onward have plotted REM sleep in cats, dogs, monkeys, chipmunks, and many other animals. Even birds demonstrate REM, though much less so than mammals. The idea quickly grew among researchers that dreaming had physical correlates and was therefore an observable phenomenon. And if it had physical correlates, was there a brain-based origin for dreaming?

As convincing as all of that sounds, it is now very apparent that REM sleep is not the physical demonstration of dreaming that researchers once thought it was. The reductionist theory it gave rise to, that there is a brain-based, neurochemical origin of REM dreaming, is also judged by many now as far too simplistic. J.F. Pagel of the University of Colorado's School of Medicine notes, for instance, "REM sleep does not equate with dreaming. REM sleep occurs without dreaming and dreaming occurs without REM sleep. The two cognitive states are doubly dissociable."[2]

In other words, dreaming also occurs during other sleep states and can only be associated very loosely with observed REM activity. The early sleep researchers' grandiose notions about the universal applicability of their theories also starts to unravel for other reasons. For instance, something of the complexity of individual differences between people has now emerged. What about the sleepers whose brain function and sleep states monitor as normal but who claim never to have dreamed—there in the sleep research center or throughout their lives? Why do they not recall their dreams? Or are they right, and they do not dream at all?

Yet REM sleep *is* important for other reasons. More recent research on it is starting to make connections between the process and activities other than dreaming. A group of sleep researchers in San Diego,[3] for instance, found a correlation between REM sleep phases in their human subjects and a subsequently enhanced level of creativity when compared to other subjects who had been asleep but had not experienced a REM sleep phase and to people who had just been resting. REM sleepers were more likely to come up with creative associations connected to a series of three words—such as *sixteen, heart,* and *cookie.* In this example, REM sleepers were more likely than the others to come up with the word *sweet.*

A Biblical Perspective on the Nature of Dreams

There is no agreed-upon definition of dreams or understanding as to where dreams come from. Although any dictionary will give you a short and concise definition, people who work professionally with dreams tend to disagree about their causes, meanings, and significance, depending on their philosophical standpoint. Scientists working in sleep clinics, psychodynamic therapists of various kinds, anthropologists, and people taking a spiritual viewpoint are going to disagree on the matter. One reason for this is the privacy of dreams.

For me, a dream is typically in full color and usually consists of a series of images but occasionally just one image. Often there are scene shifts as well in the dream, as in a play or movie. And often there is verbal dialogue between characters. The dream can frequently include emotional atmosphere, and typically this correlates with the visual content or the drama. Dreams can be immensely personal. Sometimes dreamers experience such a pleasant, comforting feeling within the dream that they do not want to wake up. Sometimes they are only too glad to awaken.

If we consider the biblical account and the dreams within it, we might say that to dream means to see something while sleeping or to have a vision while asleep. The Greek Septuagint word used is *enupnion,* as in *"pharaō eiden enupnion* ōeto *estanai epi tou potamou":* "Pharaoh dreamed: and, behold, he stood by the river" (Genesis 41:1 KJV).[4] The Greek word emphasizes the surprise nature of the dream. In addition, however, the ancient Hebrew word for dream in Scripture is חֲלוֹם, transliterated as *hha-lom* or *harlam.* Russ Parker has traced this term back to a Hebrew root word that means "to make whole or healthy."[5] In his study of dreams, he emphasizes this function: that dreams are a means by which we can grow toward inner wholeness and health—if we pay attention to them and seek to understand their meaning. The Hebrew language used originally is hinting at this.

Other modern dream interpreters, such as Herman Riffel, have reached the same conclusions—that the purpose of dreams is to bring healing, whether by correction, cautioning, or the attaining of information or wisdom previously hidden from the conscious mind. The dream advises you, invites you to move forward and to bring about change, but like a good therapist, it does so without either judging or condemning you. Riffel adds: "The great purpose of a dream . . . is to show the thoughts of the heart over against the thoughts of the mind . . . They help us set our goals. They go beyond the three dimensions."[6]

The Bible credits many different dreams, given to the godly and ungodly alike, as revelation from God. In fact, the Bible focuses on these types of dreams. When I consider these and also consider the many examples of dreams I have experienced and recorded in my dream diary, as well as the examples offered to me by friends and colleagues, I see nothing in the material that causes me to move away from the viewpoint that dreams *are* revelation. Something is being revealed to the dreaming mind.

This in itself does not necessarily identify the source of a dream. A given dream could have a spiritual source, or it could have a natural, human source from within the dreamer. Psychodynamic therapists refer to the natural source as the unconscious, while those outside this specialization may simply talk about the human heart. The dream may be formed by your own heart, your deep emotional being, wanting to communicate something to you, which it has discerned is true. It realizes it needs to communicate this revelation to you, because it knows that in the noise and confusion of living, you have failed to discern it.

When you are lying peacefully in bed, both God and your own heart have a chance to communicate with you. Although these sources are very different, the process is not so different. God can communicate a message in picture form to your heart or unconscious being, and it will present the message to your mind. As Chuck Pierce and Rebecca Sytsema point out, dreams have significance regardless of their origin, even if they come from your own unconscious.[7] Dreams from your own heart may indicate a need for healing of emotions or merely represent your own hidden desires and motivations. A dream can convey to your conscious mind the secrets lying buried in your heart.

Accurate interpretation of these dreams still requires further clarification from God rather than your own understanding. All too often, and especially in the Western postmodern world, the head or intellect can be too cut off from the heart or the emotional, deeper ways of perceiving. This modern-day split in the psyche will frequently cause a misinterpretation of the heart's dreams by the intellect. We need God to bridge the gap and heal the split. We also need to develop the required patience for this. In seeking God's further revelation, Daniel sometimes needed time to interpret dreams, and so will we. There can also be instances where the dream has an occult or false spiritual source. Hence prayer, reflection, and discernment are required when we are seeking a dream's interpretation.

Although dreams can appear unreal, they are merely another type of reality. In some ways they can be more real than our everyday lives and our limited conscious horizons. We may think we are in touch with what is going on in our lives, but a dream can present a deeper reality to us. It can inform us, through a picture like a video still or in a sequence of images, about what is really going on. I have had a number of dreams that in very economical but sometimes disturbing ways filtered down into a single image a whole, years-long relationship with someone. The image encapsulates the essence of the relationship. Dreams are accurate. They reveal how things really are, if only we can learn their language.

Dreams from the Soul

Commentators such as Jane Hamon rightly identify the distinction between spiritual or prophetic dreams and natural dreams—the various types of dreams that come from the unconscious mind. She says, "Things that have happened in our past, people we have known, situations we are currently dealing with, circumstances or people that are upsetting us, are all things that may influence us to have certain natural dreams."[8]

Many dreams are triggered by what is going on in our mind, will, and emotions. Our unconscious may be reflecting on and working through issues that we have left aside or even deny are issues at all. Your heart could say to you in a dream, for instance, "The decision you took was the wrong one. I am not happy with it. I am greatly troubled by it." It is also very possible to dream of something because you either crave it badly or fear it greatly.

At times we may have experienced a traumatic event, and the impact of it surfaces in a repetitive dream. This could be a working through of the trauma or merely a reexperiencing of it. The dream could signify an emotional burden that can only be lifted by healing through prayer or by a conscious working through of the impact by therapeutic means. Likewise, a dream could identify and alert us to areas of sin or immaturity present in our heart, character, and life. Either way, God may use dreams that are essentially natural to reveal areas in our hearts that need to be acknowledged and dealt with. If we fail to take account of what these dreams are telling us, the areas we have been alerted to are likely to trip us up in the future.

There is also a creative dimension to dreams that may have little to do with God per se. There is ample documented evidence that records numerous inventions and discoveries that came to people in their dreams. Robert Louis Stevenson wrote *Dr. Jekyll and Mr. Hyde* after a dream. Niels Bohr saw the nucleus of the atom in a dream, allowing him to solve the problem of atomic structure, a breakthrough that led to his Nobel Prize for Physics, awarded in 1922. Elias Howe, struggling with the problem of how to automate sewing, realized in 1845 that the solution lay in inventing a machine with needles, each holed at the tip. The solution came to him in a dream in which he was being boiled alive by cannibals in Africa. Each was armed with a long spear, like a sewing needle, and every spear had a hole in its tip.

CHAPTER 3

The Struggle and the Staircase

We move forward now two generations from Abraham to his grandson Jacob. Late in life, Abraham and Sarah had a son named Isaac, and Isaac married Rebekah at the age of forty. Abraham died around 1816 BC, and Isaac and his brother Ishmael buried him alongside Sarah in a cave at Machpelah, which Abraham had bought from the Hittites.

Isaac's twin sons, Jacob and Esau, were born around 1831 BC. The rivalry between them is legendary. They were very different from each other. Esau was a hunter, expert in using a bow and arrows, while Jacob was a quiet man and preferred to remain by the tents. We can assume he helped to tend the animals. Esau was technically the eldest, having been born minutes before his brother, and as such he had special status and was destined to inherit much more than his brother. This was his birthright as the firstborn.[1] Yet he lost his birthright to Jacob, whose name means "supplanter," when he sold it for the cost of a meal of wild-game stew. Jacob compelled Esau to sell him his birthright and swear an oath before handing him the stew. Famished and looking for a meal, he carelessly did what his brother demanded. The oath sealed the transaction.

Jacob is essential to the biblical narrative and to the emergence of Israel as a people. Later on when Jacob leaves home and meets Rachel, he falls in love and asks Laban, her father, for her hand in marriage. Laban seems agreeable but requires him to first work for him, herding sheep for seven years. Then when the marriage occurs at the end of the seven-year period, Laban tricks Jacob into marrying Leah instead, given that she is the elder of the sisters and custom dictates that she be married first.

When Jacob awakes the following morning to find that he has consummated a marriage to Leah and not to Rachel, the deceiver finds that he himself has been badly deceived. Yet he is still in love with Rachel. And the price has gone up. Jacob must work for another seven years in order to marry her too. In time, he fathers Joseph and Benjamin with Rachel while also fathering ten other sons with Leah, Rachel's sister, and with Bilhah and Zilpah, two servants. These twelve sons all survive, and their offspring through the succeeding generations multiply to become the twelve tribes of Israel, each tribe named after the respective son of Jacob with whom it originated.

Before all this, though, but some years after Esau sold his birthright to Jacob, their aged father was almost blind and close to death. He favored Esau rather than Jacob and asked him to go out and hunt again so that he could enjoy a meal of stew and also give him his blessing. This was a deathbed bequest and carried legal as well as spiritual force. Overhearing this, Rebekah hatched a plan with her own favored son, Jacob, who fetched two goats for her so she could prepare Isaac a tasty meal. She dressed up Jacob in Esau's clothes and even bound goatskin on his neck and hands to make it appear that he had the rough skin of his brother— their father, blind, might touch him. He then took the meal to his father, claimed to be Esau, and said he wanted the blessing. When Isaac asked him how on earth the hunt had gone so speedily, he merely said that God had granted him a quick success!

Being almost blind, Isaac was easily fooled. Jacob smelled like Esau and felt like Esau. His stew tasted as if Esau had made it himself. Isaac therefore blessed the wrong son with a complete blessing. Jacob narrowly avoided Esau as he left his father's tent. Esau arrived with his own stew only to find that his brother had stolen his blessing as well as his birthright. Esau clamored for a blessing nevertheless. What had his brother left him? What blessing could Isaac give Esau?

Isaac replied, "I have made him lord over you and have made all his relatives his servants, and I have sustained him with grain and new wine. So what can I possibly do for you, my son?" (Genesis 27:37). The blessing Jacob had received through lying and deception was irrevocable.

All Isaac could offer was the promise that after Esau tired of serving his brother, he would throw off his yoke.

From then on, Esau nursed a bitter grudge against Jacob. He said to himself that after the period of mourning for their father ended, he would kill his brother. On hearing this, Rebekah compelled Jacob to flee his brother and go to his Uncle Laban in Haran, some five hundred miles away. He was also tasked with finding a wife from among Rebekah's people there, something that Isaac approved of. The threat to Jacob's life had seemingly been kept from the old man. Blessing him again, this time knowing which son he was blessing, Isaac sent him on his way.

Jacob set out for Haran, journeying north until the sun set. When he stopped for the night, he took one of the large stones lying around to use as a pillow and settled down to sleep. But this was no ordinary place. Many years ago, Abraham had chosen this place to communicate with God, building an altar there.[2] The name means the "house of God," but to Jacob it must have appeared an unremarkable place, as good a place to stop as any. But he did not simply arrive at Bethel by chance.

Jacob's Stairway to Heaven

After Jacob lay down to sleep, "He had a dream in which he saw a stairway resting on the earth, with its top reaching to heaven, and the angels of God were ascending and descending on it" (Genesis 28:12). While commentators often draw a parallel between this image and the steps on a Babylonian ziggurat, designed to allow men to ascend toward heaven and divine beings to descend toward them, the phrase "resting on the earth" literally means "placed toward the earth."[3] That is, the stairway had been placed there by God's initiative rather than by humankind's ziggurat-building rebellion against Him. Only God has the ability and initiative to bridge the gulf that opened up at the fall between His presence in an unfallen, perfect heaven and fallen humanity.

There above it stood the Lord, and he said: "I am the Lord, the God of your father Abraham and the God of Isaac. I will give you and your descendants the land on which you are lying. Your descendants will be like the dust of the earth, and you will spread out to the west and to the east, to the north and to the south. All peoples on earth will be blessed through you and your offspring. I am with you and will watch over you wherever you go, and I will bring you back to this land. I will not leave you until I have done what I have promised you."

When Jacob awoke from his sleep, he thought, "Surely the LORD is in this place, and I was not aware of it." He was afraid and said, "How awesome is this place! This is none other than the house of God; this is the gate of heaven.'" (Genesis 28:13–17)

Lying down at nightfall, Jacob had thought himself to be entirely alone, having made an archenemy of his brother and deceived his father. He was now in the middle of nowhere, so he thought, breaking off from his journey toward a land he had never seen and relatives he had never met. And how did he see himself? Did he view his actions in a bad light? Whether he did or not, he must have been at a low ebb—yet it was then that God chose to make Himself known to Jacob. With God's presence overhead and angels ascending and descending close beside him, it transpired that Jacob was hardly in the middle of nowhere—or alone.

With no land, wife, or children to call his own, Jacob is promised all these by God in the dream, as the Lord uses the dream to underscore that, of course, all this will come to pass because of God's promises to him and to his father and grandfather. Jacob's time of exile would end as God restored him to the land he grew up in and knew so well. The God of his fathers would watch over him and protect him.

All these dream messages spoke to his needs and fears, alone in the night and sleeping on the bare ground. He knew now that God would protect him. The dream also dramatically raised his awareness toward a God who knew him intimately and had a destiny He held close to His heart for Jacob and his many offspring.

Throughout Jacob's lifetime, God appeared directly to him about eight times through a variety of means. In one famous encounter, Jacob wrestled throughout the night with God in human form. As the struggle

ended, Jacob insisted that God bless him, and God did so by changing his name from Jacob to Israel—"because you have struggled with
God and with humans and have overcome."[4] This is how the nation of
Israel got its name, and this is the meaning of the name. But in this first
encounter at Bethel, God chose a dream to reveal Himself, and we will
see that in due course, He would return to this approach.

Why did God use a dream in His first encounter with Jacob?
Presumably because it was the means that best served His purposes at
the time. He was able to communicate His promises and reassurance
to Jacob directly while also conveying the nature of spiritual reality.
There is no literal, physical staircase to and from heaven at Bethel or
anywhere else, but the dream's symbolism conveys spiritual reality.
God and His angels are constantly interacting with the fallen world,
ministering to and helping those they will help, those who are the
heirs of salvation.[5]

Yet in a more complete and perfect sense, this literal staircase *does*
exist. When Jesus began His ministry on earth, He claimed that He was
Jacob's staircase to and from heaven. After revealing to Nathanael, one of
His first disciples, things which He could only have known about him by
supernatural means, Jesus said to him, "Very truly I tell you, you will see
'heaven open, and the angels of God ascending and descending' on the
Son of Man" (John 1:51). Being familiar with the Torah and the other
early Jewish Scriptures, Nathanael would have known exactly what Jesus
was referring to and that He as God was saying He was the one means or
way to go from earth to heaven. Jesus had appeared to Jacob in a dream,
standing above His staircase, but now He was appearing to Nathanael as
an incarnated man, speaking with him face to face.

Jesus may have been saying that the angels would ascend and descend
at His command, just as He said at His arrest,[6] but He was also clearly
saying that His own ministry was like this movement and purpose of
the angels, who were given the power of heaven in order to minister to
people. Primarily, however, Jesus was saying that He Himself was the
staircase and the only mediator and true connection between God in
heaven and humankind on earth.

In his commentary on Jacob, Lance Lambert puts it like this:

> [Jesus] is God's Ladder, the ladder set up on earth whose top reaches heaven. In him, heaven and earth have been joined. By him the will of God is to be done on earth as it is in heaven. In him the kingdom of God has already come in spiritual character, and will yet come physically and publicly in great power and glory.[7]

The dream had a profound effect on Jacob. God as ruler of all things, commanding His angels as they ascend and descend at His will, was also focused on *Jacob*. So Jacob created a physical marker to commemorate the spiritual encounter and renamed the place House of God, unaware at the time, of course, that he is also going to be renamed!

> Early the next morning Jacob took the stone he had placed under his head, and set it up as a pillar and poured oil on top of it. He called that place Bethel, though the city used to be called Luz. Then Jacob made a vow, saying, "If God will be with me and will watch over me on this journey I am taking and will give me food to eat and clothes to wear so that I return safely to my father's household, then the LORD will be my God and this stone that I have set up as a pillar will be God's house, and of all that you give me I will give you a tenth." (Genesis 28:18–22)

The pillar was a witness to the staircase, to God above it, and to His promises. Jacob anointed the top of the memorial pillar as a dedication or offering to the God who stood at the top of the staircase; he commemorated the fact that the staircase led right up to heaven. Jacob then acknowledged before God the promises God had made to him, and in love and gratitude to Him, he promised back a tenth and that he would live his life with Yahweh as his God. In due time, after many years, Jacob returned to the same spot, and he built an altar there.

Jacob's dream of the staircase to heaven is one of the most famous dreams in Scripture. It has been immortalized a number of times. The ladder and the ascending angels on it exist in stone on the west front of Bath Abbey, the last of the medieval cathedrals built in England. Judaism is clear that the location of Bethel is Mount Moriah where in the past, as Jacob knew, Abraham had sought to sacrifice his son, Isaac, and where in the future King Solomon would construct his temple.

You Cannot Choose Your Relatives

In the morning, Jacob journeyed on from Bethel. After some time, he arrived at Haran in Mesopotamia, at a location now in northeastern Syria near its border with Turkey, and stopped at a well. His uncle's younger daughter, Rachel, also arrived with her father's sheep, and Jacob introduced himself. She then ran back to her home and brought her father to meet him. Laban was overjoyed to meet Jacob and insisted that he stay with them as one of the family. Suffice it to say, Jacob was the one deceived this time, echoing his conniving and deception with his brother and his father in previous years.

Bilhah and Zilpah, two of Laban's servants, were given to his daughters when they married Jacob. In time, each would give birth to two of his sons.[8] Leah gave birth to six sons, and Rachel finally gave birth to two, Joseph and Benjamin. All these sons were the "children of Israel," the twelve tribes. This multiple-wives-and-partners scenario gave rise to intense rivalry and jealousy among the women, and in due course, intense rivalry and jealousy among the sons.

Jacob remained in Laban's household, and his careful tending of his father-in-law's animals meant that Laban's prosperity grew. Eventually, though, Jacob got sick and tired of the man's exploitation of him, and they met to agree to a final settlement before Jacob removed himself and his family to return to his own land. God had promised him that he would return home, and it was now time to make the journey. As of yet, though, he had no livestock of his own, and this had to be remedied.

Jacob's Dream of Spotted and Speckled Goats

After twenty years of working tirelessly for his father-in-law, Jacob had had enough and wanted to return home. However, Laban was very reluctant to see this happen. He had no more daughters to offer Jacob by way of payment, so he asked him just to name his price for staying on and working. Perplexed by the increase in his own fortunes and flocks because of Jacob's activity, he had either consulted a sorcerer of some kind or practiced some sort of divination by himself and discovered that it was because Jacob's God had been aiding him. Jacob and whatever supernatural help he had were just too good an asset to say farewell to.

However, Jacob received a dream that enabled him to develop a strategy for outmaneuvering Laban and gaining the portion of his estate that was rightfully his. He had earned it. For now, and in the months ahead, he told no one about the dream. For payment, Jacob said he would only go through Laban's livestock and take the few animals whose markings made them less desirable: sheep and goats that had spotted or speckled markings and dark-colored lambs. In the future, all those born like this would belong to Jacob, and he would go on working for Laban as before but with livestock of his own. Laban agreed, but before Jacob could select the "flawed" animals, he removed all of them, gave them to his sons, and placed a gap of three days' journey between them and Jacob. Jacob therefore started with no animals at all, just the full-colored animals owned by Laban.

Nevertheless, Jacob set to work. He engineered a selective breeding program, retained the strong animals for breeding, gave the weak ones to Laban, sped up the animals' reproduction cycle, and vastly increased the numbers of spotted and speckled animals appearing from one generation to the next. It is clear that Jacob, through his long experience with livestock in Canaan followed by twenty years' further experience of working with animals in Haran, knew far more about them than his father-in-law did.

But the scheme was also one of craftiness. He pursued the outmanipulation of Laban by his own wisdom and cunning. Later, Jacob confessed that it was God who had blessed him, perhaps despite his machinations. In any case, and probably within five years, he accumulated huge flocks and herds of his own, along with many servants and camels through the bartering away of some of his stock. God intervened and told Jacob to leave for home.[9] It was time to get out.

Jacob secretly summoned his wives, Rachel and Leah, and as they stood together talking in Laban's fields, he told them the dream that had inspired his strategy and triggered his successful drive to accumulate their wealth. He said:

> In the breeding season I once had a dream in which I looked up and saw that the male goats mating with the flock were streaked, speckled or spotted. The angel of God said to me in the dream, "Jacob." I answered, "Here I am." And he said, "Look up and see that all the male goats mating with the flock are streaked, speckled or spotted, for I have seen all that Laban has been doing to you. I am the God of Bethel, where you anointed a pillar and where you made a vow to me. Now leave this land at once and go back to your native land." (Genesis 31:10–13)

Jacob's family was happy to leave. Taking advantage of Laban's preoccupation with his flocks elsewhere, they fled from his property with all their livestock, their camels, and their servants. Rachel also snatched some figurines[10] from her father's house. Although Laban and his sons came after them in hot pursuit, Laban was warned by God in a dream not to harm Jacob. After an extended disputation and a fruitless search for the figurines taken by his daughter, Laban allowed the caravan to proceed on. Jacob continued to head west, and Laban returned east.

At this point, some twenty-five years have passed since Jacob departed from his family home. Before he meets his brother Esau again, he first sends messengers with gifts on ahead of him. They deliver the gifts, totaling 550 animals. The messengers return alive to Jacob, but they tell him Esau is coming with an army of four hundred men. In very great distress, Jacob divides up the caravan, thinking that if Esau attacks one division, the other might be given time to escape. He then returns to both the dreams he had when God made promises to him, and he addresses God in terms that exactly repeat God's self-disclosure.

> Then Jacob prayed, "O God of my father Abraham, God of my father Isaac, Lord, you who said to me, 'Go back to your country and your relatives, and I will make you prosper,' I am unworthy of all the kindness and faithfulness you have shown your servant. I had only my staff when I crossed this Jordan, but now I have become two camps. Save me, I pray, from the hand of my brother Esau, for I am afraid he will come and attack me, and also the mothers with their children. But you have said, 'I will surely make you prosper and will make your descendants like the sand of the sea, which cannot be counted.'" (Genesis 32:9–12)

Jacob looks to the horizon and sees Esau swiftly approaching with his army of four hundred. He quickly places his children with their mothers to the rear and then goes on ahead of them. He walks on toward his brother and bows down on the ground before him seven times.

> But Esau ran to meet Jacob and embraced him; he threw his arms around his neck and kissed him. And they wept. Then Esau looked up and saw the women and children. "Who are these with you?" he asked. Jacob answered, "They are the children God has graciously given your servant." (Genesis 33:4–5)

The women and children all proceed to bow down before Esau. There is still a dispute. Esau wants to know what the gifts were for. He has more than enough already. Jacob should keep them. No, says Jacob, they are for Esau. He insists Esau must keep them. Esau accepts.

Conclusions

From the time Jacob left his brother Esau to travel to Haran, he became involved in a deep-rooted spiritual and character transformation that began during and after his first dream encounter with the living God. He discovered that God was committed to blessing him and that the greater picture had to do with his immediate forebears as well as the generations of his family line yet to be born. He was not given the *whole* picture, of course, that from one of his sons with Leah, the line of Judah would lead directly to the Messiah. But what he was given in the dream was more than enough, and with some fear, he marked the place and committed his life to the living God.

Jacob named the place of the dream the House of God and the gate of heaven, and he commemorated the staircase to heaven first with a pillar and then with an altar. As best he could, he turned the place into a temple. The altar lasted for many generations and served to remind the tribes of Israel as to what took place there. Much later, this House of God became a portable-tent shrine containing the ark of the covenant, and later still, Solomon built the first temple for the ark and for God's living presence to inhabit.

That temple would eventually be destroyed and rebuilt and then be superseded by Christ Himself and also by His church and its pilgrimage toward heaven. The church does and will host the incarnational reality of the living God indwelling it. Ultimately, in the new heaven and the new earth, no temple as such is actually needed or present: "I did not see a temple in the city, because the Lord God Almighty and the Lamb are its temple" (Revelation 21:22). But the idea and the reality began at Bethel and with Jacob because of his dream encounter with God.

The dream of the spotted and speckled goats and the message to flee at once from Laban combined to enable Jacob to take a just recompense or blessing with him when he left. His inheritance was protected further by God's intervention with Laban, who was warned in a dream to desist from any attack on Jacob, even a verbal one. It was through dreams that Jacob was able to obtain his inheritance. Perhaps today we may be guided in a dream as to how to take our rightful inheritance. However it comes to us, we will be blessed if we are able to hear God's direction and act on it.

We can infer that when Esau set out with four hundred men, he fully intended to attack Jacob's caravan and that Jacob correctly read the situation. Jacob had no military strength to counter this, and he was thrown upon God's mercy and the promises God had explicitly made to him through dreams. As well as causing a significant measure of spiritual transformation in him, the dreams also triggered his prayer of consecration and covenant, the only extended prayer to appear in Genesis. The dreams were experiences that Jacob presented back to God *in extremis*; he knew that his life was one in a succession of lives that God held close to His heart. Surely his God would stand by His word to him.

Somehow the dreams collaborated with Jacob's other experiences of God as well as the trial of living with the arch-manipulator Laban to develop his character greatly. To some extent, by the time we see him at Jabbok, Jacob has become a man of God. There are traits suddenly demonstrated that we have not seen before. He courageously steps forward to face his brother alone. He is contrite and humble with God *and* with his brother. In great humility, he bows seven times before Esau, an action that demonstrates absolute submission. Perhaps God was at work in Esau's heart as he rode toward him, but this answer to the prayer for deliverance probably caused an even greater change in Jacob's own heart. Submission and genuine humility were the way through.

At this point, Jacob was not thinking or scheming. As Esau rode toward him, he was just moving with what he needed to do and with what God enabled him to be. There was no calculation. The result was a disarming of his brother and true reconciliation. Achieving a right relationship with his brother was accomplished through first arriving at a right relationship with God and moving in it, at least at that point in time, during the crisis.

Quietly, God was behind the previous twenty-five years, watching them unfold and intervening as He willed. God's dream messages to Jacob were dreams of blessing, knowledge, guidance, and relationship—He had chosen to develop a relationship with Jacob. The dreams also gave the man a purpose, direction, and vision to rely on in a crisis. Jacob fell back on what he was promised. Prior to the dream at Bethel, he had been wandering alone in the dark, escaping a brother who wanted to kill him. We leave Jacob as the head of a very large family, truly reconciled to his brother, and aware that he is never alone.

CHAPTER 4

Psychoanalytical Interpretation of Dreams

The psychoanalyst Sigmund Freud (1856–1939) first published his book *The Interpretation of Dreams* in 1900 in German, and an expanded, revised edition was translated into English in 1913.[1] In this work, Freud presented the view that dreams represent instinctive drives escaping from the mind's repression of them and rising to surface into consciousness. These drives, through dreams, partially gratify themselves while not intruding into and disrupting the person's waking life and behavior. Dreams also serve the purposes of deliberately disguising this gratification or fulfillment and allowing sleep to continue.

For Freud, dreams could not have been more important. Along with a technique called free association, whereby the patient used dream imagery as a starting point for learning more about their thoughts and feelings, dreams were seen as *the* critical tools to a successful analysis, which invariably focused on the patient's repressed early childhood wish fulfillments.

Freud held that the unconscious dissented from the ideals and beliefs of the Enlightenment. Unlike the educated, conscious, and rational mind, one's unconscious is not rational and is not governed by rational principles. He believed that much more goes on in the unconscious than at the conscious level; powerful psychological energies deep inside a person propel or prevent decisions being made and actions being taken or not taken. On the positive side then, Freud's work succeeded in highlighting something of the true importance of dreams as messages from and outworkings of people's hidden, internal, and unconscious selves. This concept was new in the West, because the Enlightenment had largely abandoned the notion that dreams held any significance. It was a major rediscovery, and it also served as *the* starting point for Western dream research.

The Unholy Pioneer of Dream Investigation

However, as a psychological reductionist, Freud rapidly reduced the religious and emotional content of dreams to purely psychological and biological levels. He also spun an elaborate new secular and psychological mythology around the dreams his middle-class Viennese ladies told him about as he zeroed in obsessively on issues such as internal conflict, supposedly suppressed desires, and wish fulfillments of the past that were reasserting or reworking themselves in dreams. This mythology was in all likelihood driven by what Carl G. Jung later alluded to as Freud's "daimon." His former disciple viewed Freud as a tragic figure, a potentially great man who was far too overfocused on sex. It had taken possession of him, causing him to turn the sex drive into a dogma and turning him into the sex drive's archbishop.

In his practice, Freud investigated something of the hidden and psychological reality boiling and bubbling away in outwardly calm and controlled clients as they lay on his couch. Like a sort of psycho-archaeologist, he would take his patients' dreams and delve into their potential layers of meaning. He was rightly searching for the truth that was beyond reason. And although he overextended the idea, he was also partially right in his inference that some dreams are the result of psychological repression. Indeed, and to take it further, I believe that from time to time a dream is not really a dream at all but a repressed memory, something that actually happened perhaps in childhood, something that the child could not cope with or deal with at the time because there was no way to process it. What was he or she to do with it? Sometimes an event, a dreadful moment, is repressed so that life can be lived. Such things remain, though. Time does not erase them. They are still there in the heart, and the heart communicates them back up to the mind in dreams, often much later in life. Although repressed memory or dissociative amnesia is a controversial subject, I believe that spontaneous recovery of these memories is possible, for example, through the contents of dreams.

But if Freud's own mind was darkened, and if he denied the existence of an even greater unseen reality, namely God, of what ultimate use can his dream interpretive method be? No matter how many layers of meaning he succeeded in digging through, he would almost inevitably misinterpret the meaning because of his biological, naturalistic, and materialist assumptions. To accurately interpret a dream, especially one that is God-given, you need a holy rather than an unholy imagination. And since the heart is deceitful above all things,[2] you also need the discernment that only God can provide. Professor Walter Brueggemann[3] holds that Freud actually adopted a rabbinic-midrashic interpretive method to make sense of the enigmatic dream material he investigated, an ironic observation.

In the end, Freud's approach was a psychologically reductionist one, denying a transcendent God and His love for and communication with humankind. Whether Freud's investigations were scientific or not is an additional, major issue. He believed they were scientific, but the view of modern-day empirical psychology would generally hold that, for one thing, his sample of humanity—wealthy middle-class clients who both wanted his intervention and could afford him—was skewed in the extreme.

Furthermore, it also needs to be added that Freud tended to misconstrue dream dynamics as well as their interpretation. He considered for instance that dream symbolism served as a device to deliberately obscure meaning unacceptable to the conscious ego. My view is that the opposite holds true. Dream symbolism is the language of the heart. The truths that the heart intuits are communicated by it through dreams and their symbols so that the mind can perceive and understand them. Our unconscious is talking to us, and it wants to be heard—if only we learn its language.

Carl G. Jung and the Soulish Interpretation of Dreams

The system that Freud developed was primarily opposed to God because of its materialistic and biological assumptions. For these reasons, we find that people of a religious persuasion rarely find anything of real value in it. The same cannot be said of Jung and his adherents. Christians involved in counseling and other pastoral activity often wax lyrical in their acceptance of Jung's symbolic system. In its assimilation of myths and religious concepts, it would seem to be a more favorable system and approach to rely on for those who believe in spiritual and transcendent realities. However, we need to examine the question of whether this is really the case and whether we can rely on the Jungian approach as an ally as we seek to explore the nature and meaning of dreams and their symbols.

Freud's rebellious Swiss disciple, Carl Gustav Jung (1875–1961), on breaking with Freud in 1910, took dream analysis to another level. He has been arguably much more influential than Freud in the latter half of the twentieth century and into the twenty-first century. Many secular and religious-oriented dream books (including those by Christians) draw heavily from his work on dreams, as well as from his views of the unconscious and the nature of humankind.

Unlike Freud, Jung believed that the unconscious created dreams in order to be heard and understood; through dreams, the unconscious is telling the dreamer how things really are inside. He said for instance, "The dream comes in as the expression of an involuntary psychic process not controlled by the conscious outlook. It presents the subjective state as it really is."[4] If we then work constructively to understand and take on board our dream material, we are working to facilitate our own reintegration, to bring together more of what we truly are. We are drawing up and into our conscious selves those aspects that are hidden normally from our view but are active through our dreams. This is the Jungian process of *individuation*. Through it, we become more whole, more complete in ourselves.

Jung's influence today extends well beyond dreams and therapeutic psychology. Although Freud and Jung are rarely taught in undergraduate psychology in the UK or elsewhere, Jung's work has influence across a number of fields, including my own (higher education work in career advice and guidance). Psychometric instruments such as the Myers-Briggs Type Indicator are derived from Jung's theories of personality and are used extensively in academia and recruitment. These instruments elicit responses that indicate psychological preferences, for example, extroversion or introversion, which are reliable and constant and based on Jung's sometimes excellent and accurate work in the area of personality. His theories and techniques (particularly "active imagination") have also led to significant developments in areas such as art therapy and dance therapy.

Jung was also somewhat aware of the importance of religion to humankind. He was aware that a spiritual experience could achieve what therapeutic interventions and coping strategies often failed to achieve in terms of radical breakthroughs. This has been documented for addictions such as alcoholism.[5] He also realized that all of his older patients only became well psychologically if or when they reappraised and accepted a religious outlook, often the one they had rejected in their youth. They had been ill primarily because they had lost their religion. At times, it was the patients' dreams telling them this. Jung viewed the content of these dreams as spiritual or sacred.

Indeed, Jung's studies of all the major religions as well as areas such as astrology led him to view religious and mythological symbolism as the outworkings of psychological needs for self-transformation. Religious symbols appearing through dreams could symbolize unconscious archetypes at play within a person and could even symbolize the unconscious itself. His treatment of paranormal phenomena was just the same; sightings of UFOs had a creative but psychological significance for those who had ostensibly seen them.

Although Freud would not consider that he believed in a god, he had in fact deified the sex drive. For him it had a numinous power, and he would speak to Jung about it in hushed tones. In Jung's case, while he rejected the specifics of Freud's obsession, he in fact went much further in his fusion of analytical psychology and spirituality. Jung deified the unconscious and more or less everything living within it that exists autonomously to the life experienced by the conscious mind. Ultimately, this is merely a different sort of psychological reductionism.

Moreover, the position Jung and his faithful adherents take is profoundly un-Christian, even anti-Christian. The transcendent God is denied not, in their case, by the atheism of a neo-Darwinist such as Freud, but by a new or reawakened paganism and gnosticism which invariably, because of their sources of false revelation, proceed to blend together both good and evil as two complementary sides of the same being and the same reality. Ultimate truth and revelation from the transcendent God are locked out of the Jungian system. Denying the transcendent God and His living presence within humans through an indwelling Christ,[6] his system remains completely subjective and focused on a soulish or carnal interpretation of dream material. The Jungian approach also simultaneously becomes open to false, deceptive revelation because it is falsely mystical and very much open to the occult. Jung's own false dreams and revelations about the nature of good and evil, described in detail in his autobiography,[7] and his wholly uncritical acceptance of them are ample evidence of this.

In contrast to the Jungian view, which fuses good and evil together, the Christian revelation of the nature of God emphasizes His absolute goodness and His hatred of evil. As James Martin[8] points out in his study of the nature of suffering, Christ embodied and lived out both this absolute goodness and this hatred of evil. Christ dealt with sickness of mind, body, and spirit whenever He came across it. He expelled evil from the lives of all those to whom He ministered during His incarnation. He never saw sickness and evil as ever representing anything at all to do with God's nature. He saw them as the enemy of humanity and of God alike, something alien, something that never should have been but, for the present time and age, was.

Considering atheism as a dead-end in regards to meaning, Jung drew heavily from Germanic occult traditions, astrology, and pantheistic worldviews as well as the world's main religions, reducing them all to the level of a mystical but psychologically based reality, a psychological pseudo-religion. In his departure from Freud, he failed to go far enough. Jung became stuck in a midposition between atheism and an outlook that could truly embrace God as an objective, supernatural, and transcendent reality. He got stuck midway, embracing a ubiquitous life force that had no objective reality beyond the collective and individual human soul.

At the same time, Jung covered so much ground laterally that he now greatly appeals to the New Age or new spirituality, where more or less everything goes. Because he borrowed from everywhere, in Jung's writings there really is something for almost everyone, or so they may think. But his language can be very misleading. Jung borrowed from Christianity among many other religions, and he uses Christian terms from time to time just as cultists do. But the meaning and application of the terms have become un-Christian. That is, the supernatural reality they were meant to describe or define has now been reduced to only and merely a psychological reality.

We should ponder the results of this. For one thing, Christ becomes much less than God the Son, while all other Christian objective reality is also reduced to the level of the subjective. Jung's material is all, as Leanne Payne[9] points out, merely borrowed. The syncretistic Jungian approach latches on to it all, assimilates it, and feeds off it parasitically, using religious symbols to flesh out its subjective view of a psychological reality usually hidden from view.

What then of the individual patients who are much in need and seeking help and healing for their souls? Those who are seeking God could well be taken in by the Jung school's pseudo-Christian language and believe they have found the truth within a false mysticism inclusive enough to fit with individual preconceptions as well as our postmodern, globalist age. The inoculation of false revelation and soul healing could prevent such people from hearing and responding to the genuine truth if they were ever presented with it.

As a deception, Jung's modern mythology is very powerful. It has the capability to energize a seeming wholeness in a person while condemning the patient to a lost eternity. The patient of the analytical psychologist, "healed" by seeming internal integration, never found the transcendent God who willed to save. He or she only found a false redemption from within. As the addiction lost its grip, life got more functional. But unknown to the patient, now in the grip of a pseudo-religion, the soul was still not saved.

Given that Jung rejects a creative and transcendent God, there is a profound subjectivism in his approach to dream interpretation. Yet sometimes only God can interpret a dream. The truth or message conveyed lies outside human understanding. A Jungian analyst will simply offer, at best, one possible dream interpretation after another after another, until one of the options maybe strikes a chord with the patient. This is far from the certain and incisive revelation offered by, for example, Daniel in Babylon.

We also need to be aware of the fact that Jung, as a pantheist, gained much of his approach and ideas from the "gods within," forces that he considered were independent of him. He did well to objectify them—they *were* independent of him. But what were these forces? In his helpful writing on the subject, Professor Douglas Groothuis,[10] professor of philosophy at Denver Seminary, emphasizes the un-Christian nature of Jung's writings and their origins. Jung was visited for lengthy periods of time both within and without, suffering major bouts of mental illness while also experiencing a variety of poltergeist activity around his home.[11] Jung describes these forces in ways reminiscent of a haunting, and it was these, he said, which compelled him to write. They likewise inspired and drove the dreams he had that were key to the approach he formulated.

Over the many decades since Jung began to write, these forces, and the pantheistic worldview they pushed through him, have contaminated much of what has been written post-Jung about dream interpretation with an occult tincture. Some would say that his experiences were delusional or even psychotic, but on the other hand, they could have arisen from a demonic infiltration into his inner and outer worlds. It is my view that Jung derived his experience much of the time from the existential evil that he had opened himself up to through occult practices such as visualization, the process of "active imagination," and his self-initiation into a collection of early pagan religions.

In addition to Jung's drawing from occult sources, there is also a profound philosophical mismatch between Jung's approach and that of Christianity. Jung drew heavily on Georg Hegel's work and his theories of dialectical synthesis. In such theories, progress occurs from a position, argument, state of being, or thesis into its antithesis and from there to a fusion of these positions into a creative synthesis.[12] Christianity, however, does not follow this approach. As Francis Schaeffer points out in his philosophical and theological book *The God Who Is There*, Christianity requires a thesis and an antithesis that are not blended and are, in fact, irreconcilably opposed. There is within Christianity a "methodology of antithesis," as he puts it. If a belief is true, the opposite belief is false; a fusion of these will likewise be false. A lie with some truth in it is still a lie, because its purpose is still to deceive.

Antithesis also exists as a process or change in state of being before God. A human being who was lost, a sojourner in the enemy's territory, is saved through justification and thereafter exists in an antithetical state of salvation when compared to where he or she was before being saved. The Bible is full of thesis and antithesis but denies their synthesis; for instance, "Whoever believes in the Son has eternal life; whoever does not obey the Son shall not see life, but the wrath of God remains on him" (John 3:36, ESV). As Schaeffer says in his work *Escape from Reason*, a system focusing on the synthesis of a thesis with its antithesis is a relativistic system of thought that leaves truth behind.

Some of Jung's discoveries do seem to be acceptable in themselves. These would include his focus on the personae, the masks or facades many people take on to present themselves to society but which contradict much of who they really are. We may also include his work in the areas of introversion-extroversion and similar personality traits or preferences. Yet it is best not to take the rest of his system on board; that is to say, the system and outlook derived from occult sources. In the end, his mind was just as darkened as that of his erstwhile mentor. In different ways, both men worked to create their own anthropocentric, psychological religions. Freud deified the sex drive while Jung fused good and evil, deifying the archetypes and including the sex drive and the shadow, the submerged dark, amoral, and chaotic forces within, insisting they should all be incorporated into the self through individuation.

As commentators such as Groothuis point out, the Christian approach stands in stark opposition to this. In contrast to a Jungian assimilation of everything, of good and evil alike, Christ commands that we remove anything causing us to sin and throw it away, saving ourselves from the danger of hell.[13]

By deifying the unconscious, Jung deified humankind itself. But God created humans. He created our conscious and our unconscious. We are created beings made in God's image, but fallen. God exists as a wholly good, perfect being outside of His creation. If we receive the Holy Spirit, God is not only transcendent to us but immanent within us. He lives in us—but that still does not make us God.

Again, by deifying the unconscious, Jung also claimed that the *Imago Dei* or god within was both good and evil. The shadow, the dark, the chaotic were aspects of our nature and character. Yet we know from Scripture that God is infinitely good and holy, that there is no evil at all in Him. The apostle John said, "God is light; in him there is no darkness at all."[14] Similarly, Habakkuk said, "Your eyes are too pure to look on evil [with any degree of approval]; you cannot tolerate wrongdoing."[15]

Although the prophet Isaiah was talking of and to the false prophets of his day (see, for instance, Isaiah 9:15; Isaiah 44:24–25), his words also speak forward in time to the many false prophets such as Jung who live in our present time and who present reduced, misshapen, ill-conceived versions of God and His character. In Isaiah's language, Jung dared to call evil good and good evil and exchanged darkness for light and light for darkness. Those who follow after him are following a darkened, dangerous path. It is only when we have the indwelling Spirit of God that we can have true discernment: true revelation and true understanding and true interpretation of what we see.

In relation to dreams, however, both Freud and Jung were indeed pioneers. They pushed back the boundaries of the unknown as they revealed that dreams had not just a meaning that could be discovered with time and patience, but also very great importance to the life and well-being of the person. They did pay attention to the human heart and its language, and from time to time they probably did perceive the heart's meaning aright. At the same time, they both made their journeys into the mysterious interior without a light to guide them. Not seeing where they were journeying to and not cognizant of the dangers, their souls were taken captive by the dark, invasive forces they discovered within. These then corrupted the systems, psychoanalysis, and analytical psychology the psychoanalysts created. To use their valid insights wisely while rejecting the substantial error running alongside them is a challenge that few seem able to undertake successfully—either for themselves or for others they would like to help.

Contemporary Analytical Dream Interpretation

Since the days when the patriarchs of dream study, Freud and Jung, were active and developing their respective systems, a wide range of analysts and therapists have continued their investigation of dreams. In some cases, they have tended to follow the models set out by the patriarchs, amplifying or developing them but without altering the core tenets of their systems in any significant way. This is the current situation in, for example, the field of transpersonal psychology, a basically Jungian approach but with additional further influences derived from Eastern religions and from drug-induced or influenced altered states of consciousness.

More often than not, however, clinicians have ploughed their own more distinctive and creative furrows in the territories already explored. Dream interpretation has moved on. New models and approaches have been developed that are less mechanistic than Freud's approach and in many cases considerably less gnostic than Jung's, even if they are just as subjective and humanistic in their orientation. Even neo-Freudian analysts tend to dispense with the technique of free association as it was applied rigorously by Freud and are, at the same time, more concerned with dreams as constructions of and communications from the complete personality; they have moved away from viewing dreams merely as representations of repressed drives and instincts.

Psychiatrists and analysts such as Ernest Hartmann[16] who derive much of their approach from Freud also now perceive that dreams are far more connected to people's real lives than Freud had thought. In Hartmann's theory, for instance, dream images central to the content and flow of the dreams containing them are held to represent the dreamer's emotional response to a traumatic, often recent event, occurring in real life. Further, these researchers also consider that dream symbolism is really not there to deliberately disguise and obscure the meaning of dreams to the dreamer or the analyst/interpreter. The symbolism is caused instead by a strong tendency of the unconscious to link and associate ideas and images in nonrandom but fluid ways very different from the associations that the conscious mind would make. The nonrandomness is guided by the person's deep psychological and emotional concerns.

It is not my intention to review all the main contemporary analytical and humanistic theories of dream interpretation. A further example, though, comes from the work of Clara E. Hill, professor of psychology at the University of Maryland. Her work, developed over many years, is illustrative because it integrates a number of current theories into an overall structure and therapeutic approach.[17] Her overarching theory makes three assumptions. First, like Hartmann and others, she assumes that dreams reflect real life in some way and process what has occurred in reality. Second, she assumes that the dream's meaning is personal to the dreamer. The dream comes from our own unconscious; it is about us, and so we cannot simply pull out a dictionary of standard dream interpretations and look up the symbols. Third, and because the dream's meaning is a personal one, she assumes that work on the dream should be a collaboration between the therapist or dream interpreter and the dreamer. An interpretation is worked toward by discussing the dream and its context, the dreamer's life, with the dreamer.

Following Hill's dream interpretation model first involves the exploration of the different dream images, teasing them apart and considering their cognitive and emotional dimensions. At the same time, the dreamer talks about his or her life and what might have occurred to concern them emotionally and trigger these dream images. The dreamer is asked to relive and reexperience, if possible, the images as they appeared and then to word-associate from the images. The therapist discovers the different connections the dreamer makes that relate in some way to what they saw in the dream. The connections often are a mixture of life events, thoughts, and memories. This practice develops a fuller understanding for both dreamer and therapist of the actual meaning of the images for the individual.

The therapist next moves to the insight stage, which clarifies the dream's potential meaning. On the one hand, the meaning could be objective. For instance, Hill points out that a woman who dreams that her husband is having an affair could be dreaming this because he is indeed having one, in which case the therapist would work with the dreamer on the level of how she feels about this, helping her to work through the emotions. On the other hand, the dream imagery could be symbolic of issues the woman is having with her husband, in which case the therapist would work at this level. But the dream could actually be the output of things going on at a much deeper and inner level within the woman's own thinking and emotions. The therapist would then work at this more psychodynamic, subjective level. Is there, for instance, a part of the woman's personality that identifies with her husband, and is she, in fact, the one who is contemplating embarking on an affair?

Thereafter Hill recommends a final stage of dream work that either helps the client gain further and more complete insight and awareness from the dream or helps the client apply in real life the changes that the dream may be suggesting. Perhaps a dream symbolizes something out of kilter in a relationship at work or in the family. What then should the person do to rectify this? Or the dream could symbolize that a change in career direction is warranted. Whatever the locus of the change needed, the therapist would work with the client to assist a practical and behavioral change; this could be the final outworking of the dream issue or concern, but the action taken could also provide some additional insights into the dream.

Dream work which involves working with a psychoanalytic therapist or psychotherapist can produce helpful insights into the meaning of your dreams. This is at least partly because the therapist gets to know the dreamer as an individual with unique concerns and fears, hopes, family background, and personal history. Many of the images and emotions occurring in the client's dreams may be explainable in relation to any of this wider personal context along with the dreamer's unconscious desires and the relationship between their dreams and how their life is being lived. In addition to this, though, I believe in a transcendent, personal God who likes to speak through dreams and in many other ways. A therapist who holds to a psychologically reductionist or mechanistic worldview will not be able to shed light on this supernatural dimension to dreaming. Dreams are about the language of heaven as well as the language of the heart.

CHAPTER 5

A Prince Among Brothers

As the author of the first five books of the Bible, Moses recorded Joseph's birth in Genesis 30:24, where Joseph is born to Jacob's favorite wife around 1745 BC.[1] His mother, Rachel, chose his name, which means "God will add." This name primarily conveys her great desire for a second son after a lengthy and distressing time of being unable to conceive at all, and this wish was granted with the birth of Benjamin in Genesis 35, at the cost of her own life.

It is apparent that at seventeen years of age, Joseph could not get along with his ten half-brothers. They actually hated him, partly because their father Jacob loved Joseph more than them and demonstrated this by making him the now famous "richly ornamented robe" or coat of many colors, the type of robe that in future would be worn by greatly favored children of the king (see, for example, 2 Samuel 13:18) and completely unsuitable for manual work, thus setting him apart from his brothers. This unique, special gift may also have indicated that Jacob intended to make Joseph his heir at a future date.

Four of Joseph's half-brothers were born to Jacob's concubines and therefore had no rights of succession anyway. In addition, Reuben had lost his rights as male heir because of an act of incest he committed with one of Jacob's concubines.[2] In the fullness of time and after the family had migrated to Egypt, Jacob would transfer Reuben's rights to Joseph's sons. In the meantime, Joseph was also resented for overseeing his brothers and bringing a bad report of their conduct to Jacob.[3]

Joseph's Dreams

It was in the context of this complex and fractured family that Joseph suddenly had two vivid dreams and promptly told his family about them. The predictable result of this was that his half-brothers hated him all the more. It is interesting that in the early civilization and culture of Canaan, his family did not sit around and say things like "Well, that was a strange dream" or "What did you eat last night? It obviously wasn't what we had" or "Well, I reckon I'll look up that dream imagery when I get in from the fields tomorrow." To them the meaning was absolutely clear, so much so that the brothers quickly took action. They would see to it as best they could that Joseph's dreams would never come true.

In his first dream, as Joseph told his brothers, they were all:

> "binding sheaves of grain out in the field when suddenly my sheaf rose and stood upright, while your sheaves gathered around mine and bowed down to it." His brothers said to him, "Do you intend to reign over us? Will you actually rule us?" And they hated him all the more because of his dream and what he had said. (Genesis 37:7–8)

Then he had another dream and told it to his brothers:[4]

> "Listen," he said, "I had another dream, and this time the sun and moon and eleven stars were bowing down to me." When he told his father as well as his brothers, his father rebuked him and said, "What is this dream you had? Will your mother and I and your brothers actually come and bow down to the ground before you?" His brothers were jealous of him but his father kept the matter in mind. (Genesis 37:9–11)

The account reveals that—though they took them seriously—his brothers rejected Joseph's dreams out of hand, as brothers inevitably would. What brother on earth would say to another after hearing such a dream, "Well, I guess it must be prophetic and I'm to bow down to you sometime in the future; that's all right if it's God's will"? The best Joseph could have hoped for would be an ambivalent response along the lines of "Well . . . we'll see."

Jacob, his father, was initially unpleased but chose to keep the dream in mind and await understanding or illumination, perhaps because of his own experience with dreams from God. It is as if Jacob did not know for certain where the dream had come from and therefore what its significance, if any, was; so until revelation came, he would remember his son's dream from time to time and ponder it as he sat in his tent or quietly surveyed his land.

It is easy to say that one lesson we can draw from Joseph's telling of his dreams is the need for care in telling anyone a dream, especially if the dream seems to be about them. It may be that the dream should never be conveyed at all. Possibly God only wanted to provide Joseph with two prophetic dreams that would encourage him and never intended for him to share them. Yet we also see in the Genesis account that Joseph's "blabbing" of his dreams precipitated a dramatic series of events that led to the dreams' fulfillment (though arguably some of the dreams' imagery signifies a yet-future fulfillment as well).

Shortly after Joseph's precipitate recounting of his dreams, as his brothers grazed their father's flocks, they saw him approaching them in the distance, wearing that robe. Their jealousy and hatred caused them to conspire to kill him. The brothers took Joseph's robe from him, threw him into an empty cistern, and sat down to eat a meal together, callously ignoring his cries. They then saw a caravan of Ishmaelite traders on their way to Egypt and agreed to sell him to the Ishmaelites (see Genesis 37:26–27).

The brothers sold Joseph for twenty silver shekels to buyers who took him to Egypt to be sold into slavery. Joseph's ornamented robe, torn from him by his brothers, was sliced up, dipped in the blood of a slaughtered goat, and returned to Jacob, who assumed Joseph had been killed by a wild animal and mourned "many days" for his lost son. The biblical timeline indicates that Joseph was sold by his brothers around 1728 BC.

The Fulfillment of Joseph's First Dream

If we now shift twenty-one years in the story to around 1707 BC, we find that Joseph's half-brothers are all visiting him in Egypt yet are prevented initially from recognizing him, given his age (almost forty), his Egyptian court attire and shaved-down grooming, and his fluency in his new second language. They have been forced to go cap-in-hand to Egypt for food since there is a severe famine throughout the known world.

Joseph has risen to be the second most powerful man in Egypt after Pharaoh and is in complete control of the domestic and international food supply. After a period of testing his brothers, a process through which they finally reveal a remarkably positive transformation in their own motivations and characters, Joseph is so moved by the change in them that he is compelled to reveal his identity. His sobbing is so loud that news of it is carried by the Egyptians to Pharaoh. He exclaims to his brothers, "I am Joseph!" In a similar way, as commentators such as Henry Morris[5] emphasize, Jesus Christ will reveal Himself in the last days to Israel, to those who rejected Him.

Joseph's brothers are fully repentant, and they beg him to forgive them of the wrongs they did to him (see Genesis 50:17). And so he provides them and their father with food and later with large tracts of fertile land in Egypt. He even has to provide them with seed so they can plant the new ground. They all bow low on many occasions before him, first without Benjamin, his only full brother, and later with Benjamin. Finally, they offer themselves to him as his slaves, an offer he firmly declines. This is the precise fulfillment of Joseph's first dream. The sheaves of wheat in the dream symbolism actually prophesied well ahead of time that the issue that would compel his family to bow before him would concern the supply of grain.

In a moving account, Joseph's brothers return to Jacob in Canaan and eventually manage to convince him that they have discovered Joseph, now "ruler of all Egypt."

> And Israel [Jacob] said, "I'm convinced! My son Joseph is still alive. I will go and see him before I die." . . . So Israel set

out with all that was his, and when he reached Beersheba, he offered sacrifices to the God of his father Isaac. And *God spoke to Israel in a vision at night* and said, "Jacob! Jacob!" "Here I am," he replied. "I am God, the God of your father," he said. "Do not be afraid to go down to Egypt, for I will make you into a great nation there. I will go down to Egypt with you, and I will surely bring you back again. And Joseph's own hand will close your eyes." (Genesis 45:28–46:4, emphasis mine)

At the end of the journey and as the meeting approaches, the son sees his father while the latter is still some way off and rushes out to embrace him.

Why was the outworking of Joseph's first dream delayed by twenty-one years? And why was the path to its outworking so fraught, with danger including being sold into slavery, the false accusation of a serious crime in Egypt, and a long spell of imprisonment? In his lectures on dream symbols, John Paul Jackson[6] outlines the following principle regarding clarity in dreams: the greater the clarity, the greater the cost. The superficial meaning of Joseph's dream was quite apparent to Joseph and his brothers; there was no mysterious symbolism shrouding it. Yet none of them were able to take hold of a much deeper meaning and purpose also contained within the symbols.

It is also apparent that the dream was from God and that the plan of God was, through Joseph, to bless and prosper a family destined to become the ancestors of the twelve tribes of Israel, a people group God would finally bless with the incarnation of Himself. And while Joseph's family inevitably failed to see this, the enemy could easily perceive God's intention of blessing and therefore sought to thwart it—first by instigating a plot to kill Joseph and later by having him jailed.

The principle being demonstrated is that if God chooses to provide a dream that reveals His will and purpose clearly, at least at one level, the enemy will seek to thwart it. If God provides a much more opaque dream requiring prayer, discernment, and a period of time spent unraveling its meaning, the incoming dream may more or less come in under the radar and not attract substantial opposition. Dreams that are far from clear regarding their intended meaning may be a blessing for this reason alone. They are easier to accomplish. But they can also be a blessing in that they require a willingness to cooperate with God until the meaning is revealed. Faith and character can grow during this process.

Sometimes the meaning will remain obscured in a mystery until the dream has been fully outworked. At the same time, we can sense too that Joseph actually *required* a significant period of time before he himself could act to fulfill the dream. At age seventeen, he appears to have been far too ready to lord it over his brothers!

The Fulfillment of Joseph's Second Dream

One could say that perhaps the symbolism of moon, sun, and stars contrasted with sheaves of grain does not really matter and that the second dream was also fulfilled completely in Joseph's temporal position of power over and then generosity regarding his family and their rescue from starvation at a time of famine. In his commentary, James Poole considers that the dream signifies that Joseph will become a "highly exalted prince."[7]

Partly, this would be a correct interpretation of the second dream. Although Joseph's beloved mother was long dead at the time of the rescue of his family, the sun and moon imagery could well represent his parents' generation in contrast to his own generation, symbolized as stars with each star representing a brother or half-brother. The fulfillment of this aspect of the dream occurred when, with Pharaoh's permission and in response to his whole family being in great need, Joseph was able to offer sanctuary to his entire wider family—more than seventy people.

However, the second dream probably has a more profound meaning. People are not usually represented as stars in dreams. If his siblings had thought about this at all, they could have wondered about what the symbols meant, what their destinies might be. Without any complete understanding, they would have realized that it was a very positive dream! The sun, moon, and stars last through time and generations. Compared to a human lifespan and to everything we can see that is born, flourishes, and then fades away, they are just about eternal.

They also convey something of majesty and speak of their Creator who, as the psalmist says, is able to call them all by name. Joseph's dream is saying to his father and brothers that they will be honored like stars and that somehow their names will shine brightly or have unusual significance through time and eternity. This was God's word to Joseph's family, but his family did not have ears to hear; they rejected God's word.[8]

Joseph's second dream speaks possibly about a historical process progressing toward eternity, its fuller meaning to be revealed in due time with the continued revelation of Scripture written long after Joseph's life. In what sense, though, could Joseph's brothers bow to him through time and eternity?

In the first place, we find that at the end of Jacob's life, he blesses Joseph to the relative exclusion of his brothers, setting Joseph apart in the way he accords divine blessings to him as well as blessings linked to aspects of creation: "because of your father's God, who helps you, because of the Almighty, who blesses you with blessings of the skies above, blessings of the deep springs below" (Genesis 49:25). Joseph's brothers are also blessed, but in more temporal ways. Basically each is allocated a portion and future in the promised land. This speaks of differential blessings intended to be carried through many subsequent generations; it would be hundreds of years before any of their descendants would see the land. This could be one aspect of the dream's meaning.

At the same time, the dream probably also speaks of God's generosity, blessing, and very great favor to Jacob himself, renamed Israel by God early in his life in Genesis 32 and 35, a name that actually signifies struggling with God. The dream speaks too of generosity to the twelve tribes of Israel, a twelve that are similar but not identical to Joseph's original family. After Jacob has arrived in Egypt, he goes out of his way to complete the transfer of Reuben's blessings to Joseph's two sons, Ephraim and Manasseh, numbering them among his own children for blessing.[9] Reuben retains an inheritance, but the blessing of the firstborn goes to Joseph's line. Thereafter in Scripture, the descendants of Ephraim and Manasseh are named, at least sometimes, as two of the twelve tribes of Israel, thus conferring on Joseph a double portion or blessing in addition to the spiritual blessings noted already. This double portion held more than good when Canaan was conquered by the twelve tribes and apportioned out, each of the twelve receiving a share. If one examines the geographical limits of their tribal territories, it is apparent that the tribes of Ephraim and Manasseh together obtained about a quarter of the entire territory.

When the territory split into northern and southern kingdoms, the tribe of Ephraim often dominated the life of the northern kingdom, while both tribes frequently produced the northern kingdom's leaders: for example, Joshua, Samuel, and Gideon. Yet this blessing on Joseph's direct lines remained temporal. It was eventually withdrawn by God as Joseph's descendants through Ephraim and Manasseh fell into spiritual corruption and idolatry.[10] Eventually, the northern kingdom that Joseph's descendants helped to establish, Israel, was conquered by Assyria and its surviving people exiled in 772–771 BC.

However, if we shift now to the last place in Scripture where the twelve tribes are mentioned, the place of honor accorded Jacob's family has become great indeed—so much so that it is breathtaking.

> And he carried me away in the Spirit to a mountain great and high, and showed me the Holy City, Jerusalem, coming down out of heaven from God. It shone with the glory of God, and its brilliance was like that of a very precious jewel, like a jasper, clear as crystal. It had a great, high wall with twelve gates, and with twelve angels at the gates. On the gates were written the names of the twelve tribes of Israel. (Revelation 21:10–12)

It is possible that this final counting by God includes Joseph's two sons and thereby confers a double portion on Joseph for eternity compared to his brothers.[11]

Joseph gladly put aside any thought of revenge when he saw his brothers bowing before him, quite ignorant as to who he had become. He was instead able to cooperate with God, whose purpose was to bless and multiply him *and* his brothers to create the nation of Israel and advance His plan of salvation. Joseph was able to bless his brothers in such a way that they would survive a famine, and to continue the story of salvation, give rise to generations and a lineage leading directly to Christ, the Savior of the world. In the New Jerusalem, the eternal city, his brothers will continue to honor Joseph while all their names are honored greatly at the city gates. As to their original crime against him, it and their hatred of him will surely not come to mind.

Finally, and although later Scripture does not include an explicit reference to Joseph in such terms, it is true that Joseph can be considered a "type" or archetypal pattern of Christ in many different ways. For instance, they were both rejected by their people and betrayed for pieces of silver. They both saved gentiles as well as their own people. They were both filled with God's Spirit. They offered the bread of life,[12] they were made overseers,[13] they both forgave their brothers totally,[14] and they both were later crowned with glory and honor, to name just some of the parallels.

It is possible that Joseph's second dream conveys a symbolic prophecy of Joseph as a type fulfilled in Christ (Joseph's anti-type). In Joseph's dream, and in his life as it unfolded, perhaps the future incarnation of Christ was concealed and prefigured in order to be revealed at a future time. We can note, for instance, that Joseph was actually concealed in his second dream; there is no indication that he saw himself symbolically at all in the dream. Likewise, just as Joseph was concealed from his brothers but then revealed himself to them in order to save them, so too will Christ reveal Himself to Israel in the end of days: "And in this way all Israel will be saved. As it is written: 'The deliverer will come from Zion; he will turn godlessness away from Jacob'" (Romans 11:26).

The Cupbearer and the Baker

Once in Egypt and many years before his brothers arrived to seek out food, Joseph prospered for a time in Potiphar's house . . . but only until Potiphar's wife falsely accused him and he was confined in a jail, imprisoned alongside Pharaoh's own convicts. Joseph also prospered to some extent in prison, and when the prison warden realized he could trust him completely, he placed

Joseph in charge of the prisoners and the daily regimen. It is likely that the warden, like Potiphar, recognized that God was with Joseph.

At some point during Joseph's stay in jail, Pharaoh's chief baker and chief cupbearer, two senior officials, offended the king greatly and were thrown into prison. The captain of the prison guard assigned them to Joseph, who looked after them.

> After they had been in custody for some time, *each of the two men*—the cupbearer and the baker of the king of Egypt, who were being held in prison—*had a dream* the same night, and each dream had a meaning of its own. (Genesis 40:4–5, emphasis mine)

The two men were disappointed the next morning because no one was available to interpret their dreams of the previous night. But Joseph assured them that interpretations come from God and asked them both to tell him their dreams. At this point Joseph's gifting as a dream interpreter was revealed, and he proceeded to exercise the gift. Yet Joseph had also matured, and he emphasized to the prisoners that it was God who provided the meaning, not Joseph.

The Cupbearer's Dream

> So the chief cupbearer told Joseph his dream. He said to him, "In my dream I saw a vine in front of me, and on the vine were three branches. As soon as it budded, it blossomed, and its clusters ripened into grapes. Pharaoh's cup was in my hand, and I took the grapes, squeezed them into Pharaoh's cup and put the cup in his hand." (Genesis 40:9–11).

Joseph at once interpreted the man's dream for him.

> "This is what it means," Joseph said to him. "The three branches are three days. Within three days Pharaoh will lift up your head and restore you to your position, and you will put

Pharaoh's cup in his hand, just as you used to do when you were his cupbearer." (Genesis 40:12–13)

Three days later, it happened to be Pharaoh's birthday, and he lifted up his chief cupbearer's head[15] in the presence of his other officials and restored him to his former position. The cupbearer once again gave the cup to Pharaoh.

After Joseph interpreted the cupbearer's dream, he asked him to advocate on his behalf with Pharaoh to get him out of prison. He was forcibly removed to Egypt in the first place and had done nothing in Egypt to warrant imprisonment. But once released, the cupbearer promptly forgot all about Joseph.

This is the first recorded occasion in which Joseph interpreted a dream accurately and prophetically, speaking to the dreamer about the future events symbolized in the man's dream. Given that he said interpretations belong to God, we can infer that he was given supernatural revelation about the dream's symbols and their meaning as he sought their meaning out before God, much as Daniel would do hundreds of years later. This could happen because Joseph had sought God and developed a relationship with Him probably every day of his life as he waited in prison for justice at God's hand.

A further and intriguing possibility, however, is that something else was occurring here in addition to a straightforward word of knowledge from God to Joseph concerning the dream. It may be that part of Joseph's work of discernment also had to do with discerning the future in relation to the character of the dreamer. It could be that in the cupbearer, as Joseph got to know him in prison and as he heard him narrate the dream content of his heart, Joseph discerned an innocent man as Joseph himself was innocent. A like nature and situation spoke to like. He may have had confidence in the sovereignty of his God to work for this man's release even through a pagan ruler, given that what he was hearing was the dream of an innocent man dreaming of new life, future growth, and a return to his station in life.

The cupbearer's heart was representing symbolically his own confidence and hope. It was saying by means of the dream that surely the truth would win out and that he would be found innocent. Commentators such as Clay and Mary McLean[16] promote such a view. We should certainly not assume that Pharaoh's decision to reinstate the cupbearer was the result of a capricious whim on the ruler's part, particularly given the man's close proximity to the king. It could well be that the official had been found innocent of the charge made against him or that the king had realized in hindsight that the offense was more trivial than he had thought at the time and was far outweighed by the man's character and reliability.

The Baker's Dream

The cupbearer's fellow prisoner, the baker, was much encouraged by Joseph's positive interpretation and at once told Joseph his own dream. No doubt he looked forward to a similar interpretation, since apart from anything else, his dream shared some symbolism with the cupbearer's dream. Regrettably, though, the baker's dream had a sinister meaning: "He said to Joseph, 'I too had a dream: On my head were three baskets of bread. In the top basket were all kinds of baked goods for Pharaoh, but the birds were eating them out of the basket on my head'" (Genesis 40:16–17).

Unlike the cupbearer's dream, the baker's dream revealed deliberate or unintentional negligence on his part: bread meant for Pharaoh was being devoured and polluted by birds. He had failed to protect it. "'This is what it means,' Joseph said. 'The three baskets are three days. Within three days, Pharaoh will lift off your head and impale your body on a pole. And the birds will eat away your flesh'" (Genesis 40:18–19).

Three days later, this also came to pass, and the baker was killed. Again Joseph was able to reveal the future through supernatural insight given by God. And again, if Joseph was accurately reading the dreamer's heart, we could say that he realized that this dream was the dream of a guilty man whose soul was predicting loss and death. Birds in Scripture only rarely signify bringers of life; they typically represent harbingers of death.

We see too that Joseph behaved with complete integrity. It must have been much more difficult to communicate this interpretation than the one before, but he did not dress it up. To try to soften the blow would be to obscure the message, a dangerous thing to attempt given that the dream's interpretation had come from God.

Although the two prisoners' dreams shared some superficial similarities, Joseph accurately discerned between them. They were in fact opposite dreams, one of innocence leading to restoration and life and the other of guilt leading to death. Joseph was able to discern with accuracy because he was a spiritual man,[17] able to receive the things revealed by the Spirit of God.

The dreams given to the cupbearer and the baker also had a greater purpose, beyond any subconscious outworking of the servants' thoughts or consciences. They served to open two doors for Joseph: the prison door and the palace door. But this effect was delayed for a time.

Pharaoh's Dreams

After the baker's execution and the cupbearer's restoration, two years passed by. Joseph continued to languish in jail. But then Pharaoh had a dream, and in the dream, he saw himself standing on the bank of the Nile:

> . . . when out of the river there came up seven cows, sleek and fat, and they grazed among the reeds. After them, seven other cows, ugly and gaunt, came up out of the Nile and stood beside those on the riverbank. And the cows that were ugly and gaunt ate up the seven sleek, fat cows. Then Pharaoh woke up. He fell asleep again and had a second dream: Seven ears of grain, healthy and good, were growing on a single stalk. After them, seven other heads of grain sprouted—thin and scorched by the east wind. The thin heads of grain swallowed up the seven healthy, full heads. Then Pharaoh woke up; it had been a dream. (Genesis 41:2–7)

Pharaoh was troubled by these dreams and consulted all his magicians and wise men, yet despite their many papyrus books on dreams, none of them could offer him an explanation or interpretation. They were completely unfamiliar with dreams that came from God. At this point the cupbearer remembered Joseph and told Pharaoh that this man was able to interpret his dream and the baker's dream accurately. Things had turned out exactly as Joseph predicted from the telling of the two dreams.

So Pharaoh called for Joseph, who after a shave and a change of clothes appeared before him. When Pharaoh said he had heard that Joseph could interpret dreams, Joseph replied with the integrity and humility we saw him display while imprisoned—he cannot, but God can. Pharaoh then recounted his two dreams and added a few more details; he had never seen such wretched looking cows before in Egypt, and moreover, once they had eaten the fat cows, "no one could tell they had done so; they looked just as ugly as before" (Genesis 41:21).

Joseph may have been reminded of one of the dreams he told to his brothers about thirteen years prior to this encounter. Pharaoh was dreaming of crops just as Joseph had; but this time, the dreamer was dreaming of the food supply twice. Grain and cows. In fact, Joseph stated to Pharaoh that it was one and the same dream.

A series of dreams is not that unusual; people experience this today. Sometimes it is the same dream repeated,[18] and sometimes the dreams are slightly different from each other but connected into a theme. Joseph's two dreams had fallen into this latter category; the first was temporal and predicted that his family would bow before him over the issue of access to food, while his second dream had the same temporal fulfillment while also possessing a more spiritual dimension, connecting with the things of and fulfillment in eternity. Pharaoh's dreams on the other hand remained firmly in the temporal yet still had a grand scope of their own. He was dreaming of the future of Egypt.

Joseph revealed the meaning:

> The dreams of Pharaoh are one and the same. God has revealed
> to Pharaoh what he is about to do. The seven good cows are

seven years, and the seven good heads of grain are seven years;
it is one and the same dream. The seven lean, ugly cows that
came up afterward are seven years, and so are the seven worthless heads of grain scorched by the east wind: they are seven
years of famine . . . Seven years of great abundance are coming
throughout the land of Egypt, but seven years of famine will
follow them. Then all the abundance in Egypt will be forgotten, and the famine will ravage the land. The abundance in the
land will not be remembered, because the famine that follows
it will be so severe. The reason the dream was given to Pharaoh
in two forms is that the matter has been firmly decided by
God, and God will do it soon. (Genesis 41:25–27, 29–32)

Joseph then proceeded to advise Pharaoh as to how to handle these
matters; he ought to take and store up in the Egyptian cities a fifth of
every harvest during the years of abundance to be used in the famine
years. As Pete Wilcox notes,[19] Joseph exercises a true gift of prophecy,
advising Pharaoh on the correct action to take in light of an inevitable
future. In His prophetic discourse on signs of the end of the age, Jesus
does the same, as recorded in Matthew 24:15–18.

Pharaoh recognized that Joseph had shown great insight and also
demonstrated God's wisdom, revealing the true meaning of dreams that
had been closed to the minds of all Pharaoh's wise men. So he chose to
appoint Joseph not just to supervise the grain project but to rule Egypt as
his second-in-command.[20] He also gave Joseph a wife, Asenath, who bore
him two sons, Manasseh and Ephraim, during the years of abundance.

When the famine began, just as Pharaoh's dreams predicted, it affected
not only Egypt but all the surrounding countries. Learning that there
was grain in Egypt, other nations sent delegates in order to buy. Jacob,
Joseph's father, sent ten of Joseph's brothers, and they met with Joseph,
now the governor of Egypt. When Joseph finally revealed his identity to
them, they were absolutely terrified—either because they thought he had
come back from the dead or because they feared what he would now do
to them. Yet Joseph said, "And now, do not be distressed and do not be

angry with yourselves for selling me here, because it was to save lives that God sent me ahead of you . . . to save your lives by a great deliverance" (Genesis 45:5, 7).

In his study on Joseph, Liam Goligher[21] puts it like this: "Joseph is quite clear that God has overruled their sin and their evil intentions." Ultimately, complete trust is restored between Joseph and his brothers, but this trust is established slowly and painfully.

Joseph and Pharaoh agree that Joseph's entire extended family should flee the famine. They know given the dreams' timelines that there are five years of famine remaining. The only way to preserve his family from starvation and destitution is to provide land and a refuge for them in Egypt. They choose Goshen (also known as Rameses) in the Eastern Nile Delta, given that it offers a fertile region for Jacob's flocks and herds; in Goshen, Israel would be given space and time to become a nation. All Joseph's family settle in Egypt, and after meeting with and blessing Pharaoh, Jacob lives for another seventeen years. Joseph gives them all land and gives each of them food according to the number of their children and in fulfillment of the dreams he had as a teenager in Canaan.

Conclusions

We can reach a number of conclusions about dreaming given the nature and scope of the six dreams recorded here. We see for instance the dreams of four dreamers with lives and responsibilities very different from each other. But all six dreams are prophetic and given by God. They all reveal future events that could not be known already by the dreamers. Pharaoh's dreams are in a somewhat different category because they also require action; it is likely that Pharaoh was compelled to seek their interpretation because subconsciously he knew this.

Pharaoh was a ruler of a superpower with a reach right across the region. And his dreams were about the future of his nation and other nations in the region. In fact, in terms of scope, his dreams corresponded to the scope of his life and his power. He could make decisions, based on his dreams, that would preserve his own nation and at least one other nation, the Israelites. Because Pharaoh's responsibilities were big, so too were his dreams.

Of course, not all of Pharaoh's dreams would have been of this magnitude or importance. Presumably, sometimes he would be dreaming of pyramids, the Egyptian "gods," women, or the pleasant dinner he had the previous night. But the two dreams recorded for us are prophetic dreams affecting an entire global region; it is appropriate that the key ruler in that region was given the dreams, and with Joseph's help he was able to take the necessary action. On the other hand, Pharaoh's servants' dreams, while equally prophetic, were very much smaller in scope. They were simply dreaming of their own lives and destinies. The fate of nations really had nothing to do with them.

What about the relationship between our own lives and responsibilities and our dreams? It would seem likely that our own dreams operate in a similar way some of the time; that those of us who have significant responsibilities in church, secular, or political life will sometimes have dreams that reveal to us in symbolic form the present or future situations we will encounter at those levels and in those areas of authority. An entire denomination or corporation could appear to us in symbolic form in dreams. If our lives are much smaller in scope than this, our dream symbols are likely to stand for situations and people who are much more local. The dream may be about our family, our job, or a situation in our church home group.

Pharaoh realized that his dreams were unusual, and he therefore consulted his wise men. They failed to offer any enlightenment. They could not interpret dreams that had been given to Pharaoh by God. Yet God had spoken to Pharaoh, a pagan ruler. It could be that whatever time or age we consider, God sometimes, or often, speaks to people in dreams, whatever their religion happens to be. It must, therefore, be at least possible for the dreamer to understand the message and from where it has come. But Pharaoh needed a human intermediary, one who was genuinely in tune with God and how God speaks in dreams. God provided Joseph.

This situation opens up for us the possibility that if Christians prayerfully and carefully pursued the subject of dream interpretation, it would be possible for them to correctly interpret others' dreams as well as their own. What difference to the world would it make if a key policy maker, politician, or business leader could gain an understanding of a significant dream and take the necessary action? At the very least, if he or she is on the receiving end of an interpretation sensitively and accurately delivered, the response should resemble Pharaoh's. He accepted the interpretation implicitly and without question. As Herman Riffel notes,[22] Pharaoh knew Joseph's interpretation was correct when he heard it. A correct interpretation will strike a chord with the dreamer.

The story of Joseph is more than the story of the outworking of six dreams. It is the story of a family that God chose to bless despite favoritism, betrayals, imprisonment, and the adversity of famine. It begins with a family of about eighteen souls and ends with the increase of this family to about seventy as they commit to a migration from Canaan to Egypt. It is also the story of God blessing the surrounding nations through and because of this family and Joseph in particular. This prefigures the much greater blessing to all nations of a descendent of this family, Jesus Christ. At the same time, the six dreams remain key in the story, precipitating dramatic events of which ultimately, God was in full control. In the end, not one brother was lost.

We also see the development of Joseph's character through adversity. While the narrative begins with a juvenile need and striving for recognition, his response to the subsequent adversity and suffering develops his faith in God[23] and enables him to fully cooperate with the God he sees as being in control of all the events. Surely, in his times of trial, he is able to hold on to the prophetic dreams he had in Canaan. They are a promise to Joseph from God Himself.

Ultimately, Joseph's character develops to the point where he is able to fulfill his destiny and bring great good—preserving nations and averting a regional disaster—out of his brothers' evil intent. He is also able to focus entirely on this positive aspect of his experiences in all his dealings *with* his brothers in Egypt. He insists to them that God meant it all for good. He communicates God's grace to them, forgiving and restoring, remembering their crime against him no more. We can take encouragement from Joseph's life and the path he took; he patiently bore his trials as he awaited his dreams' fulfillment.

CHAPTER 6

God's Purposes in Using Dreams

During the Israelites' journey from Egypt and as they approached Canaan, God descended in a pillar of cloud and spoke to Aaron and Miriam. God said:

> When there is a prophet among you, I, the LORD, reveal myself to them in visions, I speak to them in dreams. But this is not true of my servant Moses; he is faithful in all my house. With him I speak face to face, clearly and not in riddles. (Numbers 12:6–8)

From this message from God, we can extrapolate four ways in which God chooses to speak. He is not limited to these four; He also uses many more. But in this interaction, He Himself specifies four of them, and we can lay them out, up to a point, on a continuum of indirect to direct ways of speaking.

When God speaks through dreams, He is using a very indirect method that bypasses the dreamer's conscious mind. If He chooses to speak through a waking vision, this is a little more direct in that the person's mind is conscious. In this case we see a picture shown to us or we see into the realm of the Spirit.

Next up we have speaking in riddles, parables, and other figurative ways. We have God speaking in verbal symbolism.[1] Although He chose not to speak to Aaron and Miriam in that way, He tends to speak in this way very often; Jesus used this approach *a lot* in His parables.

Finally we have clear and direct speech without the use of symbolism. Either we hear God's words inaudibly word for word in our spirit, or He speaks audibly to us as He did with Aaron and Miriam, and we simply hear with our ears what He says.

Dreams and visions transcend speech since they are primarily visual and nonverbal, while verbal symbolism and direct literal speech are both exclusively verbal. As we have seen, of course, God will speak through dreams in different ways. In some He uses both imagery and words; in others it appears that He only uses one or the other.

It would be wrong and too simplistic just to label these methods of communication as separated out one from another on a continuum. Symbolic dreams, for instance, can be very like the enigmatic parables that Jesus spoke. In fact, the way He interpreted the parable of the sower[2] (the preacher of the good news) can teach us a lot about how to interpret dreams containing symbols. Each symbol Jesus uses in the parable or indirect riddle has, like a dream symbol, a different meaning, and the meaning relates very closely to the symbol. Without his explanation, though, the parable would require a lot of reflection, and for many who pondered it, the meaning would remain obscured. Only the literal sense would be clearly understood. Jesus wants the hearers to be spurred into reflection by what they hear and achieve a right interpretation. The God who creates at least some of our dreams wants us to engage with them, engage with Him, and understand the message.

The Biblical Account

Scripture clearly shows that God uses dreams as one of His methods for communicating with men and women. The people who experience this are a mixture of those who have faith in Him (such as Joseph and Daniel) and those who have no faith at all in Him and no knowledge or understanding of Him (such as Abimelek and Pharaoh). The Bible presents the truth that God will speak in this way at times, and it reiterates this over a period of thousands of years.

The book of Job says, "For God does speak—now one way, now another—though no one perceives it. In a dream, in a vision of the night, when deep sleep falls on people as they slumber in their beds, he may speak in their ears and terrify them with warnings" (Job 33:14–16).

Much later, in the New Testament, we read, "In the last days, God says, I will pour out my Spirit on all people. Your sons and daughters will prophesy, your young men will see visions, your old men will dream dreams" (Acts 2:17).

One of the patterns to emerge from our consideration of the various dreams from God detailed in Scripture is their context of crisis. Many dreams are given in times of oppression, exile, famine, imminent battle, or immense spiritual danger. Pharaoh is given guidance by God for getting his people and the surrounding peoples out of a famine that has yet to strike. Gideon is given guidance and encouragement immediately prior to his engagement with enemy forces greatly superior to his own. Later in Matthew's gospel, Joseph and the wise men are given dreams that guide them in their dealings with Christ as an infant; in the former case, dreams are given on several occasions prior to Christ's birth and after it. A dream also prevents the wise men from revealing Christ's whereabouts to Herod, an event that would have triggered an attack on Him.

Generally, God uses dreams in Scripture for a wide range of reasons, always to communicate. On the negative side, He announces His provisional judgments, which are certain to be executed unless the dreamer radically changes direction. Abimelek and Nebuchadnezzar are prime examples. On the positive side, He warns, promises, guides, and directs. This is sometimes linked to prophetic revelation of future events. In this case there is consolation within the prophecy, whether it is to Jacob being told he will take Laban's flocks, or to tribes, nations, and believers living close in time to the dream or afar off, even yet to be born thousands of years later. God informed Daniel in dreams and visions that the times of the gentiles would one day come to an end. God can see the end from the beginning, and He is never surprised by the way things go. He has predicted it all already.

In the New Testament, God continues to use dreams to do many of these things. As detailed already, He directs, warns, and promises the key people involved in Jesus' very early life. Later He communicates through visions given to believers and unbelievers who seek Him. For instance, the apostle Peter is given a vision that communicates to him that he should consider no man, no gentile, unclean. He should share the gospel with all those who will hear, respond, and believe. Likewise, the Roman centurion Cornelius is given a vision in which he is instructed to send men to fetch Peter.[3] The visions themselves do not present the gospel, the good news of salvation. As George Martin[4] comments, Cornelius is not saved because of a dream he had. Rather, he is put in touch with Peter, who is able to share the good news with him. Meanwhile, by providing another vision, God prepares Peter to share the gospel with him. In other words, it is the preaching of the truth that is the primary means of salvation rather than a dream or a vision. But God is using a variety of means to communicate.

Does God Speak Through Dreams Today?

Even if all this is true, perhaps God has ceased engaging with people through their dreams. At a time when the revelation of Scripture is complete, perhaps the Word replaces the former ways God used to speak to people. This would be the hyper-Calvinistic viewpoint. God speaks to us in Scripture. Why would He need to speak through dreams as well?

However, God Himself states plainly that He does not change: "I the LORD do not change."[5] Again, He says through the letter to the Hebrews, "Jesus Christ is the same yesterday and today and forever."[6] He is immutable and constant in all His purposes and ways. We can surmise that just as He acted in the past in love and concern to warn, save, and guide through dreams, He will do so again.

At the same time, has humanity changed? It is true that we are subject to change and decay individually and as a race. For instance, a gradual accumulation of DNA mutations has, over the generations, brought about an increasing range of inherited diseases and conditions. Our cultures and civilizations rise and fall too; they rise only to be destroyed in war or through moral and spiritual decline, and now and then, they are wiped out in a cataclysmic disaster. Again, this is because everything, including the earth itself, is subject to the fall and to decay.

Yet we are still the same spiritual creatures we always were. We consist of and function as body, soul, and spirit just as our ancestors did. We are dreamers just as they were. If God does not change at all and we have not changed in terms of our basic nature and makeup, why would God stop speaking to us in dreams? Does the Bible not legitimize the fact that God wants to speak to us in this way by using the same symbolic language in parables and visions (such as the Revelation) that He chose to use in times long past in Daniel's or Joseph's time?

There are many recent accounts of non-Christians throughout the world having vivid dreams of Christ in which He appears and communicates verbally. Usually, He appears in white robes and is surrounded by light. He states clearly to the dreamer that He is the truth, the God whom the dreamer has been searching for.

In one report cited by Professor George Martin, an African man who had just torn up a Bible tract fell asleep only to be confronted by Jesus who explained, "You have torn up the truth."[7] Another account reports in detail how the Holy Spirit focused on a single village in Algeria and moved from one dreamer to the next, going from house to house, convicting people of the truth and the need for salvation. Such reports seem to come mainly from African and Middle Eastern countries such as Nigeria, Algeria, Iran, and Iraq, and are reported to local Christian radio stations and missionary groups with people writing in or visiting to talk about the dreams they have had. It is interesting that in African and Middle Eastern cultures, there has been a great respect for and focus on dreaming for many hundreds of years, far more so than in the secularized, post-Enlightenment West. It may well be that far more significant numbers of dreamers across this vast area are more attuned to their dreams than we are in the West. They take their dreams seriously anyway. They are open to God speaking to them in this way.

At the same time, though, there *are* vivid and detailed accounts in the West of God speaking through dreams. In his book *Encounters,* John Woolner[8] describes one of them:

Elizabeth Brazell founded Word of Life Trust, a UK-based mission and healing ministry, in 1997. Her team sought a location for a base and resource center for the ministry, and during a time of prayer and silence, a "word" given to one of them said, "Do not be surprised at the site of this special place. It will be called 'Bethlehem' (or the house of bread)."

From then on, the team hunted for this house, looking at place after place along England's south coast. Yet whenever a deal was about to be completed on a building, the whole thing would fall through. In 2002, they received another word again about the house of bread. They widened their search, basically touring England.

After praying for guidance one night, Elizabeth fell asleep but was awakened some hours later by a vivid dream. In her dream, she was walking through a building made of a very distinctive colored stone. It also possessed an unusual and intricate series of stained glass windows picturing creation. She got up to write down these details, and again she drifted off to sleep. She woke shortly afterward as an inner voice said clearly to her, "Go to Monmouth, find the statue in the town square, go to the estate agent behind the statue, witness to Me, and tell them you have come to buy the House of Bread." After praying, she felt that it was indeed God who had spoken to her, confirming His earlier words to the group.

Elizabeth got in her car and traveled to Monmouth, a little town in southeast Wales, and looked for the statue. Finding it, she looked for the estate agent. It turned out that the estate agent was currently involved in the selling of a property called "The Old Bakery," which, when it was built in 1752, was originally called "The House of Bread." When she viewed the property, she found exactly what she had seen in her dream. The color of stonework was identical, as were the stained glass windows featuring creation. The move was completed shortly afterward, and the House of Bread became a major healing and renewal center.

This dream is an example of a prophetic dream given by God. Prophetic dreams are but one type of dream, and their definition, according to Paula Price's extensive resource, could be given as follows: "dreams where the dreamer is told or shown something while asleep that pertains to or affects his or her waking sphere of life . . . Initially cryptic, the prophetic dream ends up being decidedly predictive or revelatory."[9]

A prophetic dream authored by God, however, could remain cryptic and its meaning be lost entirely to the dreamer if it is not interpreted correctly. We saw this in a number of examples in previous chapters. Pharaoh was at a complete loss as to interpretation of his dream, even though it was God who was speaking revelation to him. The situation required the interpretive gifts of Joseph and a further revelation by God, this time of the dream's meaning. At times, we may be in the same position. Unless we pray for the interpretation of a prophetic dream, its content and meaning will slip away.

In her book *Listening Prayer*,[10] Leanne Payne outlines a wide variety of means through which God chooses to speak to us in the current day. To name just some: the Bible; His still, small voice; other people; creation—and dreams. She describes God's dreams approach as something that enables us to receive messages that go beyond the limitations imposed by words: truths that are sweeping in scope or timeline and have to be conveyed through symbols and vivid imagery. These messages are sometimes about what is wrong within ourselves or others we are caring for, something God can heal when a true interpretation of the dreams is achieved as opposed to a false interpretation, which will either be too literal or too pagan.

In a later chapter, I have collected a number of case studies of leading Christians past and present, including Leanne Payne, whose ministries have been greatly influenced by dreams from God. These dreams have not been of a uniform type. At times, for instance in the case of Jackie Pullinger, the dream has had a clear and literal element. Jackie dreamed of Hong Kong, and in her case, Hong Kong simply meant Hong Kong. In other cases, such as the dream of John Newton, powerful and disturbing symbolism has been present. Dreams from God can have literal or symbolic content, or indeed, could contain direct verbal communication, such as the warning dreams given in the Old and New Testaments. As I say, God has not changed, and neither have we.

We have seen that dreams can come from within ourselves and are not necessarily direct communication from God. So if a dream *is* coming from God rather than from within ourselves, will it carry a distinctive with it, given its author? Will it have an authority to it and demand a response from us, a turning toward Him as we seek to understand the dream and obey the One who sent it? At times this will be the case. But there are potentially many dreams from God that appear at first remembrance to be "ordinary dreams," only to reveal their authorship when a right interpretation is given. If the correct interpretation also reveals a consistency between the dream and the revealed character of God in Scripture, then the dream, most likely, is from Him. Does the dream indicate a decision or outworking fully consistent with the God of the Bible?

In his commentary on dreams, Benny Thomas[11] rightly points to the wisdom in Proverbs that speaks of many advisers or counselors making victory sure. Listening to dreams and learning how to correctly interpret them establishes one of these potential sources of guidance. Thomas also emphasizes the potential of dreams to guide us at several different stages when it comes to an issue or problem. They can offer initial, interim, or final guidance. Initial guidance can inform us prophetically of a situation that will unfold for us many years in the future. Joseph's dreams as a teenager of rulership and authority are good examples of this. In the last scenario of final guidance, a dream can confirm a decision you have already come to by taking advice from some of your *other* advisers or counselors. For instance, in the next chapter, you will read about how the Midianite soldier's dream confirmed to Gideon that his course of action would meet with great success.

At the same time, a dream may cut across a decision you have reached through limited knowledge or understanding and recommend a U-turn. In either respect, if the dream comes from the God who is love, it is given in order to bless.

Of course, we do not *have* to listen to God in our dreams. As a loving Father, God will use whatever communication channels are open to Him. Within these, He will choose the most appropriate ones. When we are open to His speaking through dreams, we are choosing by our own free will an additional means for Him to speak to us.

CHAPTER 7

The Soldier's Dream

We now move forward in time about five hundred years, to the period of the judges ruling over the tribes of Israel. This era began after Joshua conquered much of the territory and ended with the rise of King Saul to rule over a unified kingdom. The book of Judges records that these judges exercised both judicial and military authority and details twelve in number, beginning with Othniel from the tribe of Judah and ending with Samson from the tribe of Dan.

Gideon, the subject of this chapter, is the fifth in number and came from the tribe of Manasseh. Two later judges, Eli and Samuel, are also recorded in the first book of Samuel, with the timeline running into King Saul's rule as well as King David's lifetime. Only six of the first twelve judges featured in the book of Judges are considered major, Gideon being one of them. Gideon's name means "destroyer"[1] or "mighty warrior," and he reigned as judge over the tribes of Israel for forty years.

Judges were not kings. Only one judge tended to rule at any one time, and there were sometimes breaks of many years in the continuation of rule. Judges arose as circumstances and crises required. There were different times of oppression when invading peoples conquered the tribes. A judge would arise to successfully rally the tribes against the occupying power. Gideon arose after a seven-year period when the Midianites, the Amalekites, and their allies had made annual raids throughout the tribes' land, sweeping in from the east to plunder it of its produce and animals. Their combined armies were simply too great in number for the Israelites to resist.

Although the dating of individuals and events is difficult during the judges' period, the following events probably occurred around 1194 BC.

The Very Reluctant Hero

As Gideon went about the daily labors of a man whose people were under siege, God appeared in person to him. Although God Himself is described initially as "the angel of the LORD," it is clear enough as the story progresses that this is not a created angel but a theophany of the eternal, preexisting Christ, that is to say, a manifestation of Jesus Christ, the second Person of the Trinity, before His incarnation. Although there is some debate about this, the majority of evangelical, conservative commentators agree that it is God Himself who makes contact with Gideon.[2] We take up the story at Judges 6.

> The angel of the LORD came and sat down under the oak in Ophrah that belonged to Joash the Abiezrite,[3] where his son Gideon was threshing wheat in a winepress to keep it from the Midianites. When the angel of the LORD appeared to Gideon, he said, "The LORD is with you, mighty warrior."
>
> "Pardon me, my lord," Gideon replied, "but if the LORD is with us, why has all this happened to us? Where are all his wonders that our ancestors told us about when they said, 'Did not the Lord bring us up out of Egypt?' But now the LORD has abandoned us and put us into the hand of Midian."
>
> The LORD turned to him and said, "Go in the strength you have and save Israel out of Midian's hand. Am I not sending you?"
>
> "Pardon me, my lord," Gideon replied, "but how can I save Israel? My clan is the weakest in Manasseh, and I am the least in my family."
>
> The LORD answered, "I will be with you, and you will strike down all the Midianites, leaving none alive." (Judges 6:11–16)

Gideon's initial response to God shows a man lacking in faith and courage. Then follows a series of events in which Gideon entreats God to show him signs that He is with him. Because of God's patience with him in fulfilling the signs, Gideon's courage begins to take hold. In the first of these, he asks permission to bring God an offering. God accedes to this. When Gideon returns with it, probably about an hour later, the angel of the LORD causes fire to flare up from the rock where the offering of meat and unleavened bread is placed by touching the rock with His staff. God then suddenly disappears.

Later that same night, God again speaks to Gideon, commanding him to tear down his father Joash's altar to Baal, chop down the Asherah pole beside it, sacrifice a bull from his father's herd as a burnt offering, and build an altar to God to replace his father's altar. God is specific about which bull he should kill and that Gideon is to use the chopped-up wood for the fire.

God starts to train Gideon for battle by assigning him a task at home: before facing an enemy army, he needs to defeat the occult shrine that has taken up residence inside his own estate, along with the demonic power behind it. Gideon accepts the command, and without asking for further signs from God at this point, he does all that is commanded with the help of ten servants. Gideon does it under cover of darkness because of his fear of his family and the townsfolk, but he does it and lives up to his name. His unprecedented and destructive act leads to a careful investigation, and after the people discover that Gideon is responsible, a hostile crowd demands his life. Yet his father Joash refuses to hand him over, saying that if Baal is a powerful god, surely Baal can deal with Gideon himself!

The next event we learn of is that the Midianite coalition has suddenly crossed the Jordan, invaded Israel's territory once more, and camped nearby in the Valley of Jezreel. The invasion army stands at more than 135,000 men.[4]

God empowers Gideon suddenly by "causing his Holy Spirit to fall on him," and this enables Gideon to blow a ram's horn shofar, a war trumpet, and send messengers throughout the northern tribes to assemble their men for battle. Jeff Lucas puts it like this: that the Holy Spirit's wisdom directed Gideon's actions, enabling him to do what God required, an experience similar to the Holy Spirit's energizing of the early church at Pentecost.[5]

Yet even now, Gideon still looks for further signs of God's favor! In a famous double request to God, he lays out a wool fleece on the threshing floor on two consecutive nights.[6] For the first night, he requests that the sign of God's favor will be that in the morning, there is dew only on the fleece with all the surrounding ground dry. In the morning, it is so, and Gideon examines the sign. He wrings out the dew from the fleece and gathers a bowlful of it. But he is still anxious. So he pleads permission to reverse the sign. When the morning comes around again, let the fleece be dry and all the surrounding ground be covered with dew. Again it is so when morning comes.

God's Counterintuitive Way of Battle

At this point in the story, Gideon had assembled an army of thirty-two thousand men, an impressive number but an army that would be hugely outnumbered by the invading force. The numbers just did not stack up for the battle. Many of his men were fearful. Very probably they were all ill-equipped, having been robbed by the Midianites time and time again of weaponry and material. They were also on foot, whereas the Midianite force was cavalry.[7] The Midianites and their allies were therefore mobile and adaptable, and their archers and spear throwers could shoot at Gideon's forces from high up on their camel mounts. The camels themselves were tall, heavy, and ideal as weapons of war, able to trample and disorientate Gideon's soldiers. With no battle experience whatsoever, who knows how Gideon would need to deploy and utilize his men to have any chance at all? Then God tells him that, in fact, he has far too many men.

> The LORD said to Gideon, "You have too many men. I cannot deliver Midian into their hands, or Israel would boast against me, 'My own strength has saved me.' Now announce to the army, 'Anyone who trembles with fear may turn back and leave Mount Gilead.'" So twenty-two thousand men left, while ten thousand remained.
>
> But the LORD said to Gideon, "There are still too many men. Take them down to the water, and I will thin them out

for you there. If I say, 'This one shall go with you,' he shall go; but if I say, 'This one shall not go with you,' he shall not go."

So Gideon took the men down to the water. There the LORD told him, "Separate those who lap the water with their tongues as a dog laps from those who kneel down to drink." Three hundred of them drank from cupped hands, lapping like dogs. All the rest got down on their knees to drink.

The LORD said to Gideon, "With the three hundred men that lapped I will save you and give the Midianites into your hands. Let all the others go home." So Gideon sent the rest of the Israelites home but kept the three hundred, who took over the provisions and trumpets of the others.

Now the camp of Midian lay below him in the valley. (Judges 7:2–8a)

The odds, which had been 4 to 1 against, had now become 450 to 1. The weapons they would use were strange indeed: each would need a trumpet, a jar, and a torch.

The Soldier's Dream and Interpretation

God then instructed Gideon to take his force and move down from the hills to approach the Midianite camp that night, because He was going to give the camp over to him. If he was fearful, he was to take his servant on ahead with him, go down into the camp, and listen to what the enemy troops were saying to each other. That would give him the encouragement he needed to launch the attack. The book of Judges gives the following account of what took place.

The Midianites, the Amalekites and all the other eastern peoples had settled in the valley, thick as locusts. Their camels could no more be counted than the sand on the seashore.

Gideon arrived [at a camp outpost] just as a man was telling a friend *his dream.* "I had a dream," he was saying. "A round loaf of barley bread came tumbling into the Midianite camp. It struck the tent with such force that the tent over-turned and collapsed."

His friend responded, "This can be nothing other than the sword of Gideon son of Joash, the Israelite. God has given the Midianites and the whole camp into his hands."

When *Gideon heard the dream and its interpretation,* he bowed down and worshiped. He returned to the camp of Israel and called out, "Get up! The Lord has given the Midianite camp into your hands." (Judges 7:12–15, emphasis mine)

The soldier who gave the quick interpretation was not unlocking a complicated symbolism. The dream's meaning was reasonably obvious. For a long time, the loaf of bread had symbolized Israel, a fact that no doubt greatly underwhelmed the surrounding peoples. They probably thought it was a prosaic and foolish symbol for a nation to use. In the dream, the loaf was a barley loaf. Only the poor ate bread made from barley, and this no doubt symbolized Gideon's peasant army and the oppressed, impoverished people from which it had been drawn.

Then there was the tent in the Midianite camp that the loaf rolled toward and demolished. The tent symbolized the camp itself, but it also symbolized the whole nomadic way of life of these raiders, even life itself. The tent symbolized the life of the army, and their life was going to be ended.

Again, just as we have seen in previous chapters, the dream as well as its interpretation were from God. Only this time, He had ensured that He gave it to just the right dreamer so that Gideon and his servant, crouching in the dark, could overhear. It was a dream of encouragement for Gideon, strengthening him to undertake what he might otherwise have been too fearful to do.

The Valley of Jezreel Battle

Gideon had been encouraged by the dream. Yet given the numbers, how could such a battle ever be won? Gideon divided his troops into three companies of one hundred and gave each soldier a ram's horn trumpet and a torch inside an empty jar. When they approached the enemy camp, they all had to do exactly what Gideon did. They surrounded the camp in the middle of the night with their torches hidden. Then they sounded their trumpets, shouted a war cry, and smashed the jars to reveal the torches, shouting, "A sword for the LORD and for Gideon!" The sudden, piercing shofar sounds, the shattering sound of smashed jars, the shouts and the sudden appearance of torchlight spread out all around, occurred just after the "start of the middle watch." That is to say, it happened when the new sentries had just been posted to the outposts. They were probably not fully awake yet, and their eyesight still had to acclimatize to the night conditions. Also, who was in charge if there was a sudden attack? Was it those who had just come on duty or those who had just retired?

When the clamor occurred, the blackness of night prevented any Midianite from seeing behind the surrounding fires and the noise. Their instant assumption was that they had been surprised by a massive force surrounding their camp, that their enemy was already *in* the camp, and that the battle had commenced. Blind panic broke out among them, and tens of thousands slaughtered each other with their swords, slashing around wildly as they barged into and collided with each other. Panicked, braying, charging camels would only add to the chaos sweeping through the camp.

The carnage would have gone on for hours. And all Gideon and his men had to do was stand and watch. They would then move forward to plunder the camp for abandoned weapons and start to pick off the terrified, retreating enemy from the rear as they sought to escape.

Of the combined force of 135,000 in the camp, 120,000 men were killed in the initial bloodbath, combined with the ongoing skirmishes with Gideon's wider forces, troops other than the three hundred who were activated by messengers sent quickly throughout the territory by Gideon. One skirmish followed another as the surviving Midianites retreated in a disorganized flight southeast toward the Jordan. The Midianite generals were killed. Just fifteen thousand of the original enemy force were able to escape east beyond the Jordan. Gideon's victory, God's victory of course, brought His people peace for forty years.

Conclusions

God spoke many times to Gideon during this account. He appeared directly before him and communicated with him face to face. He acceded to Gideon's many requests for signs. All this helped to shape Gideon as well as his fighting force. Gradually, a warrior emerged from all the preparation that he went through.

It is quite a journey of development to go from cowering in a winepress to destroying the family's pagan altar to marching into battle facing impossible odds, and with very few weapons of war, at least when it comes to swords, shields, and spears. Yet of all the interventions made by God, only one thing caused Gideon's fear to flee away entirely. That one thing was God's intervention with a strategically placed dream that He dropped into a Midianite soldier's sleeping mind. Not just any soldier, but one who happened to be sleeping at exactly the right location on the outskirts of the camp. God then inspired the soldier's comrade's accurate and alarming interpretation of it.

This type of dream is an encouragement dream. Usually it strengthens and encourages the dreamer; but in this case, it encouraged a listener. Perhaps it was because he heard it from the enemy. No doubt part of its dramatic effect on him was that it built on the many prior encounters Gideon had with God. Whatever the exact reason, the dream enabled him to take action he would otherwise have been too fearful to take. His faith was strengthened. All fear was dispelled. Gideon knew it was God who let him hear the dream. He knew it was God who has caused it to occur. He knew he would have a total victory before the night was over.

Did God use the same dream to cause the panic? It is likely that in the time it took for Gideon and his servant to return four miles or so in the dark to prepare and bring the war party to the camp and surround it, the sentries continued to talk among themselves. The only topic was their comrade's dream. The dream was passed from sentry to sentry, outpost to outpost, Midianite whispers late at night.

Perhaps in our own day, God will use a dream to show us a vision of the victory we are hoping for before it has even occurred and indeed, when the odds seem so greatly stacked against us. Our enemies can be within our own hearts, individuals close to us or farther afield, or they can be largely or completely unseen, spiritual forces encamped in the darkness and seeking our end. A dream can give us the courage and vision to press on with renewed faith, knowing that God will give us the victory.

Has God shared a dream or a vision with you about what He is going to bring to pass?

CHAPTER 8

False and Ungodly Dreams

We know that not all dreams come from God. Even the Bible tells us this. The dreams in Scripture we consider in this book were dreams given by God. Yet the Bible also includes many references to dreams that are not from God. There are many places in Scripture where warnings are given concerning dreams that are false, idolatrous, and ungodly in some way or other.

False Dreams and Dreamers

At least four books in Scripture refer to a serious category of false and ungodly dreams through which people are led astray toward their destruction. Often this is in the sense of an entire nation that is in danger of being deceived at a time of critical national danger. The key word here is *deception.*

The first book to warn of this is Deuteronomy, the fifth book of the Jewish Torah, which can be dated to about 1406 BC. The title of the book means "words" (*devarim* in Hebrew), as in spoken words. In a passage titled "Worshiping Other Gods" in the NIV translation, we read:

> If a prophet or one who foretells by dreams, appears among you and announces to you a miraculous sign or wonder, and if the sign or wonder of which he has spoken takes place, and he says, "Let us follow other gods," (gods you have not known) "and let us worship them," you must not listen to the words of that prophet or dreamer. The Lord your God is testing you to find out whether you love him with all your heart and with all your soul. It is the Lord your God you must follow, and him

you must revere. Keep his commands and obey him; serve him and hold fast to him. That prophet or dreamer must be put to death, because he has preached rebellion against the Lord your God, who brought you out of Egypt and redeemed you from the land of slavery; he has tried to turn you from the way the Lord your God commanded you to follow. You must purge the evil from among you. (Deuteronomy 13:1–5)

This category of false dreams promoted by false dreamers has to do with demonic deception. Humans are not capable by themselves of producing a false miraculous sign or wonder such as a dream that accurately foretells the future. If the dreamer is also advocating false gods or false religious practices such as shamanism or New Age mysticism, practices and beliefs which contradict Hebrew and Christian Scripture, the dream has to have originated with a fallen, disembodied spirit. The false dreamer has channeled the communication.

In our current era, sometimes an evil spirit masquerades as a spirit guide. Increasingly, and given the world's preoccupation with science fiction, these spirits also masquerade as benign aliens from another dimension or solar system. This falsehood merely fits into other widespread deceptions and false belief systems of the present age. The channeling of false revelation can also occur while the dreamer or medium has voluntarily entered into a trance or similar altered state of consciousness to establish contact with a deceiving evil spirit.[1]

Deuteronomy reveals that the main purpose of such false dreams is one of testing. God permits sources of supernatural evil to communicate with humanity for a time to test whether false dreamers and those they seek to influence will choose to seek and remain in fellowship with the one true God or whether they are eager to depart from the truth and believe lies instead. If they have opened themselves up to sources of supernatural evil, will they turn away from this activity, or will they continue to embrace it?

At the same time, God is angry with all such false dreamers who embrace evil and entice others to do the same. He does not want anyone to end up in a spiritual gutter.

In the present age of grace, there is no ongoing command to put false dreamers to death, but in the age of the law, such a command was given as one of a lengthy series of *mitzvot* (commands, injunctions, and laws) to preserve the Israelites' spiritual health and communion with God within the bad neighborhood that surrounded them, a sea of nations completely committed to idolatrous pagan superstition.

Dreamers Who Falsely Ascribe Their Dreams to God

A later book records the ministry and prophecies of the prophet Jeremiah, who preached from 627 BC to 586 BC. In three different chapters, he urges the southern kingdom of Judah not to listen to false dreams and false dreamers. In what follows, the prophet quotes directly from what he hears God say to him.

> "I have heard what the prophets say who prophesy lies in my name. They say, 'I had a dream! I had a dream!' How long will this continue in the hearts of these lying prophets, who prophesy the delusions of their own minds? They think the dreams they tell one another will make my people forget my name, just as their fathers forgot my name through Baal worship. Let the prophet who has a dream tell his dream, but let the one who has my word speak it faithfully. For what has straw to do with grain?" declares the LORD . . .
>
> "Indeed, I am against those who prophesy false dreams," declares the LORD. "They tell them and lead my people astray with their reckless lies, yet I did not send or appoint them." . . .
>
> So do not listen to your prophets, your diviners, your interpreters of dreams, your mediums or your sorcerers who tell you, 'You will not serve the king of Babylon.' They prophesy lies to you that will only serve to remove you far from your lands; I will banish you and you will perish. But if any nation will bow its neck under the yoke of the king of Babylon and serve him, I will let that nation remain in its own land to till it and to live there," declares the LORD. (Jeremiah 23:25–28, 32; 27:9–11)

This is a slightly different situation from the one proscribed in Deuteronomy. Here the false dreamers deceive the people in God's name; they falsely ascribe to God what God has not said. The deception is just as deadly. The false dreamers are encouraging the people to rebel against God's will for them. He has stated clearly through His true prophet that they must bow to Nebuchadnezzar because they have been so unfaithful to God. If they do this, they will be shown some mercy. But if they listen to the false hopes and dreams of sorcerers in their land, to those who are directly in touch with fallen evil spirits, their fate as rebels against Babylon will be much worse.

It is likely that in some cases, these lying prophets were merely pretending to have had a dream or revelation. They were simply using dreams as a device to flatter their rulers. In other cases, they probably had dreamed of successful rebellion against Nebuchadnezzar. But the dream was false; it arose out of their hearts' evil desires or from the nightly whispers of evil spirits. In any event, their false dreams flew in the face of what God had already said. Instead they said, no judgment has come, no calamity will occur. Just continue living as you are. We will see off this Nebuchadnezzar. But God had proclaimed the end of their kingdom.

When the Jews were exiled, their false dreamers were deported too and continued to deceive the people, causing the true prophet to say:

> Yes, this is what the Lord Almighty, the God of Israel, says:
> "Do not let the prophets and diviners among you deceive you.
> Do not listen to the dreams you encourage them to have. They
> are prophesying lies to you in my name. I have not sent them,"
> declares the Lord. (Jeremiah 29:8–9)

Joe Ibojie[2] points out that in Jeremiah's time, prophets were sometimes sent on dream and vision quests and were required to come back with something substantial to confirm that they were indeed prophets. The pressure of this could lead them into making rash proclamations in order to hold on to their title and office.

Another Jewish prophet, Zechariah, gave a very similar warning to Jeremiah's, though he was preaching after the Jewish captivity in Babylon, as the people were returning to Jerusalem. Much of his teaching from around 520 BC to 516 BC is apocalyptic and Messianic. He prophesied Christ's humanity, His betrayal for thirty pieces of silver, His crucifixion, and His rule over and judgment of the nations. He says, "The idols speak deceit, diviners see visions that lie; they tell dreams that are false, they give comfort in vain. Therefore the people wander like sheep oppressed for lack of a shepherd" (Zechariah 10:2).

Again we have false dreamers in view here: those who consult the *teraphim* or household gods in occult divination of the future. They could only offer false comfort, since anything good they promised as a result of dreams and visions would come to nothing.

Although false dreamers and their lies were still something of a problem after the Israelites' exile in Babylon, it does seem that over the next several hundred years, the Jewish people did turn their backs on the types of false gods and occult practices to which Zechariah was referring. He had prophesied that this would occur as well, that the idols would be banished from the land (see Zechariah 13:2).

It is also worth mentioning the phrase used by Jude, the author of the Bible's penultimate book and one of Jesus' half-brothers (Jude's parents were Joseph and Mary[3]). In his short but incisive book, Jude also speaks against the type of false prophets spoken against by Jeremiah hundreds of years earlier, but this time, he speaks against those who have now infiltrated the early church. These "dreamers" have false words for the church. They claim that their words are inspired and from God, but they are misrepresenting Him. In reality, they are rejecting God and the apostles and teachers who have genuine gifts and authority. It seems that the added danger in this situation was that the ordinary people were undiscerning and just did not notice: "In the very same way, on the strength of their dreams these ungodly people pollute their own bodies, reject authority and heap abuse on celestial beings" (Jude 1:8).

Examples of False Dreams Today

That is the history. What would be the parallels today? Many parallels exist at a national level, but in our globalized, twenty-first-century world, the majority of nations can be enthralled by false dreams and dreamers within six months of the release of a film or book. Surprisingly often, contemporary horror writers report that their inspiration arose when they were asleep. Stephanie Meyer, for instance, told Oprah Winfrey in 2009 that her fiction was triggered by a dream sequence about a vampire boy and a girl meeting in a beautiful meadow.[4] Similar acknowledgments to dreams have been made by Stephen King for a number of his novels, as well as Charlee Jacob and others. Modern media can easily take an individual writer's ungodly subconscious fantasies, provide a multimillion-dollar budget, and portray the fantasy for hundreds of millions of people to see on the cinema screen. Spin-off industries, aimed particularly at children, then continue to market the fantasies to perpetuate their longevity further. The money has to be recouped. A handsome profit must be achieved.

Having said that, not all modern-day fantasies are ungodly. Children's stories by, among others, C.S. Lewis and Elizabeth Goudge have been well-portrayed in recent film adaptations that help point people toward Christian reality. They portray with some accuracy a correct differentiation between good and evil, and in this case modern media can perpetuate truth.

In contrast though, and just for example, "paranormal romance" is a recently invented genre encompassing the current flood of vampire-related movies streaming out of Hollywood. This movie and literary subgenre fuses horror and romance and is a modern media phenomenon featuring human romances with vampires, werewolves, and various demonic hybrids, including demonic dead or half-dead creatures. The lead occult character, often a vampire, is sometimes portrayed as heroic in some way. Yet the demonic reality this misrepresents is completely the opposite. No disembodied occult entity can be heroic in any way; their focus on and desires for humanity are wholly evil, and they are all destined to be thrown into hell. The fires of hell are being stoked up for them, and no evil spirits will escape (see Matthew 13:41–42; 25:41).[5]

The producers of this kind of sinister and degenerate fiction pander to the millions who long for an erotic encounter with the demonic or to indulge in some other sort of indiscriminate sensual pleasure. These works, involving books, movies, and computer games, constitute just one cluster of modern-day dark dreams, and they speak also of an occult and demonic reality that inspires them.

Although the "other gods" spoken against by Moses were insensate, useless idols of stone and wood, there was nevertheless an unseen reality inspiring them, and they too were worshiped: evil spirits who sought humanity's destruction and who demanded sacrifice and death, sometimes on an epic scale. In the present day, the images and symbols are given movement and apparent life through film, and they too speak of an unseen reality, of evil spirits who are forever separated from God and who seek to drag as much of humanity down with them as possible.

Often in such movies, there is also the unleashing of carnage on an epic scale in a sort of vicarious replay of the real-world ritualized slaughter of old. Many modern-day writers and producers have made their fortunes on such topics, and perhaps to them, it was only ever about the money, cashing in on the trend. But it is not really about the money—there are human souls and eternities at stake.

We need to flee from such dark and morbid preoccupations as well as from all other types of horror and evil. We have to both walk in God's light *and* flee from evil. As Paul, speaking of the light who is Christ, said:

> And do this, understanding the present time: The hour has already come for you to wake up from your slumber, because our salvation is nearer now than when we first believed. The night is nearly over; the day is almost here. So let us put aside the deeds of darkness and put on the armor of light. Let us behave decently, as in the daytime, not in carousing and drunkenness, not in sexual immorality and debauchery, not in dissension and jealousy. Rather, clothe yourselves with the

> Lord Jesus Christ, and do not think about how to gratify the
> desires of the flesh. (Romans 13:11–14)

Today there are other types of false dreams and visions. These have to do with the real and material world as opposed to fiction and the movie screen. Just as with the biblical situations previously described, they will always deceive and lead people further away from God. Modern media plays a part in this. Sometimes it attests to what seems demonstrably to be true—that is, it is not fiction. For example, from time to time there is a documentary on television that considers scientific evidence for the bizarre; that, for instance, weeping icons in a church in Brooklyn really have oozed oil. Likewise, in the former Yugoslavia, now Bosnia, about forty-five thousand people in the small village of Medjugorje all apparently witnessed the sun spin like a disk in the sky before careening earthward in a zigzag trajectory on October 13, 1917. Wet clothes hanging on clotheslines and balconies were dried instantly.

Christ prophesied that in the end times, there would be great deception. Some of this will be caused by delusion: people thinking they saw what they did not actually see. Medjugorje basically fits this category of false vision. The sun did not in reality spin or careen earthward. Scientists are absolutely agreed on that. Thousands of people merely witnessed an impressive but localized illusion, a lying vision. Yet sometimes the false miraculous will, in fact, occur alongside the illusions. Were wet clothes instantly dried? If so, or if an icon really does weep oil from time to time in Brooklyn, it is a false sign designed to obscure the true God and His desire for repentance and salvation in Christ. The God of the Bible would not be behind such signs and wonders, just as He would not be behind spoon bending.

We live in a time when illusions, cults, and false religions abound. The increasing frequency of illusions and their perpetrators in our day may well indicate that the time spoken of by Christ is already with us. "For false messiahs and false prophets will appear and perform great signs and wonders to deceive, if possible, even the elect. See, I have told you ahead of time" (Matthew 24:24–25).

Along with illusions, there has been a sharp increase in the number of false christs, people actually claiming explicitly to be Christ, who have often gone down in flames and taken large numbers of their followers with them. High school dropout David Koresh, aka Vernon Wayne Howell, and his Branch Davidians—a group somehow utterly deceived by Howell's extreme and self-serving pseudo-theological agenda—are typical. Other types of false prophets not claiming specifically to be Christ have also abounded, often birthing movements and false religions that have grown rapidly and internationally within the past 150 years—far too many in number to list. Yet, by and large, we have not seen such people perform great false signs and miracles. That is still to come.

Insubstantial, Meaningless Fantasies

Other books in Scripture focus from time to time on a lesser category of ungodly dreams that we could term *insubstantial fantasies*. An extensive piece of writing about dreams (among other things) appears in Ecclesiastes, a book possibly written by King Solomon toward the very end of his reign, though there is some dispute about both authorship and date.[6] Much of the book delineates the limits of humankind and what men and women are capable of, including the limits of those who believe in God and have a measure of godly wisdom.

To accept God and humankind's true position in the scheme of things is to live carefully and accept one's limitations with equanimity, enjoying the good that life provides. All too often, though, humankind pursues vain, godless ambitions and hopes that are meaningless. These pursuits are a "chasing after the wind; nothing was gained under the sun" (Ecclesiastes 2:11b). This applies ultimately to those who do not trust in God. By not trusting in Him, people seek to trust instead in what is false and meaningless.

But Ecclesiastes also concludes by asserting that there is a final meaning that humankind cannot escape: "For God will bring every deed into judgment, including every hidden thing, whether it is good or evil" (Ecclesiastes 12:14).

In quite a well-known section the author says the following:

> Do not be quick with your mouth, do not be hasty in your
> heart to utter anything before God. God is in heaven and you
> are on earth, so let your words be few. A dream comes when
> there are many cares, and many words mark the speech of a
> fool. When you make a vow to God, do not delay to fulfill it.
> He has no pleasure in fools; fulfill your vow . . . Much dream-
> ing and many words are meaningless. Therefore fear God.
> (Ecclesiastes 5:2–4, 7)

Here a comparison is being made between two things. First there
are "fools," who use many words rashly and without care or thought in
a religious setting, church perhaps. Their words stream out, and they go
beyond any intention of fulfillment. These people are babblers unaware
of the nature of the God they are supposedly addressing. Paralleled with
this, there are dreams that are daydreams: idle, unreal fantasies that can
occur when we are awake but our thoughts are wandering. Some of these
can be very troubling. They are rooted in and caused by excess work,
stress, and care, which overload one's heart and mind.

Foolish chatterers are not false dreamers in the sense that they are
deliberately seeking to lead others astray, nor are they seeking to worship
false gods. But their pious chatter is still false. It is like the chatter of troubling dreams. These people are not at peace with themselves or with God.
Their torrents of words spill out wherever they happen to be, whether it
is at home, work, or church; but in church, it is not God whom they are
truly addressing. There is a meaninglessness to their worship. It is foolish,
and as the author says, God has no pleasure in fools!

A passage about insubstantial fantasies appears in Isaiah, where the
prophet prophesies:

> Then the hordes of all the nations that fight against Ariel, that
> attack her and her fortress and besiege her, will be as it is with
> a dream, with a vision in the night—as when a hungry man
> dreams of eating, but awakens hungry still; as when a thirsty

person dreams of drinking, but awakens faint and thirsty still.
So will it be with the hordes of all the nations that fight against
Mount Zion. (Isaiah 29:7–8)

This message to Israel is about God dispersing the enemies who rise up to attack them. *Ariel,* a reference to Jerusalem, means a religious altar-hearth, the place of God's ever-burning fire and wrath.[7] Although the enemy armies appear at first to have complete victory, they will be swept away by God's intervention. Thus their victory is an insubstantial fantasy. It departs as swiftly as a dream, and in its own way, it is a false dream: it has nothing to do with reality. God intervenes to disappoint the enemy hordes just as a hungry or thirsty person dreams of what he longs for but finds the fulfillment of his wish is empty. He awakes hungrier or thirstier than before he fell asleep.

Isaiah's prophecy may concern a number of attacks on Jerusalem rather than a single event. Assyria's attack on Jerusalem occurred in 701 BC and resulted in the death of 185,000 besieging Assyrian troops, killed supernaturally by the angel of the Lord (see Isaiah 37:36–37). It is this event that certainly best fits the sudden reversal of fortunes the prophet has in mind. But could the prophecy also concern Nebuchadnezzar's successful siege of the city in 586 BC, with God's wrath now falling directly on the city whose people had rebelled against Him for so long? Is Nebuchadnezzar's torching of the city what the prophet had in view when he used the unusual term *Ariel?*

The prophecy also seems to be one of the many biblical prophecies that pans forward to the end of days. It has partial fulfillments in the not-too-distant future from the time of the prophet, but it also looks ahead to the culmination of God's dealings with Jerusalem, His people, and the surrounding nations. As Barry Webb points out, it "presents the long view of God's plan for Zion."[8] It is this long view that the later prophet Zechariah picks up on, many years after the above attacks.

I will gather all the nations to Jerusalem to fight against it . . .
Then the LORD will go out and fight against those nations, as
he fights on a day of battle. On that day his feet will stand on

the Mount of Olives, east of Jerusalem . . . The Lord will be king over the whole earth. On that day there will be one Lord, and his name the only name." (Zechariah 14:2–4, 9)

The Lord will then, as Brian Papworth reminds us,[9] enter Jerusalem once more by the Eastern Gate, which faces the Mount of Olives, a gate He often passed through when He was last on earth.

So we return to the nations' false dreams of conquest, to *all* the nations with their destructive intentions, and to the sudden sweeping away of their armies when Christ returns to earth. The death of 185,000 Assyrians is itself prophetic of the far greater plague with which God will strike the surrounding nations in an event yet to occur. Their soldiers' eyes will rot in their sockets, and their flesh will rot while they are still standing up (see Zechariah 14:12–15). Modern readers may wonder: does this prophesy the results of thermonuclear war occurring in the vicinity of Jerusalem?

Soulish Dreams

A number of Isaiah's prophecies use false dreams as metaphors for illusory achievements. The type of false dreams portrayed in such prophecy is the soulish dream. Each such dream arises out of the body's or soul's cravings and has no meaning beyond these cravings. For instance, we may dream we are marrying someone we are greatly attracted to, yet it does not come to pass. We may somehow feel that our dream gives our longings some additional, even supernatural validation, and we may intensify our pursuit of the person of desire. But they marry someone else. Not only that, but the dream provided false comfort at the time and possibly also led to a lot of useless wasting of energy in the pursuit of something that was never going to come about. There was nothing supernatural about that dream. The body or the soul was merely expressing itself in dreams. One's heart was creating pictures out of the overflow of desires it was aware of. Such dreams have nothing to do with what should be, could be, or will be.

Dreams can also be influenced by the body and what is going on in it. They can be affected by injury or illness as well as by medication taken for an illness. Some medications, such as antidepressants, can radically alter one's dreaming in terms of frequency and intensity of recalled dreams. Soulish dreams can also arise out of overwork and exhaustion, as the writer of Ecclesiastes said. The mind cannot settle at night. It is overburdened or overstimulated and "just keeps going" all night. These kinds of dreams are not necessarily false dreams in the sense of deception brought about by evil spirits, but they still fall within the context of soulish dreams. They are dream events triggered and determined by physical and chemical variables such as tiredness or stress. They are therefore largely meaningless. They can also be misinterpreted.

Dreams also appear in a number of other books in Scripture as negative metaphors. One of Job's "friends," Zophar, says of the wicked whose pride may reach up to heaven for the briefest of moments: "Like a dream he flies away, no more to be found, banished like a vision of the night" (Job 20:8). In a very similar passage, the psalmist says of the ungodly whose scoffing and wealth seem always just to increase, "They are like a dream when one awakes; when you arise, Lord, you will despise them as fantasies" (Psalm 73:20). Here the prosperity of the wicked is characterized as illusory. Their very lives are insubstantial and not built on solid ground. Like soulish dreams, they are but shadowy fantasies, not grounded in reality.

Conclusions

The frequent warnings in Scripture regarding false prophets and dreamers are not given to those people themselves. It is assumed that false dreamers are very unlikely to change and seek to know the truth. They would first need to humble themselves. They would need to cast the false dreams aside. All too often, they have invested their whole lives in a false reality. They would need to drop it all in order to start again—from scratch. Rather, God is warning His people at large, and anyone else who might listen: you will be, or you already are, living in perilous times when false dreamers abound. Their works will either be characterized by the false miraculous, miracles presented alongside a call to worship other gods, or by fantasies and illusions, deceptions designed to misrepresent God and to blind people as they walk unknowingly toward their destruction.

We are currently living in such a time. The warnings again are given to the people at large rather than to the false christs and other false teachers who are, it has to be said, very unlikely to repent. In the main, they have already deluded themselves. They themselves live on the inside of their false dream, a false and destructive human aspiration or fantasy. They have woven themselves into it, and now they are eager to draw in a following. They want the attention and affirmation, even the worship of others. They want others to bolster up the dream, and, of course, they want their money too. In fact, there is a tendency for them to become greedy for money since there can be no genuine, deep-rooted security in a life built on lies.

Any dream or vision, and any revealed "secret" that contradicts God's revealed will and character in Scripture, is not from God and must be rejected. Such dreams or revelations are not underpinned by reality but by illusion, falsehood, and deception. While some false dreams are characterized simply by their meaninglessness, others will in due time be revealed as evil and inspired by evil. Either way, all false dreams and the works they inspire will be revealed for what they are and will be burned up by fire[10] when God judges all things.

Yet God *is* a revealer of secrets by His Spirit, and sometimes He may choose to do this through a dream for His perfect purposes and glory. Jesus Christ is the chief cornerstone, the foundation stone of a living temple, and God's chosen people are its living stones. We are required to build on the right foundation, on Christ Himself and His life and revelation, including godly dreams, which flow directly from Him by His Spirit living within us.

We must exercise discernment and test the spirits. Are we hearing from God, from the enemy clothed in false light, or from our own unconscious? What is the spirit of what is being said to us? The current New Age cults and teachers do not exalt Christ, even if they mention

Him. They do not portray Him as uniquely God and man or as savior of humankind. He is viewed as one of many who are happy to help humankind evolve to a higher consciousness. But this is a lie. To quote Paul in his correspondence with Timothy: "For there is one God and one mediator between God and mankind, the man Christ Jesus, who gave himself as a ransom for all people" (1 Timothy 2:5–6).

To turn people away from this truth is as serious an error as it is possible to make. In leading people astray from Christ, false prophets are coming under Christ's stern warning recorded in Mark's gospel: "If anyone causes one of these little ones—those who believe in me—to stumble, it would be better for them if a large millstone were hung around their neck and they were thrown into the sea" (Mark 9:42).

PART II

SYMBOLISM AND TYPES
OF DREAMS

CHAPTER 9

The Intuitive and Symbolic Language of Dreams

The language of dreams is quite unlike the mind's rational language because of where dreams come from within a person. Most rise up from the heart, the hidden depths within ourselves. Our heart speaks to us, sharing its concerns with us but using its own language of symbols and pictures to communicate its concerns to our mind.

In other cases, dreams originate with God rather than with the heart; we have seen that in numerous biblical examples. But in these cases, the message is still often presented in symbolic ways, because it is the heart that is receiving the dream message, not the wakened, conscious intellect. The heart perceives and knows in a different way than the rational way. It intuits psychological, emotional, and spiritual truth. If we ignore intuitive and symbolic ways of knowing, if we ignore our dreams, we are at best partially sighted.

The symbolic language of dreams is both universal and personal. It is universal in that some dream symbols can be common to all humanity or to the dreamer's society; within a particular culture, the symbol means a particular thing. But whatever the culture surrounding the dreamer, his or her emotions and thoughts can be communicated and experienced in dreams as if they were actual events within the real and sensory world. This is something that some psychodynamic therapists are realizing when they, for instance, pick up on a wide variety of people in a society all dreaming in similar ways about the same kinds of events they encountered. This is especially clear with major traumatic events. In the case of the September 11, 2001, bombings of the Twin Towers in New York, which affected thousands of people who *survived* the attacks, many victims who were unknown to each other dreamed subsequently of being overwhelmed by a tidal wave. Ernest Hartmann, professor of psychiatry at Tufts University School of Medicine, investigated this phenomenon. He argued that this type of dream and the imagery in it may be symbolic of the emotional intensity or trauma experienced by the dreamer both during and after such a devastating and unexpected event. The imagery may also symbolize the emotional aftermath of a personal and traumatic life event such as an accident or bereavement. The symbolic associations in such dreams need to be understood as formed by the heart as it uses a natural and a cultural, sometimes universal, human symbolic language.

At the same time, though, the symbols in some dreams can have a much more personal meaning defined by the context. Whether a symbol such as a cat, a tree, or a doll symbolizes something benign or malign will depend on how the symbol appears within the overall dream as well as the dreamer's life experience with cats, trees, or dolls and what the dreamer associates intuitively at a deep level with such symbols.

When someone or something appears in a dream, they or it tend to be symbolic. Actions in dreams also tend to be symbols. Sometimes the dream *is* about your brother or sister, your job or your house. But much more often than not, the person or object symbolizes something else entirely. Dreams tend to use situations, people, and things we are readily familiar with to talk to us about other things, often aspects of ourselves that are normally hidden away from our awareness.

God will often use dreams to talk to us about spiritual things. John and Paula Sandford assert that God does this because there is minimal to no interference from the dreamer's own mind *and* to stir us, through indirect communication, into seeking and discovering the truths He wants us to understand. Yet just as the people often could not understand Christ's parables when He taught them spiritual truths in symbolic terms, we often misinterpret the symbolism of dreams. We tend to interpret them literally. But most dreams are not meant to be interpreted in this way! When in any doubt about a dream's interpretation, the default position needs to be a symbolic meaning rather than a literal one.

Most dreams recorded in Scripture required interpretation of their symbolic language. Pharaoh, the cupbearer, and the baker simply could not interpret their own dreams, causing Joseph to say, "Do not interpretations belong to God? Tell me your dreams" (Genesis 40:8). Only a few dreams in Scripture are literal, for example Jacob's dream in Haran or the warning and guidance dreams given by the angel to Joseph in Palestine and Egypt in Matthew's gospel. Such dreams contain literal messages of revelation, warning, or guidance.

Dreams can sometimes contain some literal elements as well as some symbolic elements. An individual such as a colleague or family member might appear as themselves, while other colleagues or family members might be symbolized as other people or even as animals or objects. Similarly, your car or your workplace might appear as they really are in life and not as symbols for anything else. The dream is really about your car or your workplace. Sometimes an entire dream is literal, as Abimelek's dream was when God accused him of taking Abraham's wife and said he was as good as dead.

However, the majority of dreams use symbols only. These can seem so real that our tendency is to take them literally. We simply use our own understanding to interpret them, and it falls short.[1] We should always take such dreams before God and ask Him for revelation as to their symbolic meaning. What are You saying to me? What is my own heart saying to me? We also need the involvement of others who are likewise open to God. A true interpretation revealed by God will usually be received with relief. The dreamer's heart already knows the truth. The interpretation needs to strike a chord with knowledge already present but held at a subconscious level deep within.

Pharaoh's dream is a prime example. The seven fat cows and the seven gaunt cows appeared vividly to him, but the dream was not about cows. Each cow symbolized a year, and God had to reveal this. When God gave the interpretation to Pharaoh, he accepted it at once. Although Pharaoh's heart communicated the dream to his sleeping mind, the dream had not originated within his heart; it had originated with God. The dream was God's revelation to Pharaoh. But Joseph's interpretation still struck a chord with the message as it had been received within the ruler's heart.

Many books about dreams are little more than lists of symbols on one side and standard interpretations of them on the other. Some of these books, such as Ira Milligan's *Understanding the Dreams You Dream* and Thompson and Beale's *The Divinity Code* with its extensive dream symbols dictionary, can be helpful at times, but they are never helpful all the time. The meaning of some of the symbols in your dreams will not fall within standard definitions, and as Jim Driscoll and Zach Mapes point out,[2] the same dream symbol featured several times in one person's dreams could have a different meaning each time depending on the context and how prominently it is featured.

Dream dictionary definitions of symbols all depend on the world-view of the author and the relative level of insight they have gained. A book that lists dream interpretations may be helpful at times, but only as long as you read the possible interpretations as guidelines at best and not as locked-in definitions. These guidelines do not replace in any way the seeking-and-finding approach that you as the dreamer need to embark on and commit yourself to. Some of the dream language may be unique to you; it may be unique to your life experience.

For instance, suppose two people dream of the same type of dog approaching them. Does this mean they have had the same dream? Not at all. A lot would depend on these dreamers' perceptions and experiences, if any, of this type of dog. One dreamer may have bred this dog in the past, showed it at dog shows, and had a great affinity with it. Another dreamer could have been bitten by one as a child. In the former case, the dog could symbolize loyalty or something of quality. In the latter's case, it could symbolize something that was a psychological, spiritual, or physical threat currently in or about to enter the dreamer's life.

No book on dreams will be able to interpret your dream's symbols in a way that accounts for the context of your life, and neither can it replace God's guidance if you take your dream before Him. Furthermore, it could be that in the former case, the dreamer is having a symbolic dream, the more common type, while in the latter case, they are having a literal dream. They are really dreaming about the dog. They could in fact not be dreaming at all per se. Although it is a relatively uncommon experience, some dreams are repressed memories rising up from the unconscious into awareness.

Interpreting the Language of Dreams

The key task is to interpret the language of dreams from the symbolic to what the symbolic represents and communicates. What do the dream symbols and events signify, and what is the message? As Daniel said to the king, "Your Majesty, you are that tree!"[3]

If we are in a situation where our help is sought in an interpretation, we must take the greatest care. Chuck Pierce and Rebecca Sytsema put it well when they say, "we should not impose our interpretation of symbols if it does not bear witness with the dreamer."[4] In other words, if the interpretation does not strike a chord with the dreamer's own heart, the likelihood is that the interpretation is wrong. We may, like an analytical psychologist, be in the situation where we offer a number of possible interpretations to the same dream and see which strikes the chord of truthfulness in the heart of the dreamer.

At times, the correct interpretation of a dream's symbol will relate that symbol to humanity's universal symbolic language. At other times, it will relate the meaning to a shared cultural understanding: the cultural symbols, metaphors, and aphorisms shared by the dreamer and millions of others from his or her culture. In many other cases, the correct understanding will only be reached when the dreamer's life context is considered; the meaning lies in the events, circumstances, and memories in the dreamer's experience.

Still at other times, as Ira Milligan[5] points out, the answer will actually lie in the Bible. The God who sent dreams in the past has not changed. How has God used symbols already in Scripture? If it is God who is alerting your spirit through a dream to a truth you need to hear, and the dream is symbolic, you need to be aware of how He has already used symbols such as animals, trees, crops, and numbers in His Word— in dreams, parables, visions, and other types of revelation. His communication through Scripture needs to be part of our perspective for accurate dream interpretation.

Interpretations through Listening Prayer

Benny Thomas provides some practical and helpful advice when it comes to interpreting dreams. He says we should break them up into manageable chunks or elements. Just as we deal with complex tasks by breaking them down into simpler ones, we need to separate a dream's symbolic content into individual symbols or parts. If the dream provides a sequence of scenes or acts, the changes in scenery or environment should make it obvious as to which sections to separate out. Then we can divide each section into separate symbols. If the dream is simpler and contains just one scene, just divide that into individual symbols. As we understand each of the pieces, the full meaning of the dream will unfold.[6]

It is important to ask God what each of the symbols means, and to do this, we need to get into listening mode. In Scripture, prophets and disciples alike would receive revelation when they had first settled into prayer and away from daily life with its often innumerable priorities or burdens. This focusing on God is a focusing up and out to God rather than a focusing into self and on self. While God indwells believers by His Spirit, He is also other than us. Prayer is not an emptying of ourselves, however. There are significant dangers attached to meditative practices that utilize breath prayers and other mystical techniques.[7]

Focusing on God is the opposite of focusing on a single word or mantra or on a natural process such as breathing, since we are focusing on a Being far greater than us. We are focusing on the unseen real, on God as the ultimate reality. This activity is sometimes referred to as listening prayer[8] or as getting into the Spirit. For instance, the disciple John while in exile on Patmos said, "On the Lord's day, I was in the Spirit, and I heard behind me a loud voice like a trumpet . . ."[9] He was in the Spirit *first* and then clearly heard Christ's voice.

God is likely to speak to us about our dream's symbolic content in a still, small voice or simply give us revelation, and we therefore need to be quiet and still in order to hear this. His voice may be so quiet that after we receive an impression or a surprising thought, we ask, "Is that You, God? Are You speaking to my heart?"

Conscious Reflection and Personal Events

Another way to seek insights and interpretations is to consciously reflect on the dream's content, again by first breaking it down into the different symbolic elements. Even if you are completely perplexed by a dream, pondering it for a while may well bring revelation. Daniel was perplexed for a time by Nebuchadnezzar's dream of a tree; the King James Version translates his response as being "astonished for one hour."[10] But then a complete revelation of the dream's meaning was given to him. This could happen to us, or our dream's meaning could gradually unfold as part after part becomes clear to us. You could ask yourself questions such as, what could this symbol mean, what do I associate with it, and why is it in the dream?

Meanings for dream symbols can usually be found through relating them to what has just happened in your life. What happened just before or during the days or weeks leading up to the dream? Mennonite pastor and expert on dream interpretation Herman Riffel goes as far as to say that the dreamer's past and present serves as the setting for every dream he or she has. No interpretation should be arrived at without bearing this context in mind.

Another key, however, is what then occurs in the days and weeks *after* the dream has occurred. What is on the dreamer's conscious horizon? Placing the dream against the dreamer's past-present-immediate future life context can really help to make its meaning clear, enabling you to discern which aspect of life the dream relates to. Riffel makes the point that the scope of one's dreams usually relates closely to the scope of life. If you are a world ruler such as Pharaoh or Nebuchadnezzar, you may well dream of the rise and fall of nations. If you are a typical citizen, the scope of your dreams will probably reflect that status. Your dreams symbolize your experiences, the extent of your world.

We also need to reflect on how we felt in the dream. Accurately recalling different feelings we had while dreaming may allow us to avoid a lot of misinterpretation of the dream's symbols. An emotion we experienced while dreaming can act as a bridge to the life event or situation the dream was about. In terms of what has recently happened or what is currently happening in our lives, when have we felt what we felt in the dream? Who or what is associated with these feelings during our waking lives?

Further, the feelings could relate to events and the feelings they caused longer ago, for example in childhood. The dream could be about a childhood event or longer term situation that still has not been resolved. The event could be holding us back in some way, and the dream could therefore be pushing us toward refocusing on it in order to work through it and move forward.

Thankfully, we do not need to undertake all this alone. As we reflect on our dreams, we can approach God both for insight and revelation, and then, with the revelation and clarity we arrive at, He can help us not just with the unveiling of what our dreams are saying to us but also in moving forward in response to our dreams.

CHAPTER 10

Wisdom and Warning Dreams

King Solomon was the third and last ruler of united Israel during biblical times. He was born in Jerusalem about 991 BC. He ascended the throne after his father, King David, died in about 970 BC, and he reigned for forty years. His mother was Bathsheba, and he was the couple's second son. His reign was completely unlike that of Saul and of his father David in that it was characterized by peace.

During Solomon's reign, Israel became a regional superpower stretching from its border with Egypt to the Euphrates River; it entered something of a golden age. It was a time of commercial prosperity, architectural and artistic activity, and great accumulation of wealth. In one of his references to Solomon, for instance, Christ compares the lilies of the field to "Solomon in all his splendor."[1] Yet after Solomon's death, the kingdom experienced rebellion and was quickly divided, also losing its various vassal territories and peoples. The Bible recounts that this was because of the sins the king committed during his reign and particularly because Solomon turned away from God to follow after false gods, despite the fact that God had appeared to him twice.[2]

Yet Solomon was also renowned for his many displays of outstanding wisdom, an attribute that takes us to a dream the king had and a request he made to God. In response to his request to God, he was given such unique and incisive wisdom that "the whole world sought audience with Solomon" in order to hear it (1 Kings 10:24). The queen of Sheba was but one of many who sought out his wisdom and justice. Those who sought it would meet with Solomon in a magnificent building covered in cedar from floor to ceiling, variously known as the Hall of Justice or the Throne Hall, which stood in front of his royal palace.[3]

Solomon's Dream at Gibeon

The following is the account of Solomon's initial dream and his conversation with God within it. The dream occurred early on in Solomon's reign during his visit to the ceremonial worship center at Gibeon and immediately after he sacrificed one thousand burnt offerings there.

> At Gibeon the Lord appeared to Solomon during the night in a dream, and God said, "Ask for whatever you want me to give you."
>
> Solomon answered, "You have shown great kindness to your servant, my father David, because he was faithful to you and righteous and upright in heart. You have continued this great kindness to him and have given him a son to sit on his throne this very day. Now, Lord my God, you have made your servant king in place of my father David. But I am only a little child and do not know how to carry out my duties. Your servant is here among the people you have chosen, a great people, too numerous to count or number. So give your servant a discerning heart to govern your people and to distinguish between right and wrong. For who is able to govern this great people of yours?"
>
> The Lord was pleased that Solomon had asked for this. So God said to him, "Since you have asked for this and not for long life or wealth for yourself, nor have asked for the death of your enemies but for discernment in administering justice, I will do what you have asked. I will give you a wise and discerning heart, so that there will never have been anyone like you, nor will there ever be. Moreover, I will give you what you have not asked for—both wealth and honor—so that in your lifetime you will have no equal among kings. And if you walk in obedience to me and keep my decrees and commands as David your father did, I will give you a long life." Then Solomon awoke—and he realized *it had been a dream*. (1 Kings 3:5–15, emphasis mine)

Interpreting the Dream

In this case, the dream is a highly literal one—a conversation between Solomon and God. The dream reveals that Solomon thinks of himself as a child unequal to the mantle and the role he has been handed by his father. He feels the task is too great for him and he is too young for it. This would be a substantial burden in itself. But if we briefly consider the wider context for the young king, we realize that the burden may have been scarcely bearable at all. Solomon had recently had to deal with two different forms of coup d'état, both caused by his older half-brother Adonijah; after the second attempt, he had Adonijah executed along with two coconspirators. Moreover, Solomon had just married Pharaoh's daughter and was building a palace for her. He was also concerned about the completion of the temple complex in Jerusalem, a project he had been commissioned by his father to undertake.

At the same time, Solomon's approach to this multitude of difficulties and concerns was to seek God's favor, hence his visit to Gibeon. It may be this prioritizing that God was responding to,[4] but we can also see from Solomon's request for wisdom that his heart was not self-seeking but sought wisdom and discernment that he might rule and judge among his people aright. Solomon was primarily concerned with the welfare of his people rather than himself. He also ensured that he first praised God for what He had already promised and delivered. He acknowledged God's faithfulness to that which He promised Solomon's father David. He also referred back to God's promise to his ancestor Abraham[5] a thousand years ago: that his offspring would be as numerous and uncountable as the dust of the earth. By association he also alluded to the rest of that promise, the land, north, south, east, and west of where Abraham was standing, the land that God had promised to Abraham's offspring.

In Solomon's lifetime and at the start of his reign, both these promises were now fulfilled. Standing on the high place at Gibeon, he was surveying the land. His praise was not self-seeking in any sense either. God is worthy of praise. He had fulfilled the promises He made to a landless man who was without any offspring at all at the time. Surely the living God would also fulfill any promises He now made to the king during this encounter.

God's response to this request from Solomon is right from His character; He is generous with gifts that prove to last a lifetime—even though Solomon falls far short in many areas. The empire cannot endure beyond the king's death, but the evidence suggests that his wisdom did endure throughout his reign.

We can surely take comfort from this revelation of what God is like. The divine characteristic of generosity is confirmed, of course, many times in Scripture and in God's various dealings with humanity. As the apostle James says, "If any of you lacks wisdom, you should ask God, who gives generously to all without finding fault, and it will be given to you."[6] Neither is God's generosity confined to the here and now. It lasts forever. As Jesus said, "In my Father's house are many mansions: if it were not so, I would have told you. I go to prepare a place for you."[7]

In the new king of Israel's case, as Russ Parker comments,[8] God presents Solomon with a blank check; he can have whatever he wants. But this offer is a test as well. Solomon's answer will reveal his heart and what he most desires. In fact, his answer pleases God, who grants him what he asks for, but to such a degree that his exercise of it will give him a name and a reputation above any other mortal king, past, present, and future. Added to this will be wealth, honor, and longevity, with the long life conditional on the extent to which he chooses to continue to follow God's ways.

On awaking, Solomon seems surprised that it was a dream—it was as real as if he'd had an audience, perhaps in a waking vision, with God. But he accepts that it was an audience in a dream instead. At once he returns to Jerusalem and stands before the ark of the covenant, located in its temporary residence inside a sacred tent. His prayers and worship before God at this point are unrecorded, but the ark represents a place of meeting that God had used in the past to meet with Moses and Joshua. It was also a holy object closely connected to the miraculous. The river Jordan parted when the priests carried it to the river,[9] and this was quickly followed by the sudden and complete destruction of Jericho after the ark was paraded around its walls for seven days, again by the priests.[10] Back in Jerusalem, Solomon decides to give a feast and celebration for his entire court. He wants his friends and officials to share in his joy over his meeting with God and in what He has been promised.

The Judgment of Solomon

The account in 1 Kings then immediately shifts forward to a case of Solomon exercising wise judgment at court. This case impressed Israel so much that all the people heard about it. It has become famous even to the modern day. Raphael painted a fresco of it, the French artist Gustave Doré made an etching of it, and Andrea Mantegna painted it, to name a few European examples from art. This scene has also influenced plays, such as the *Caucasian Chalk Circle* by Bertolt Brecht, and even some television series episodes. Expressions and judgments arising from it are used today by the legal profession in areas such as compromise awards and arbitration.[11]

Solomon is now armed with the God-given wisdom promised to him in the dream. Perhaps you are familiar with the event. Two prostitutes appear before Solomon with one live baby boy. They squabble and fight before the king as they both claim to be the mother of the child. Regrettably, it is one woman's story against the other's. Solomon summarizes the intractable situation in the following way: "This one says, 'My son is alive and your son is dead,' while that one says, 'No! Your son is dead and mine is alive'" (1 Kings 3:23).

He then swiftly moves to the judgment:

> Then the king said, "Bring me a sword." So they brought a sword for the king. He then gave an order: "Cut the living child in two and give half to one and half to the other." The woman whose son was alive was deeply moved out of love for her son and said to the king, "Please, my lord, give her the living baby! Don't kill him!" But the other said, "Neither I nor you shall have him. Cut him in two!" Then the king gave his ruling: "Give the living baby to the first woman. Do not kill him; she is his mother." (1 Kings 3:24–27)

Solomon detects the true mother by forcing the sudden stirring up of her true mother love. In her view, if she is to be denied a just outcome, at least she can still save her child's life. Her accuser, however, will have none of it. She has antipathy toward the child and is hostile toward his mother. Her position is one of spitefulness. If she cannot gain in the situation, she will ensure that the other woman cannot gain either.

News of the events spilled out beyond the court: "When all Israel heard the verdict the king had given, they held the king in awe, because they saw that he had wisdom from God to administer justice" (1 Kings 3:28). In his insightful commentary on these proceedings, Dale Ralph Davis[12] notes that if this encounter is projected back to Solomon's dream and what he asked for, a number of fulfillments can be seen just in this one example of justice. He was now able to exercise a discerning heart; he was able to distinguish between right and wrong; he was able to govern the people; and the people saw that his wisdom came from God. Davis also notes that if we project forward regarding this type of justice, we see a coming messianic king who will also discern accurately beneath the surface in his administering of justice and who will greatly supersede Solomon: "He will delight in the fear of the Lord. He will not judge by what he sees with his eyes, or decide by what he hears with his ears; but with righteousness he will judge the needy, with justice he will give decisions for the poor of the earth" (Isaiah 11:3–4).

Solomon's Second Dream

There is another dream detailed in 1 Kings that is often overlooked because the word "dream" is never used. The text, however, clearly signifies that the encounter with God happens by means of a dream. Given that this later event occurred after Solomon completed the building of the temple as well as the royal palace complex in Jerusalem, it would seem to be about twenty-four years into his reign, in around 946 BC; in other words, about halfway into the king's reign. The text states: "When Solomon had finished building the temple of the Lord and the royal palace, and had achieved all he had desired to do, the Lord appeared to him a second time, as he had appeared to him at Gibeon" (1 Kings 9:1–2).

The context of the dream appears in the previous chapter. All the key building works Solomon had undertaken had come to their completion. He instructed the priests to move the ark of the covenant into the finished temple, and this suddenly caused God's presence to descend visibly into the temple as it had done when the people journeyed through Sinai with the ark: "When the priests withdrew from the Holy Place, the cloud filled the temple of the LORD" (1 Kings 8:10). Having blessed all the people assembled in Jerusalem for the temple's dedication, Solomon then gave a lengthy prayer of dedication.

Even though God's presence was visible and palpable, Solomon rightly prayed: "But will God really dwell on earth? The heavens, even the highest heaven, cannot contain you. How much less this temple I have built! Yet give attention to your servant's prayer and his plea for mercy, LORD my God" (1 Kings 8:27–28). He then went on to outline a whole series of circumstances in which the people would inevitably sin against God in the future and the repercussions this would invoke— Solomon remembered the curses as well as the blessings communicated by God through Moses. He prayed that after they repented, God would forgive them, aid them in the crisis whatever it might be—drought, disease, defeat in battle, captivity, or exile—and restore them.

However, the dream that follows this dedication and petition is very different from the one the king experienced at the start of his reign. It is largely a warning dream. God says He has consecrated the temple Solomon has built. But there are no unconditional, positive promises this time for the king. In fact, the dream speaks explicitly about disaster:

> But if you or your sons turn away from me and do not observe the commands and decrees I have given you and go off to serve other gods and worship them, then I will cut off Israel from the land I have given them and will reject this temple I have consecrated for my Name. Israel will then become a byword and an object of ridicule among all peoples. This temple will become a heap of rubble. All who pass by will be appalled and will scoff. (1 Kings 9:6–8)

God also implies that if the king does not walk with integrity, the throne he sits on will be cut off, it will not endure through the generations. There is no sense given that the king was about to fall away drastically from serving God. He continues to keep the main Jewish festivals and the temple runs as it is meant to do, serving as a location and focus for the burnt offerings and fellowship offerings to God.

But Solomon does not heed the dream's warnings and turns away from God despite them. His heart is not fixed on God as David's had been. Perhaps there is a hint of this where the narrative states that in his temple offerings, the king ensures that he "fulfilled the temple obligations." There is no mention of love or devotion, merely the fulfilling of obligations—of someone who is perhaps going through the motions. But if this is so, much worse is to follow. The king is led astray by the gods of the many pagan wives he takes to himself. This turning away is subtle, gradual over many years, but Solomon ends up worshipping gods that require human sacrifice.[13]

Ultimately, everything disintegrates. Rebellions mar Solomon's last years in power, and after the king's death, the empire falls apart, shrinks, and divides. The pagan influences Solomon introduced through his many marriages mar the cultures, religious practices, and fortunes of both successive kingdoms, and the majority of their kings prove to be evil. In due time, both kingdoms are swept away. Israel is cut off from the land—the people are killed or exiled. The temple is attacked and destroyed, its treasures taken as plunder.

Conclusions

In his first dream, Solomon comes to God knowing that he lacks the wisdom to rule the nation. God is pleased to give wisdom as an attribute to him, so much so that not one temporal ruler then or since has matched him. Solomon's character and rulership are utterly transformed. But is there something being described that has direct relevance to us here and now? In her commentary on dreams and visions, pastor Jane Hamon is quite clear about this. She says, "When the Lord speaks in a spiritual dream to an area of need in our lives it can yield an impartation of God's

Spirit which releases a new power and revelation which can vastly alter our character and abilities."[14]

The second dream is given at a critical turning point for Solomon. Outwardly, his reign is successful. He is doing what kings do, he has accomplished the building works that were required, and he is rapidly forging an empire by peaceful means. Yet inwardly, despite his God-given wisdom, his heart is no longer humble. Unlike his humility at Gibeon, he no longer comes to God with nothing. Rather, he comes to God with all his building accomplishments and other achievements: international treaties, alliances, and quickly accumulating trade wealth. Now he is a successful king, and his reign is secure.

But surely Solomon is deceived, since it is only God's blessing and gifts that have enabled him to accomplish what he has. In addition, there is a flaw in his heart that was not in his father's and of which he is presumably unaware. The dream is a warning of where the flaw could lead. This second dream is acknowledged and recorded, but there is no record of a response. It appears that the king just carries on as normal in religious practice, building works, and commerce. At this critical juncture and despite his wisdom when it comes to the affairs of others, Solomon ignores his own dream's meaning. The warning and the turning point fade into the past. He has not turned back to the right path, and he consigns the rest of his life to an ever-increasing proliferation of darkness.

When God speaks to Solomon again, we are not told whether this is in a dream or by means of a prophet or waking revelation. God will tear the kingdom from Solomon, but because of His love for David, He postpones the judgment to the years just beyond Solomon's lifetime.

The main conclusion we can draw from Solomon's dreams really has to do with the love of God. Initially, God is responding to Solomon's needs and devotion to God, giving exactly what Solomon prayed for and beyond it. Then later, at mid reign, God responds again to Solomon's need. He again gives what Solomon needs to hear, a series of warnings exactly when he needs to hear them. But the successful king, perhaps because of pride, refuses to acknowledge his need.

Have we been warned by a dream? If so, we need to take heed, since the dream's timing is critical. Our conscious mind may not be aware of the danger, whether it is in ourselves or in the events and circumstances of our lives. For Solomon, the opportunity to turn back to God was lost. The amount of drift in his life accumulated, and ultimately, everything was lost. Indeed, the ark of the covenant is still lost![15]

CHAPTER 11

Dream Symbolism and Types of Dreams

It is impossible to provide any comprehensive listing of dream symbol interpretations for two reasons. First, the language is too vast and complex. There are just too many symbols. And second, as we have already seen, many of the symbols are unique to the dreamer in terms of their meaning. Their context lies in the dreamer's life and the individual's unique outlook and perspective on their own life and on life being lived round about them.

Yet at the same time, we are all fundamentally wired the same way. We all belong to the same unique species, the only spiritual creatures God has made for the earth. We are made a little lower than the angels[1] and with spirits created for eternity. We also all share a recent, common human ancestry, and so-called racial differences between ethnic groups are biologically negligible. Among human beings, there is really only one race, the human race. Although cultural differences do exist and affect our outlook on life, we all have a lot in common, however deep into the heart and psyche you choose to go. This includes the function and meaning of dreams. It is possible, therefore, to outline in reasonably broad and flexible terms the significance and possible meaning of some of the common themes we often encounter in the language of our dreams.

Vehicles in Dreams

When you dream of driving your car, the car typically represents your life. All sorts of things can happen in this type of dream, and they will be symbolic of what has recently happened, what is currently happening, or what is about to or likely to happen. You can dream of being stuck in a pothole or of taking a wrong turn. Perhaps someone else is driving your car. For instance, I once dreamed that I had just been given a new company car. It was small, but it was mine. Yet I dreamed that my line manager at work was the one who was driving it. At the time, I was feeling disempowered by some sudden and dramatic changes in my workplace. My heart was saying to me: this is how you are feeling, and it is not how you are meant to be working. I was able to apply the dream and bring about constructive change in my new workplace so that I regained some needed space and autonomy.

Houses in Dreams

Likewise, a dream of a house may represent your life as well as your psychological, emotional, and spiritual condition. The rooms in the house can represent different aspects of your life, such as the upstairs section and/or the bathroom relating to your spiritual life: washing yourself in the bathroom may symbolize prayer and repentance. The bedroom will tend to represent your personal life. If something in your dream is occurring in your basement, the location could refer to aspects of your life that you normally keep hidden or to circumstances and situations that are hidden from you; for instance, your heart may harbor a deep-seated suspicion or fear about someone in your family, which you have not so far consciously admitted to or come to terms with.

In all these rooms and sections of the dream house, what is going on? Are the rooms well-decorated and attractive, or are they dilapidated and run-down? Is there anything in the house that should not be there?

Dreaming of a familial home no longer ours, our home during childhood, for instance, could signify that the dream is about unresolved issues, concerns, or events that are rooted in our childhood. The dream is about our past and something located there that is affecting our present life. Sometimes it is possible to experience an unfocused fear or even an addiction that makes no sense and defies explanation or resolution. A dream about a childhood home may, depending on its symbolic content, indicate a root cause to the fear or addiction planted decades ago. Even using the dream's metaphors to make a conscious, mental connection between past events and present disturbance may weaken its hold.

As with all dreams, it is important to take time to reflect on and pray through all of this symbolism, since some of the symbols may be quite unique to you and where you are in life.

Colors in Dreams

If an object is colored white in a dream, the meaning often has to do with righteousness or being blameless—yet there are exceptions. For instance, the King James Version and the New King James Version of the Genesis account of the baker's dream[2] (as opposed to the New International Version, which mentions no color) record that the three baskets on the baker's head were white. Joseph interpreted this as signifying that in three days he would be executed, the wider context of the dream conveying the full meaning. The white in the baker's dream has more to do with bleached bones in the desert than with righteousness.

If something is colored black, the meaning usually, though not always, has to do with evil, suffering, or mourning. Yet most colors and shades of colors have a wide variety of potential meanings, both good and bad, depending on the dreamer and the context of the dream. The best treatments of this that I have come across are by Ira Milligan,[3] who outlines many variations in meaning, and by John Paul Jackson in his courses on dreams. His course 201 delves into many of the foundational elements found in dreams, such as colors, people, methods of transport, and animals. He points out that every color has both positive and negative metaphorical meanings, depending on whether the dream is a good and positive dream for the dreamer or a darker, unpleasant dream.[4]

Some colors, such as blue and green, are usually positive, signifying the heavens, peace or healing, and eternal or resurrected life respectively. Brown can signify death or barrenness and is therefore usually a negative color, but at the same time, it can denote humility. Red often denotes passion or danger: life or the potential loss of it.

People in Dreams

When we dream of someone known to us, we tend to assume that the dream is about that person. At times, when the dream of someone we know is closely consistent with our experience of that person, this assumption can be correct. But as with all dream symbolism, the person appearing will, more often than not, be symbolic. The likelihood is that the dream is either about an aspect of yourself or is about what that person means to you. Herman Riffel estimates that more than 90 percent of dreams about people are dreams about aspects of yourself, which those people symbolize.[5] These can be considered subjective dreams: they are about the subject, the dreamer.

Dreaming of your pastor, for instance, could be a dream about God, or it could be a dream about your attitude toward your pastor or authority figures more generally, or it could be about a pastoral quality in you. Key questions to ask yourself regarding the dream's meaning would have to do with what the person represents or means to you, what was happening in the dream, and how you felt in the dream about that. If you dream of an authority figure, whether it be a pastor, judge, policeman, or doctor, what was the authority figure doing? For instance, was he or she supporting or obstructing you? Then the next questions you might need to ask yourself could be: When am *I* actually doing that? When do I behave like that? Is that helpful and right, or do I need to change how I am behaving?

Dreaming of your youngest or eldest same-sex sibling could be a dream about your own youth or where you see yourself in the future. So much depends, though, on what the person or relative means to you individually. What do you perceive as their main characteristics and traits? Do you view them in a positive or negative light? Have they been someone who has condemned and ridiculed you, or have they been a true friend, someone who has sought to support and encourage you?

Of course, there is a complication here, because from time to time you will have a dream about, say, your brother, and it is just exactly that. Your brother appears as himself, and the dream is a literal rather than a symbolic dream. It is also true that occasionally a dream will mix the literal and the symbolic together. For instance, I once dreamt of a couple whom I had known well for several years. The husband appeared as himself, but his wife was absent. Nevertheless, in my dream, she had caused some damage to a door in my parents' home. The damage was a series of deep gouge marks scraped into the wood, low down toward the floor, the sort of damage a feral animal such as a weasel would have caused. In the dream, I knew that the culprit was the man's wife, who had caused the damage before leaving!

A number of commentators have highlighted that dreams of male or female people known or unknown to us can be about God seeking our cooperation in a rebalancing and development of our personalities. Jane Hamon, for instance, summarizes some of the symbolism like this: "Dreams involving our mother or our sister or our grandmother might be addressing traits referred to as feminine while dreams involving fathers, brothers or other male family figures may deal with masculine traits."[6]

We should all have a healthy internal balance of truly masculine and truly feminine qualities in order to both respond to others (a feminine attribute) and initiate with and be intentional with others (a masculine attribute) and to cooperate as fully as possible with God, something that requires both sets of attributes. Because of faulty and inadequate upbringing and development, aspects of our personalities are typically repressed. They were never affirmed or called into being, so they exist within us as unrealized potential that God seeks to bless and call forth. A dream about a same-sex or opposite-sex character could be about further development of same-sex or opposite-sex traits and qualities, depending on the dreamer's need or deficit. God encourages our growth toward whole personalities. Among other things, this requires the proper balancing within ourselves of masculine and feminine traits.

In many instances, the people we dream of symbolize aspects of ourselves, aspects that are unrecognized, weak, and seek integration into our personality. But rather than engage in some kind of self-help, we should offer these aspects of our hidden selves to God and ask Him to do the healing work required, redeeming the parts of ourselves that were unknown to us prior to the dream but which have risen up to speak to us. By seeking God's help when it comes to personality integration, we allow Him to do the work and transform or correct the hidden aspects of ourselves that have risen up from our heart to meet us in the dream. Such cooperation with God can actually change how we relate to other people. We also become stronger, our personalities become more balanced, and we become more authentically ourselves.

An extreme but not uncommon type of dream is to dream that a male or female relative has just died or is about to die. This can at times be symbolic of the truth being revealed to the dreamer that a repressed part of themselves is being so cut off by the dreamer that it fears death or nonbeing.

In this day and age, there is a very common head-heart split in humankind. The emotional self of genuine emotions, one's heart if you will, can be repressed by a conscious and ultra-rational thinking self and by its approach to life and living. The cognitive and rational have been elevated into a position of sole rule over life and experience that they were never meant to have. We were not created to function that way, but both education and familial upbringing in the West can reinforce the rational in a positive but exclusive way at the expense of the emotional, feeling functions. This slow strangulation of the heart can continue into adulthood and become an ossified, mentally rigid state of being and experience. In such a situation, it is not surprising that the heart will at times call out through dreams, communicating its fear of death through its own heart language of symbols. Recognizing the meaning of such dreams can be the beginning of a journey toward inner healing—the healing of head and heart, the start of a life lived in color rather than black and white.

An interesting aside is the evidence that from time to time, loved ones who are believers and who have died may appear in our dreams. Steve and Sarah Berger[7] relate a fascinating collection of dreams in which their son, who died in an auto accident in 2009, appeared to them, his sister, and some of his friends to assure them that he is doing just fine where he is! These dreams were not sought, and certainly none of the dreamers took the step of consulting a spiritist or medium—actions clearly condemned in Scripture. Rather, the dreams just happened, and they greatly helped the dreamers to break through intense grieving and move on. Such occurrences are examples of objective or literal dreams and are devoid of symbolism.

Dreaming of a baby often indicates something new that has started to happen or is about to happen in your life. For instance, healer and writer Leanne Payne dreamed several times of a baby, sometimes male and sometimes female, each baby symbolizing a book that was developing within her and needed to be written. Likewise, a baby could symbolize a new idea to be developed, an idea that will change your life and the lives of others.

Animals in Dreams

Animals in dreams can often symbolize our traits and emotions. They can also symbolize good or evil forces. Dreaming of rats infesting a basement, spiders crawling along the ceiling, or snakes may symbolize the presence of evil. Other animals present in dreams can symbolize much more positive forces or traits. Dreaming of a horned animal such as a bull is often a dream about authority or power, but this could be either legitimate or false authority. Sometimes the bull can symbolize persecution or false religion.

Likewise, dreaming about a horse could be positive or negative. It could be a dream about one's own life energy or strength. It could, like the horses of the biblical Revelation,[8] be a dream about a length of time, with several dream horses equating to several periods of time in the future—each representing its own period of time whether it be a week, a month, a year, or longer. But a dream of a horse could also be a dream about conflict or war, even if it is conflict just in your own life or workplace. With such a dream animal, the color can be very significant and help with gaining an accurate interpretation.

The presence in a dream of an aggressive animal that chases us, such as a lion or bear, may symbolize an aggression that has been suppressed in us because of the way we were raised or for many other reasons. It is still there, taking energy to suppress while at the same time threatening to rise up and burst through destructively, perhaps in road rage or in a destructive outburst with our family. If this is so, it is something that must be faced in the dream and in waking life. If we can find ways to constructively be angry rather than suppressing our anger, the aggressive dream animal will shrink or just disappear altogether. Ultimately, this kind of dream is an invitation toward inner healing and a healthier way of living.

At the same time, a lion has a potential positive or negative spiritual meaning in a dream. In John's vision, Christ is termed "the Lion of the tribe of Judah,"[9] while the Bible also likens the enemy to a "roaring lion"[10] searching out prey. Commentators such as Perry Stone emphasize that some symbols, such as snakes, virtually always denote negative circumstances or events. Snakes often denote lies or trials of various kinds.

The exact psychological, emotional, or spiritual significance of a dream animal depends on its own characteristics in real life. Some animals tend to be destructive and aggressive while others tend to be industrious. Some are gregarious and hunt in packs while others are solitary and independent. But at the same time, the animal's significance also depends on its meaning to the person who has dreamed of it. What does the person freely associate with that animal?

Dreams of Water

Dreaming of water often has emotional and spiritual significance. Depending on the dream's content and narrative, the water could represent something good and refreshing, even the presence of the Holy Spirit. Rivers can represent many different things to different dreamers depending on their experiences and what they associate with them, though at times dreaming about a river is a dream about a boundary that can or cannot be crossed. Being able to cross it on a bridge or in a boat can symbolize a new phase of life, a new adventure, new territory to explore. Dreams of deep waters such as the ocean often symbolize the deep heart or unconscious. Typically we do not know ourselves, and we have very little or any idea as to what may be down there.

People's dreams of water can be very disturbing at times. They are taken off course in their travels because of a sudden and dangerous flood, or they dream of perching on a rock, perhaps attempting to rescue their children while a stormy sea batters the rock and attempts to dislodge them. Such dreams may represent an intense emotional or spiritual battle within the family and the dreamer's attempts to rescue or protect loved ones from others who are unsafe.

Timescale in Dreams

Dreams are often about the here and now and about what has just occurred as well as that which is about to occur. On the other hand, a dream can also give a commentary on the medium-to long-range future that a set of circumstances will lead to.

In terms of the here and now, God may provide a dream to convey a message to you that addresses a problem you are currently grappling with. He seeks to give you guidance about your present concerns. He wants you to understand the dream, receive the guidance, and then take action. As we have seen, this was often the case in biblical times. The dream was given so that danger could be avoided and the right path taken, sometimes literally as in the various cases in Matthew's gospel. At other times, a crisis could not be avoided, but the dream gave instruction as to how to prepare for and manage the crisis. The dreams given to Pharaoh, as interpreted by Joseph, are great examples of this.

Unless you are a world leader, God will not give guidance on how to overcome a crisis on that scale. But He may well give guidance as to the choices and challenges you are facing. The dream will have the same scope and territory as the life you lead.

Types of Dreams

As we seek to interpret our dreams as accurately as possible, it will help if we can discern what type of dreams we have been having. The following list is certainly not exhaustive, but it does include many of the main types.

Discernment Dreams

Some dreams contain genuine discernment. In such cases, the dream conveys to you more information about a person or situation than your conscious mind is aware of. Accurate interpretation may well cause you to change a decision or a course of action. The dream contains new information that either supplements what you knew or contradicts what you thought was the case.

I have experienced such dreams every now and again, and in my experience, they have tended to contradict what I thought was the case. In the dreams, I typically see a person, such as a friend or family member, and a detailed representation of their inner condition or perspective, their heart if you will. I see in the dream the person's true character or what the person truly feels about a difficult situation.

Healing Dreams

Some dreams can be used for the purposes of healing. Many dreams contain either literal or symbolic manifestations of unfinished personal business that has been pushed down into the unconscious. The heart is burdened by this content and is pushing it back up, but often in symbolic form, telling you as the dreamer that the issue has not gone far away. It is there and should be resolved. Otherwise you will remain troubled, even become ill. Such dreams are often about broken or troubled relationships.

Once we are clear about what the dream is conveying, it is possible to move into a process that results in healing. This should mean that we take the contents of the dream before God, placing them at the foot of the cross and, for instance, asking for the grace to forgive someone, even someone who has died. This process can be gone through as part of a more extended process involving counseling where the counselor is familiar with dream work. In his book *Healing Dreams,*[11] Russ Parker explores the therapeutic effects of dream work much further, and I recommend it to you.

Dreams About Death

Because dreams are mainly symbolic, a dream about your own death may symbolize transition into something new or symbolize the likely crushing or death of some aspect of your personality unless you take steps to alleviate the stressful circumstances. At the same time, though, such dreams can be about a *fear* of death.

At other times, as Perry Stone points out in his book on dreams and visions, the dream about your own death may be a call to pray so that danger is averted. This certainly extends to intercessory prayer for others if the dream concerns them rather than the dreamer. There are numerous documented instances of people praying as a result of dreaming of someone's death, followed by death being averted, while some of the details of the warning dream still come to pass. A dream about someone's death can therefore be a call to prayer so that God can transform a present or impending situation into blessing. As John and Paula Sandford point out, the dream about death is not something that should be or is meant to be interpreted in a fatalistic way.

Nightmares

Nightmares are often signs of emotional distress, often repressed, and may repeat themselves, sometimes over years, in every detail. The emotional intensity and the threat will typically build as the nightmare progresses. In the main, nightmares are caused either by traumatic real-life events or by fears of one's own possible responses. Key questions for the dreamer: When did the nightmares start? Where were you? Who were you with, and what was happening?

In cases where the nightmare contains symbolic imagery, it is important as always to arrive at a valid interpretation, including through prayer, before bringing the now understood situation to the cross, asking God for deep healing for the emotional distress and, in many cases, for the real-life trauma that created the disturbance. Greg Cynaumon's book[12] has many detailed cases of clients with nightmares, often repeating themselves for years, that only ceased through dream work, an accurate interpretation of the symbols and a grounding of the nightmare in the life events that precipitated it. In some of these cases, the dreamers were able to pray this revelation through and offer the dream and its causes to God. By opening themselves up to God, they were able to gain further insight and the ability and emotional freedom to move forward again.

Not infrequently, nightmares symbolize one's fears. The fear may be chasing you in the dream and be symbolized as an animal or a stranger.

In the dream, the fear must be confronted, and in all likelihood, the confrontation will diminish it. If we have the interpretation of the dream's symbolic content, we can then also confront the fear in real life by the decisions we make and thereby overcome it.

Another possible cause or factor with nightmares may be medication. J.F. Pagel,[13] for instance, gives a very detailed listing of the medications known to increase the reporting of nightmares in both case studies and clinical trials. Nevertheless, what is really going on? Is the medication causing nightmares or simply bringing them further into our consciousness? It could well be that many such medications are mainly affecting the ability to recall nightmares that are caused by the real life events or fears mentioned.

In many cases of post-traumatic stress disorder, nightmares can continue over the very long term as the person continues to relive a situation where they were in immediate danger or were actually under attack. These dreamers need an intervention, someone who can work with them therapeutically to help them walk along a road toward inner peace and healing.

We should also include here the possibility that a series of nightmares indicates a need for deliverance. The word *nightmare* stems from the Old English word *maere,* which meant incubus or goblin, an evil spirit that afflicted the sleeper with a sense of being suffocated. In such scenarios, the dreamer is actually under attack while asleep, typically because of an involvement in the occult or perhaps because of a familial history of involvement. These nightmares do not tend to follow the more usual progression of a building up in the sense of threat and danger but may instead actually involve a strong sensation of suffocation, choking, or dark oppression. If you can connect these attacks to involvements or associations you have had in the past, it is best to seek help from a minister or someone else in the church with expertise in this area.

Prophetic Dreams

Prophetic dreams are dreams that reveal the word of God to the dreamer's heart. The word can be for the individual concerned, for his or her family, business or church, or they could, as in the cases of Pharaoh's and

Daniel's dreams, concern the future and fate of kingdoms and nations. They may as Paula Price notes[14] convey something already happening at a spiritual level but still to manifest in the physical realm. The symbolism in such dreams relates to the dreamer's own life, but it takes a prophetic gifting to unveil the meaning, which otherwise would remain sealed.

Reminder Dreams

Some dreams remind us of things we need to do and should have done by now. We have pushed a matter aside, or rather down, into the unconscious. For instance, I could dream about my car having a repair or breaking down by the roadside. This *could* infer that it has been too long since the car was last checked over, or that the service report I intend to deal with at some point needs to be given a much higher priority. Likewise I could dream of relatives or friends at a time when I have neglected them for too long, or as Russ Parker comments,[15] because they need my prayers of intercession on their behalf. They are in some sort of trouble, and it is, in fact, God who is reminding me of them.

Warning Dreams

We consider a number of warning dreams already in this book, such as Abimelek's warning of death and the various warning dreams to Joseph and the wise men in Matthew's gospel. Modern-day warning dreams can warn of ill-health if the dreamer has, for instance, been working too hard for a long time, or the dream could even warn of death unless a course of action is abandoned in favor of another. Yet real discernment is required, because usually a dream about one's own death or the death of someone known to the dreamer is not about physical death but about psychological change, even about personal growth and development. To progress, something has to die. If we know the person in the dream who has died and we can discern what they signify to us, we can potentially work out which part of our personality is about to die.

A dream that symbolizes psychological death could be a warning dream. If the dreamer does not change how he or she lives, a significant part of the person's personality is about to be finally extinguished. This could be either an aspect of true masculinity (such as creativity or proactivity) or true femininity (such as empathy or intuition). Has someone been stifling the dreamer for so long that part of their personality is about to actually die unless something is done?

According to the book of Job, God will often choose to speak through a warning dream. If the warning dream is ignored, as Nebuchadnezzar ignored his dream of the tree cut down to its stump, God may switch tactics away from warning dreams to real-life pain:

> For God does speak—now one way, now another—though no one perceives it. In a dream, in a vision of the night, when deep sleep falls on people as they slumber in their beds, he may speak in their ears and terrify them with warnings, to turn them from wrongdoing and keep him from pride, to preserve them from the pit, their lives from perishing by the sword. Or someone may be chastened on a bed of pain . . . (Job 33:14–19).

Repeated Dreams

There are many recorded instances of people having the same dream over and over again, sometimes for years, even for decades. It is true to say that time by itself does not heal. If the cause of the dream is something traumatic or deeply disturbing in one's past, the memory of the event and its emotional impact is held within the dreamer. It is carried around day in and day out. The repeated dream may simply indicate that the person is stuck—he or she has refused to acknowledge the pain and work through the event's impact. When the person is able to accurately interpret the dream and take positive steps toward healing, the dream ceases, since it has finally been heard and understood. A dream often comes from the unacknowledged or blind spots in one's deep self.

If the repeated dream is from God, He is giving the dreamer repeated opportunities to hear His voice and His message to them. Once the dream is finally understood and acted upon, God can shift the focus to other matters on His agenda. A repeated dream should cease when it has been understood and correctly acted on.

This year I have had a repeated dream. The first dream was one in which I was walking quickly through the building I once lived in when in my late twenties and early thirties. I was looking for my apartment. As I was hunting for it, going up one set of stairs and down another, walking along corridors, people came at me with different needs. With one lot, I needed to work with them as a group. With another individual I needed to have a one-to-one appointment with her. I told them all to come along with me; I'd fit them all in once I had found my apartment. I awoke without finding it, feeling frustrated.

In the second occurrence, I was searching for my old office in a university, although I was not a member of the university staff. This was my work situation in the mid-1990s. In the dream, I was due to attend a meeting there. I walked all through the university buildings searching for my office, walking along long corridors and up some stairs and down some others. From time to time, I came across university staff whom I tried to enlist to help me in the search, but most were just too busy, dealing with students in the library or in the refectory. One man did try to help me. In fact, he told me that I was in the wrong building. I needed to exit and walk around to the correct location. In the dream, my cell phone rang, and a client's secretary told me that the meeting I was due to attend had to be delayed. My client couldn't make it, and I should rebook the meeting for early September.

Although some of the specifics are different, the dreams are basically the same. Having both dreams enabled me to make some sense of the meaning, since both related to a short period of time during the mid-1990s when I both lived in the apartment and worked out of a university office. They were drawing me back to that time, yet somehow they were commenting on my current life. The main impressions I had on waking both times were frustration and expending too much energy on a fruitless search.

I believe the dreams probably have more than one meaning, but one of these relates to the time they referred back to, when I was working much longer hours and bringing in a greater salary, relatively speaking, than I am now. I have a better work-life balance now; for instance, I am able to write more freely now and have quality time to do that. Yet at work this year, I have been seeking out opportunities to increase my hours—as if I am trying to recreate the work conditions of an earlier time in my life. The dreams were saying that this search is a fruitless one and something that has already been frustrating. It will become increasingly frustrating if I continue with it. The past has gone, and it cannot be returned to. Rather, I should accept my current work-life balance and enjoy it. I should accept what many would seek to have. For those who come to me now with different needs, I work with them with a stronger focus and energy.

How to Begin to Interpret Dreams

If you want to be able to interpret dreams, the first step is to believe that dreams have importance. Any dream is likely to have significance, whatever its cause. It is also good and scriptural to pray for God to reveal things to you in dreams, just as you would pray for Him to reveal Himself through Scripture or through a house group fellowship or within a church service.

In his letter, James says, "You do not have because you do not ask God."[16] Similarly Christ says, "Ask and it will be given to you; seek and you will find; knock and the door will be opened to you."[17] Then you need to *expect* to receive dreams. Placing a journal at your bedside is a working out of this expectation.

Buy a journal and keep it by your bedside. When you awaken, you need to be still and reflect on the dream you just experienced. Whether it is vivid or vague, focus on what you remember of it, and other details or parts of the dream sequence will often present themselves to you as well. As you are doing this, it is important to write down the details. Often in the act of writing, more of the dream's details will come to mind, and you can record these as you go until you have captured the entire dream. Record the setting, colors, symbols, scene changes, and how you felt in the dream.

If when you awake you think that there is no need to record all this because you will remember it, you are probably mistaken. The dream will almost certainly evaporate, even if its symbolism and impact really affect you at the time. You need to write it down. Later you can go back to it, pray over it, or refer to it when twists and turns in ongoing circumstances bring it to mind. Clarity and revelation as to the dream's meaning are likely to come but be somewhat delayed.

Daniel wrote his dreams down, and that is a good enough precedent: "In the first year of Belshazzar king of Babylon, Daniel had a dream, and visions passed through his mind as he was lying in bed. He wrote down the substance of his dream" (Daniel 7:1). We also see from this reference that Daniel dated his dreams, and we need to do that too. It could well be that the dream speaks into what has just occurred or will shortly occur in your life. Dating the dream allows you to go back to it, to see exactly when it occurred and use its context in life to help you unravel the meaning of its symbolism.

Herman Riffel says, "Look at the setting of the dream. What were you thinking about, or in what were you emotionally involved when you had the dream?"[18] This is sound advice. At the same time, though, some dreams are not about the here and now. Like Daniel's dreams of the end times, they could be about a future that is still far off. There is a chance that an occasional dream of yours could be about *your* future and a time in your own life many years ahead.

Does a dream's vividness correlate with its importance? At times it will, and it is important to pay attention to any dream that leaves a strong emotional impression on waking. But there is no absolute correlation. For instance, while God revealed to Nebuchadnezzar what was to occur in the end times by means of his dream of a statue and its final destruction, the symbolism did not stay with the king. About Nebuchadnezzar's dream the text says, "The king answered and said to the Chaldeans, 'The thing is gone from me.'"[19] God had to reveal the whole dream again to Daniel along with its meaning. We have already noted that God can speak vividly and clearly through words and images, but He can also choose to speak in "dark speech," communicating in more subtle ways. Neither does vividness seem to aid recall much. If you do not write a vivid dream down, the likelihood remains that in the morning, you will still have forgotten it.

When you record a dream, more of it often appears before you as you write, and you will record a much more detailed description than you thought you would when you reluctantly picked up the pen. During this time, or at another time when you can be more focused, you then need to take the dream before God in prayer and contemplate each of the elements in the dream. Which ones are literal and which are symbolic? What are they symbolic of? This can then lead to action. Once you believe you have understood the dream, you can take the steps you need to take.

To record your dreams faithfully takes determination and effort right from the initial decision to take time to recall at least one dream as soon as you awaken. Then there is the added self-discipline of writing it down. Finally, even when people decide to do this and have initial success in recalling, recording, and interpreting, many people fall away from their commitment because of the pressures of life or because their initial enthusiasm wanes. Yet if we believe that dreaming is a genuine way of hearing personally from God, it should spur us on to develop and maintain the practice. As in so many things, we will reap in proportion to what we sow.

If the dream is about future events, such as a challenge that is not yet on the horizon, you will probably struggle in vain for its meaning. The best thing to do at such times is to keep the record of it and periodically review it until events line up with the dream. Its meaning may suddenly unfold before you when the events it predicts have become a reality.

Clearly, it is important to understand the types of dreams and the principles of dream interpretive methods in order to begin to interpret dreams well. Is a dream spiritual, natural, or a type of false dream as previously described? What is the symbolism possibly conveying to the dreamer, and is it entirely or mainly subjective—that is, is it entirely or mainly about the dreamer's outer and inner life? Or is the dream about someone else? What in that case is the dream concerning the other person about? Most people will have dreams about themselves 90 to 95 percent of the time and will only occasionally dream objective dreams about someone or something else.

John Paul Jackson[20] provides helpful starting points for differentiating types of dreams through his basic principles of interpretation. One principle is your location in your dream. Are you an observer of events in the dream and not participating in them? If so, the dream is about people and situations and not about you. But if you are participating or the main focus, then the dream is about you. Dreams in which you are the main focus are far more common than other types of dreams. It is then worthwhile to work out how many subfocuses there are, that is, the other elements necessary for the dream to work and have meaning. These will usually number two to four and relate directly to the dream's focus. Last, you may have a few residual details that are not significant and do not affect the dream's meaning. You therefore assign status to each dream element: is it a focus, a subfocus, or a detail belonging to a focus or subfocus?

You will then need to evaluate the context and tone of the dream. Are the attitudes of those in the dream hostile or friendly? What emotions did the dream create in you? The dream's atmosphere is also important: was it exhilarating, neutral, foreboding? Colors as details are important and will reveal a symbol's meaning once it is clear whether the dream is a good dream or a dark and negative dream.

It is often helpful initially to write down a number of possible meanings against each of the symbols. At times this list may include both positive and negative interpretations. Over time, it should be possible to eliminate some of the possibilities in favor of the ones that make the clearest and most consistent sense. It may be that the meanings of some of the symbols remain obscure to the last until you can first interpret the setting of the dream and some of the more obvious symbols within that. What does the dream seem to be about? How did you as the dreamer feel during the dream and on waking from it? What life situation or event has similarly affected you at an emotional level? Scanning across your life experience, is the dream's context perhaps something to do with your family, your work, your relationships, or your church? Given that, what or who could some of the symbols signify?

In their book *The Divinity Code,* Adam Thompson and Adrian Beale describe the process of dream interpretation as very similar to connecting the dots, the drawing game for children. The overall picture is only revealed when all the dots are successfully joined. Often a dream interpretation is possible only after each dream element has first been interpreted correctly. The authors emphasize the Holy Spirit as the one who can help us to accurately choose and then link the individual element meanings together to discover a dream's overall meaning.

All these questions and issues are crucial. Yet at the same time, we need to be aware that at least some dreams are spiritual or prophetic. They are pictures and images that essentially exist beyond rational, human-based approaches to interpretation. In other words, if they originate with God, only God will know their meaning. Therefore, we must in humility approach their Creator and ours and ask Him to tell us what they mean. We need to hear from God just as Daniel did, knowing that the Lord says:

> "For my thoughts are not your thoughts, neither are your ways my ways," declares the LORD. "As the heavens are higher than the earth, so are my ways higher than your ways and my thoughts than your thoughts." (Isaiah 55:8–9).

The final stage in interpretation is being confident enough with the dream and its meaning to take whatever action is called for. Not all dreams require action, but many do. Many dreams originate in a dissatisfaction with how things are or how they have been recently. The unconscious is not happy with where life has led or with actions you have taken. If a dream is at least flagging up some further considerations for you to take account of, that reappraisal may then require a decision or even the overturning of a decision.

With the reappraisal done, has a goal now changed? Or perhaps the dream is more about the balance of things and a need to be less driven. Or was the dream sending you a clear warning about something or someone? What sort of danger is the dream saying you are in, and what can you do to heed such a warning?

Before taking action, though, it is vital to assess the change you think is warranted initially by prayer and also against God's Word—whether the change could be judged as scriptural and whether it could be sanctioned by Scripture. It could be that the revealed will of God is opposed to the action you are thinking of taking as a result of a soulish, self-centered dream. Alternatively, it could also be that a fundamental mismatch with God's revealed will highlights a *misinterpretation* of a spiritual dream. However, if there is complete consistency, you can then move to working out how and when to make the change. It is often the case that confirmations come from other sources of guidance, whether they be other people, further personal insights, or a revelation from Scripture where God's Word becomes living and active for you as an individual—the *rhema* or living word.

The Mystery Can Remain

Sometimes the meaning of a dream eludes us no matter how hard we try to reach a true interpretation. The mystery remains, and behind it is God's silence and His love. Sometimes God gives a dream that He does not interpret because His purpose has to do with drawing us nearer to Him. If a dream's mystery can draw us closer to His heart, this, as Michal Ann Goll points out in the book *Dream Language,* is more important by far than always getting the answer. If we always receive the answers, we might just sit down with them, content in the place we have reached. God wants us always to get closer to Him, to keep praying, to keep walking toward the city of angels and redeemed spirits, to His infinite heart of love.

CHAPTER 12

A Babylonian King's Dreams

The events recorded in Daniel's book of prophecy begin during 605 BC with the Babylonian crown prince, Nebuchadnezzar,[1] besieging Jerusalem. The crown prince was moving west, in charge of his father's[2] army. He had just defeated an Egyptian army at Carchemish and had then swiftly moved against Judah. The siege is successful, and Jerusalem and the Jewish temple there are overrun. Judah remains nominally independent but as a vassal state paying tribute to the empire. In 586 BC, however, after an unsuccessful revolt against foreign domination, Judah is conquered systematically and completely, again by Nebuchadnezzar. The Jews' period of exile as a nation has begun.

There were actually three successive waves of Jewish deportations after three separate attacks on Judah by Babylon, each one more destructive than the last: in 605 BC, 597 BC (when Ezekiel was deported), and finally in 586 BC. We know that Daniel and various other young Jewish noblemen were captured after the empire's first siege of Jerusalem and taken as prisoners to the Babylonian court in 605 BC. Daniel, whose Jewish name means "God is (my) Judge," is renamed Belteshazzar or "Protect the king"[3] by a Babylonian court official but is still clearly known as Daniel[4] as the years go by.

We know too that Daniel remained at Babylon until after Darius the Mede conquered the empire in 539 BC. At that time, Darius changed Babylonian policy radically and permitted Jews to return to their former territory, thereby ending their period of exile. But God certainly gave Daniel longevity in his service at the Babylonian court. Daniel was a court official through the reigns of five different Babylonian emperors, of whom Nebuchadnezzar was the first.

After their forced removal as captives from Judah to Babylon, Daniel and his three Jewish companions found favor at the Babylonian court and were trained up for three years to then enter the emperor's service as royal officials. They also underwent a test, detailed in the first chapter of Daniel, to do with lifestyle. In an act of faithfulness to God, they held out successfully against a diet of rich fare from the king's table and lived much more frugally instead. After the three years of training, they were summoned to appear before the king, and he talked freely with them.

After they entered his service, Nebuchadnezzar, now reigning as emperor, made a discovery: "In every matter of wisdom and understanding about which the king questioned them, he found them ten times better than all the magicians and enchanters in his whole kingdom" (Daniel 1:20).

We find in the narrative that God gave all four Jewish officials "knowledge and understanding of all kinds of literature and learning. And Daniel could understand visions and dreams of all kinds" (Daniel 1:17b). Why was that? There would seem to be a clear link between the gifting Daniel received from God and his character. Daniel had already firmly decided that even though he must live in Babylon, he would not defile himself with its lifestyle. He had decided to keep his mind and body holy even in the midst of the empire's pagan temples and worship. God gave a special understanding of visions and dreams to someone who had already shown a singular commitment to his relationship with his God. The first chapter of Daniel's book gives the detail of this and the testing he underwent. His later trial in the lions' den gives a further illustration of his commitment and devotion (see Daniel 6:16–23).

God singled out Daniel for a unique gifting, and we find that after the first chapter, his whole book is structured around the gift's operation. The uniqueness of the gift has some parallels in Joseph's gift hundreds of years earlier. Daniel was also positioned in a similar way to Joseph. He was a key adviser to the king and was there at court when needed to interpret the king's dreams. And like Joseph's dream of the sun, moon, and stars, we find that a number of the dreams and visions Daniel interpreted have to do with a very long timescale indeed, stretching far beyond the life of the empire in which he was living.

The Statue Dream and Interpretation

The following events occurred in 603 or 602 BC, in the second year of Nebuchadnezzar's reign over Babylon. In a very close parallel, at least initially, with the Pharaoh whom Joseph dealt with, Nebuchadnezzar had a disturbing dream, could not sleep because of it, and demanded that his wise men (enchanters, astrologers, and various others) interpret it for him. However, the emperor decided to be a lot more exacting of his wise men's powers than Pharaoh was. He not only wants them to interpret his dream, he wants them to tell it to him first—he will divulge no details. In what becomes a bit of a circus, more amusing for us than it would have been for the wise men no doubt, the whole thing goes round in circles for some time. The wise men just do not appreciate what Nebuchadnezzar has chosen to do.

Several times his wise men say, just tell us your dream, O king, tell us it *whatever* it is, and we will happily interpret it for you. We are not told why the king did not go down that path. It may be that he was so disturbed by the dream that he wanted to apply a stringent test of his wise men's abilities in order to be able to truly trust their interpretation. Or it may be that in the past, he had asked for advice and had as many types of advice as the number of wise men he asked. It could be that what they have prophesied in the past has not come true. In other words, he may think the wise men have fobbed him off in the past and have no real wisdom. Just conceivably, however, it's possible that although he remained very disturbed by the dream, he genuinely could not remember it. As may happen to us, it's possible that a lot of it had been forgotten, and it was just its atmosphere rather than the detail that remained with him still. In any case, he insisted to them: You must first tell me my dream. Then tell me what it means. If you fail in this, you will all be killed. You will all be torn to bits. And your houses will be turned into piles of rubble.

The wise men exclaimed: What the king demands is too hard for us; no king has *ever* asked a wise man to do such a thing. It is unreasonable of you. Nebuchadnezzar was furious, and the decree went out—put all the wise men to death. The sweeping decree included Babylonians and foreign wise-men-in-training alike. But on hearing of it, Daniel went before the king and appealed successfully to him: Give me time to seek the answer. He had faith in his God who would deliver him and the others from a death sentence. He and his Jewish companions then prayed to God for the answer.

We read the following account of what happened next:

> During the night the mystery was revealed to Daniel in a vision. Then Daniel praised the God of heaven and said: "Praise be to the name of God for ever and ever; wisdom and power are his . . . I thank and praise you, O God of my ancestors: you have given me wisdom and power, you have made known to me what we asked of you, you have made known to us the dream of the king." (Daniel 2:19–20, 23)

Although the answer came at night, we can assume that the revelation came in a waking vision of the dream rather than *in* a dream, and that it came even as Daniel was praying.

This vision is the first example of the apocalyptic occurring in Daniel's book. A mystery inaccessible by all other means is revealed directly to a chosen person, Daniel, by God. In other instances, as we will see, such mysteries were revealed by a divine intermediary, an angel, acting on God's commands. This is the first hallmark of the apocalyptic. A second hallmark has to do with revelation of future salvation in the midst of chaotic and dangerous future events, often in the distant future in terms of when the mystery is being communicated. This is really what "apocalyptic" means. Christ gives a very good example of the apocalyptic when He describes what it will be like in the end times, just before He returns to earth, and how He will appear like lightning flashing across the sky (see Luke 17:20–36).

Like Joseph before him, Daniel begins by saying to the king that no one can explain Nebuchadnezzar's dream to him. The dream is a mystery that only God can reveal, because it is God who has given the dream to the king. It is also God's will that the king fully understand its meaning.

Daniel first recounts to Nebuchadnezzar all the detail contained in his dream. In the dream, the king's mind had turned to things that were to come in the "end of the days." The dream's timeline therefore includes the yet far distant future. The use of the phrase "end of the days" in Scripture typically means the close of the present age *and* the ushering in of the Messianic Age. But the dream's timeline includes the king's immediate future too.

> Your Majesty looked, and there before you stood a large statue—an enormous, dazzling statue, awesome in appearance. The head of the statue was made of pure gold, its chest and arms of silver, its belly and thighs of bronze, its legs of iron, its feet partly of iron and partly of baked clay. While you were watching, a rock was cut out, but not by human hands. It struck the statue on its feet of iron and clay and smashed them. Then the iron, the clay, the bronze, the silver and the gold were all broken to pieces and became like chaff on a threshing floor in the summer. The wind swept them away without leaving a trace. But the rock that struck the statue became a huge mountain and filled the whole earth. (Daniel 2:31–35)

The king had seen an awesomely impressive statue, but at the same time, it was also one that was made of materials of ever-decreasing value as his gaze slowly went from head to feet. Then a rock which had nothing to do with humankind's creative powers struck the feet he was gazing at, and the effect was to destroy the entire statue. As the rock became a mountain large enough to fill the whole earth, it was as if the statue had never been.

In his interpretation of the king's dream, Daniel states that Nebuchadnezzar and his kingdom constitute the head of gold. God has given him and his empire great power, strength, and glory. After him, another, "silver" empire, inferior to his, will arise. Then a third empire, this time symbolized as bronze, inferior still, will arise; and finally a fourth empire will arise in its place. Symbolized as partly iron and partly clay, this fourth empire will have the strength of iron and smash all other earthly powers, but it will be a divided kingdom and as weak as clay in some respects. Just as iron and clay cannot mix, the people will be a mixed people, and they will become disunited. All four empires will successively rule the whole world; that is, the whole of the known world in that time. We are not told the names of the empires symbolized here, only that the golden empire is Babylon.

Daniel states that while these kings or kingdoms are ruling, God will establish a heavenly kingdom, symbolized by the rock. It will crush all four human kingdoms or powers while it will never be crushed. The kingdom it represents will rule forever. Daniel concludes by saying, "The great God has shown the king what will take place in the future. The dream is true and its interpretation is trustworthy" (Daniel 2:45b).

Daniel accurately narrated the king's own dream back to him and provided its interpretation. The effect of this? Nebuchadnezzar was completely overcome, got off his throne, and fell prostrate before Daniel. He said to him, "Surely your God is the God of gods and the Lord of kings and a revealer of mysteries, for you were able to reveal this mystery" (Daniel 2:47). The king then promoted Daniel to rule as governor over the province of Babylon and over all the court wise men. Daniel was not yet twenty years old, and his rise was meteoric.

What were the purposes of the dream? One purpose seems to have been to communicate a message to Nebuchadnezzar very early on in his reign, to check his belief in his own power and his empire's power. The dream is saying clearly that it is God who permits gentile powers to rise and fall, and compared to God's power, they are nothing and have nothing. They *appear* powerful and glorious for a season of time, but in the end, they will be crushed utterly and be blown away by the kingdom of God. It alone will last.

We have to remember that Nebuchadnezzar had recently withdrawn from a successful invasion of Judah and that his business with Judah was unfinished. He would mount two additional attacks on God's chosen people and on Jerusalem, the city God had chosen for His temple. It is interesting that after the dream, interpreted for him by a Jewish prophet from Judah, he delayed the first of these attacks for about seven years and the final onslaught for eighteen years. The dream was perhaps something of a warning to the king.

The dream had other purposes too. As Gordon McConville[5] points out, it would have encouraged Daniel and the other Jewish exiles he was associated with. The dream gave them knowledge and understanding that God was in control of world events. The timeline given to Nebuchadnezzar's empire was limited and would end at the time of God's choosing. In addition, Gentile kingdoms standing in the way of God's kingdom would be swiftly removed by God Himself at the appointed time. God would still fulfill all the promises He had made to the Jewish patriarchs and prophets. And Daniel was happy to share that truth with a pagan king.

The rock that grows into a mountain symbolizes Christ's visible return to earth, still future for us, to crush all human opposition to His eternal kingdom. Since the time of Daniel, Gentile kingdoms such as those seen by Nebuchadnezzar have ruled over the earth and dominated Israel. But even as they reign at the height of their powers, Christ is the rock who will grow in power, making people stumble and fall[6] unless they trust in Him and make Him the cornerstone. Likewise, as Christ said, "but on whomsoever [this stone] shall fall, it will grind him to powder" (Matthew 21:44, KJV).

For now, the kingdom of God is hidden for those who do not have eyes to see it—but its arrival in power is sure and certain. It will destroy all that is vanity and self-centeredness, all the false kingdoms and rule that humankind has established without the will of God in families, business, politics, empty and false religions, nations, and empires. Human power can look solid, but in reality, it is insubstantial and often flawed with internal contradictions or tensions. Therefore it can only last for a time and season. The mountain of God will replace it with healing, joy, and everlasting peace. In the meantime, all that is false is tottering on feet of clay.

Some commentators today attribute great prophetic significance to the statue's two legs and ten toes, for example, attributing the legs to the Roman Empire split between east and west. Yet no particular meaning is attributed by Daniel to the legs. They are merely characteristics of the statue. The statue's toes, however, do seem to symbolize ten kings who are reigning over their tenfold division of the world just prior to Christ's sudden return. Daniel mentions these kings in his interpretation immediately after he describes the toes.

Babylon is the only empire to be mentioned by name at this stage. The other three empires remain unnamed. Yet all four are Gentile powers. In his commentary *The Coming Prince*, Sir Robert Anderson[7] emphasizes that for Daniel, this is a very key part of God's revelation by means of the dream. The scepter of sovereignty over the nations has been passed by God to Gentile powers because of Israel's idolatry and unbelief. It is the Gentile powers, four in particular, who will hold this scepter, but only until the God of heaven intervenes to establish His kingdom that will last forever.

The Tree Dream and Interpretation

Many years later, possibly in 586 BC,[8] Nebuchadnezzar had another dream that terrified him, this time of a tree, and in writing himself about the experience, he preludes his first-person account in Scripture with a greeting and a brief psalm in praise of God. He says:

> It is my pleasure to tell you about the miraculous signs and wonders that the Most High God has performed for me. How great are his signs, how mighty his wonders! His kingdom is an eternal kingdom; his dominion endures from generation to generation. (Daniel 4:2–3)

The signs Nebuchadnezzar alludes to are the two remarkable dreams he was given, the one just considered and the one we are about to consider. The wonders he is proclaiming include the precise fulfillment of his second dream, both in his descent into insanity and in his full recovery, exactly as the dream predicted. A pagan king until his conversion, he is now compelled to worship the true God, a major step forward from his brief, emotional obeisance before Daniel some years before.

This time Nebuchadnezzar initially tells the court magicians, astrologers, and various others the dream. He is so concerned that this time he does not hold back. The dream seems to envisage some dark nemesis for him, something that is going to remove his greatness, power, and majesty from him, but just as with Pharaoh's courtiers, they are unable to interpret it. It has been sent by God, and the mystery is sealed.

In addition, there is perhaps something of self-interest in their ignorance. They would not want to be out of their depth regarding a dream that does seem to presage something dark about the dreamer, a man who could order their execution (again) if he does not accept their interpretation. Eventually their chief, Daniel, arrives, and Nebuchadnezzar says, "Ah, Daniel, I know no mystery is too difficult for you—so interpret my dream." Nebuchadnezzar describes the dream to him just as it happened, and it is interesting that he also relates his condition when the dream occurred: he was in his palace at the time, feeling contented and prosperous. Nebuchadnezzar says:

> These are the visions I saw while lying in bed: I looked, and there before me stood a tree in the middle of the land. Its height was enormous. The tree grew large and strong and its top touched the sky; it was visible to the ends of the earth. Its leaves were beautiful, its fruit abundant, and on it was food for all. Under it the wild animals found shelter, and the birds lived in its branches; from it every creature was fed. In the visions I saw while lying in bed, I looked, and there before me was a holy one, a messenger, coming down from heaven.
>
> He called in a loud voice: "Cut down the tree and trim off its branches; strip off its leaves and scatter its fruit. Let the animals flee from under it and the birds from its branches. But let the stump and its roots, bound with iron and bronze, remain

in the ground, in the grass of the field. Let him be drenched with the dew of heaven, and let him live with the animals among the plants of the earth. Let his mind be changed from that of a man and let him be given the mind of an animal, till seven times pass by for him. The decision is announced by messengers, the holy ones declare the verdict, so that the living may know that the Most High is sovereign over all kingdoms on earth and gives them to anyone he wishes and sets over them the lowliest of people."

This is the dream that I, King Nebuchadnezzar, had. (Daniel 4:10–18)

The language used in the original indicates that the messenger, or "watcher," characterized as holy and seen by Nebuchadnezzar as coming down from heaven, refers to an angel.[9] The angel commands that the tree be cut down but not altogether removed. The remains are to be bound, protected, and hemmed in to their confined space. Then he, the king—because the dream is certainly about him—will be so incredibly altered that he will be like and live like some sort of desolate animal for "seven times." This has been decreed by God; the angels, now plural, are merely seeing to it that the decree is stated publicly in heaven, stated on earth at Nebuchadnezzar's court through this exchange about his dream, and in due time executed on earth.

Even before Daniel gives the interpretation, we sense that God intends to humble the king in a very dramatic way. If his first dream served as an early warning, at least in a subtle way, this new dream delivers a very stark warning to him much later in his reign. Unless he changes his ways and forsakes his pride, his fortunes are going to suffer a sudden and unprecedented decline.

Daniel pauses for some time, greatly concerned as to how to relay the interpretation of such a dream to the king. Nebuchadnezzar reassures him not to be disturbed either by the dream or by its interpretation. Daniel also shows some tact before he launches into the interpretation, wishing aloud that it would be far better if the dream did *not* apply to the king but to his enemies instead. Yet it is Daniel's task to hold nothing back from the king, because to do so would be unfair. It would be false comfort. The king has to know what God is saying—in case he decides to do whatever it takes to avert such a calamity.

Daniel begins by stating what Nebuchadnezzar must already suspect—that the strong, beautiful tree represents the king himself. He continues by restating what the king has already said about the angel coming down from heaven and the angel's proclamation about what is to happen to the tree. Daniel bypasses the angel, though, and ascribes the decree as coming directly from God Himself. God has pronounced judgment on the proud and boastful king; he will be caused to acknowledge that God is King of kings and that human kingdoms are only allowed to rise up and rule within God's sovereign will.

Then there is nothing else for it. Daniel proceeds to interpret the dream:

> This is the interpretation, Your Majesty, and this is the decree the Most High has issued against my lord the king: You will be driven away from people and will live with the wild animals; you will eat grass like the ox and be drenched with the dew of heaven. Seven times will pass by for you until you acknowledge that the Most High is sovereign over all kingdoms on earth and gives them to anyone he wishes. The command to leave the stump of the tree with its roots means that your kingdom will be restored to you when you acknowledge that Heaven rules. Therefore, Your Majesty, be pleased to accept my advice: Renounce your sins by doing what is right, and your wickedness by being kind to the oppressed. It may be that then your prosperity will continue. (Daniel 4:24–27)

The king will be banished from his fine palace and eat grass in the fields for "seven times." He will lose his sanity for that time. Yet he will return to sanity and to power after the experience causes him to acknowledge

God's sovereignty. The metal band protecting the tree stump signifies that the king's throne will remain available for him. As Charles Ozanne[10] notes, its composition of iron and bronze signifies durability, hardness, and power. The band would also protect the king from death, decay, and the advances of undergrowth and predatory animals, that is to say, from death and the advances of those who would usurp the kingdom from him. The "seven times" almost certainly alludes to a period of seven years and is linked to the protection of the king's throne for his return. The dream has predicted the exact time his insanity will last to the day, and thus, Daniel and others can prepare for his return, perhaps setting up a regency government to rule the kingdom in his stead.

However, in the meantime, Daniel's advice is that if the king changes his behavior drastically for the better by being merciful to the dispossessed and downtrodden, God may perhaps lift the judgment from the king's life and not bring to pass the events the dream has predicted. Perhaps even now, late in his reign, he can escape the judgment. Such a radical change in conduct could be the evidence that he is willing to do more than merely pay God lip service. The king would need to do more than simply add the Most High to his pantheon of innumerable gods. He would need to turn wholeheartedly to God.

This time, there is no record at all of any positive response by the king to Daniel's interpretation and advice. Perhaps it was met instead with a stony, stern silence. We do know, though, that the king chose to ignore the warning and admonition.

The Fulfillment of Nebuchadnezzar's Dream of a Tree

We learn in the same chapter of Daniel that from the time of the dream, God gave the king a year in which to repent and change his behavior, to do what was right instead. But he did not do it. We find Nebuchadnezzar one year later as he walks on the Babylonian palace rooftop, and he beholds the splendor of all that he sees before him, saying:

> "Is not this the great Babylon I have built as the royal residence, by *my* mighty power and for the glory of *my* majesty?"
> Even as the words were on his lips, a voice came from heaven,

"This is what is decreed for you, King Nebuchadnezzar: Your royal authority has been taken from you. You will be driven away from people and will live with the wild animals; you will eat grass like the ox. Seven times will pass by for you until you acknowledge that the Most High is sovereign over all kingdoms on earth and gives them to anyone he wishes." (Daniel 4:31–32, emphasis mine)

God's judgment happened at once, and Nebuchadnezzar went mad instantly. He lived in isolation from humanity, living peaceably alongside the wild animals, eating grass like cattle. His hair grew like feathers around him, and his nails became like a bird's claws. The entire prophecy came to pass, and it would indeed take "seven times"—seven full years—for him to become humbled enough to acknowledge God as sovereign.

Yet the narrative has a positive ending. At the end of the period of time given in his dream, Nebuchadnezzar lifted his eyes to the God of heaven, and his sanity was restored. He praised God and honored him. At the same time, his sovereignty and majesty as king were restored to him. And in an outcome somewhat like the outcome for Job after his time of severe testing and suffering,[11] Nebuchadnezzar's life and kingdom become even greater than before, greater than they were before calamity overtook him.

At this time and as a truly humbled king, Nebuchadnezzar turned his back on the false Babylonian gods he had worshipped in the past and instead praised God, the King of heaven. Scripture records his words for us:

Then I praised the Most High; I honored and glorified him who lives forever. His dominion is an eternal dominion; his kingdom endures from generation to generation. All the peoples of the earth are regarded as nothing. He does as he pleases with the powers of heaven and the peoples of the earth. No one can hold back his hand or say to him: "What have you done?" Now I, Nebuchadnezzar, praise and exalt and glorify the King of heaven, because everything he does is right and all his ways are just. And those who walk in pride he is able to humble." (Daniel 4:34–35, 37)

The language Nebuchadnezzar uses is interesting. Much of it has parallels in the Psalms, Isaiah, and Job.[12] Perhaps he has access to these Scriptures through Daniel and other high-ranking Jewish courtiers at the Babylonian palace. Perhaps he is moved also by the Holy Spirit as God blesses him; he prays and worships from a position of genuine repentance. Yet occasionally the language is unique to Nebuchadnezzar. God is only referred to once in Scripture, here, as the King of heaven, although He is referred to as king in Scripture from time to time. The reason we are so familiar with Nebuchadnezzar's unique expression is that the Irish hymn "Be Thou My Vision" contains the line, "High king of heaven, after victory won." Nebuchadnezzar has a unique perspective of God because of his former standing and the humbling experience from which, in God's mercy and sovereignty, he has been delivered. In his meekness, Nebuchadnezzar can now reinherit his earthly kingdom, given to the lowliest of men, as God decreed through an angel in his dream. In a future time, Christ will allow the meek to inherit the kingdom of God.[13]

By understanding the dream from heaven and coming through his ordeal to a place of repentance before the God of heaven, Nebuchadnezzar was actually saved from losing his life. Had he not undergone this experience, he would have gained the whole world, as he saw it—the beautiful hanging gardens, the temples, the territory gained through outstanding military conquests—but would have lost his soul.[14] As it was, he came to repentance and found real life. God was then pleased to add to him even more than he had when he walked the palace roof arrogantly surveying all that was before him. As Joyce Baldwin[15] succinctly puts it, God afflicted the king in order to be able to bless him. As God said through the dream, He exalts the lowliest of men.

Conclusions

By refusing point-blank to describe his dream of a statue to anyone while also demanding the dream's interpretation, Nebuchadnezzar created a unique and potentially fatal situation for all around him. And as we have seen, it led to an even more remarkable turn of events, unique in

Scripture, in which God provided His prophet with a vision that completely encapsulated and explained an earlier dream by someone else. It seems that God utilized this approach to instruct and teach Nebuchadnezzar that while he perceived himself as a semi-divine ruler, he was merely a man, albeit one who had been given an earthly kingdom and glory. Moreover, his kingdom was destined not to last. The territory it contained would be conquered again and again by future powers inferior in various ways to his kingdom of gold.

The young king reacted at once to this revelation and elevated Daniel to a position of power and influence. Nebuchadnezzar also acknowledged Daniel's God, but merely added him to all the others. And it may be that he decided to be much more careful of Daniel's country, Judah, than he otherwise would have been. Certainly, his conquest of Judah, a very much weaker neighboring kingdom, was very protracted. He would surely have seen Daniel's God, the God who provided him with so much revelation, as the God of Judah and its capital, Jerusalem.

But who was this God to Nebuchadnezzar, really? Perhaps merely one of so many territorial gods operating in the region . . . and had he not conquered most of the other gods along with their territories? Were the gods of Babylon not more powerful?

In a revealing and again potentially fatal turn of events, the king then focused on the "head of gold" idea and extended it to a whole statue! In pride, he rebelled against the truth conveyed in his dream that his power to rule was merely given by God. No, he the king had power to rule, and *he* must be worshipped: "King Nebuchadnezzar made a gold statue ninety feet tall and nine feet wide and set it up on the plain of Dura in the province of Babylon" (Daniel 3:1, NLT). The statue probably either represented himself, the god Nabu, from whom his name was derived, or a conflation of the two into one image.

The decree went out. All people had to bow down before the golden image and worship it or face the pain of death in a blazing furnace. Daniel's three Jewish associates refused, were thrown into the furnace, and were supernaturally protected by God, who appeared in the furnace as a fourth person but also as "a son of the gods," according to the astonished king who was looking on. This time Nebuchadnezzar called God "the Most High God."

Yet this vision of God and His saving power, along with Daniel's faithful witness of God in the Babylonian court, was still insufficient for Nebuchadnezzar. He did not repent of his despotic wielding of sovereign power. It took a further dream from God to achieve that. We see him much later in his reign when he receives the second dream. Again it is about himself, but this time, he truly gives praise to God. His recounting of this dream is part of his testimony as to how, through signs and wonders, God chose to humble him but also to bring him back up from the depths as soon as he looked up to heaven, silently repenting and crying out to God. This time Nebuchadnezzar is profoundly changed. Now he is one who fully acknowledges and worships God as ruler of all while gladly accepting the place God has given him in the scheme of things.

In our own day, God is perfectly capable of giving us in dreams the same type of prophetic warning He gave to Nebuchadnezzar in his dream of a tree brought down. God had warned the king that he must repent of his pride and idolatry. If we get such a warning, we would do well to repent and seek after God who, as eternally and unchangeably good, will spare us the kind of catastrophic fate that befell the king of Babylon. Otherwise, pride and idolatry lead inevitably to the destruction of the soul.

The timeline of Nebuchadnezzar's dream of the unfolding statue sweeps on through subsequent history, and the end of the dream has not been reached. We are still in the days when Gentile powers rule on earth. Although the major fulfillment of the emperor's dream of two feet with ten toes of iron mixed with clay still has not unfolded fully, it is possible that a number of minor fulfillments have already occurred. In 2003, for instance, a coalition of forty nations, led by the United States, invaded Iraq, the heartland of Nebuchadnezzar's empire. In 2004, the United States interim military formation was replaced by the Multi-National Force-Iraq (MNF-I). In the media, this tended to be referred to as the "coalition forces." The MNF-1, the command authority operational between 2004 and 2011, consisted of ten nations, as per Nebuchadnezzar's dream. The iron and clay in this composition of nations was so short term and politically divided that Spain pulled out in 2004, shortly after arriving on the battlefield, its newly elected Prime Minister Zapatero fulfilling a key election pledge to remove Spanish troops. Italy followed likewise in 2006 with Prime Minister Prodi announcing that the invasion had been "a huge mistake." Only the USA and UK remained until 2011.

CHAPTER 13

Cautionary Notes

I started this book with a series of chapters that focused on the Bible's accounts of how and when God spoke to various people through dreams. I wanted to show that in Scripture, dreams are recorded time and time again as one of the ways God has used to communicate with us. I follow up this focus in the penultimate chapter of this book with a number of recent and contemporary accounts of God speaking through dreams.

Clearly, I am not a cessationist. I believe that if God communicated in certain ways in the past, then He is very likely to do the same now and in the future. We have not changed, and neither has God. Jesus is the same always. The consistency of God is part of the case for and part of the test of the validity of a lot of contemporary spiritual experiences, whether they be dreams possibly from God, visions of angels, experiences of heaven, miracles of healing, and so on.

In these days of rationalism, materialism, reductionism, and super-ficiality, a significant danger is that we will avoid paying any attention to our dreams and thus miss out on warnings, guidance, and insights that God may be giving us in this way. If our thinking is a by-product of a godless educational system, there is also a more general danger that our overall worldview and critical stance will be completely rational and skeptical. This stance is likely to dismiss the possibility of heaven touch-ing us, of the more real breaking in on us and the world surrounding us—a world that, in fact, is less real than the heavenly one. It is this world, the fallen earth, which contains illusion and deception, not the heavenly world which, as we know, is perfect.

Why was it, after all, that when Jesus returned to earth in His resur-rected body He was able to appear miraculously in a room to speak with

His disciples? Was it because He was ghost-like? Far from it. He was able to appear because His was, and is, the greater reality. In comparison to His omnipotence and His greatest reality, the walls of the room He appeared in were very much less solid.

However, if we have not fallen into over-rationalism, we must rely on Scripture much more fully when it comes to dreams (and any other possible source of revelation), since we need to use Scripture to test our experience. This has less to do with whether God ever speaks through dreams; Scripture attests to the fact that He has. It has much more to do with whether or not God could have spoken through *this* dream now.

We really must have a solid grounding in Scripture so that we are familiar with the character of God as it has already been revealed to us. If a dream contradicts scriptural revelation, clearly it is the former which somehow is in error. It could even be deliberately deceptive. Anything that speaks of a non-biblical, "other" Jesus or other gospel must be rejected, whether it comes through a dream, a false prophet, or the demonic masquerading as the angelic.

At the same time, if we are open to God's communication with us, there is a danger that we will stray into an over-focus on dreams at the expense of being open to God in other ways. This over-focus could quite easily send us off course and into error and deception. We should not rely only on a dream for guidance on major decisions, and we should look for confirmation from other sources. It may be that the dream we had was a soulish dream created by the carnal longings of our heart. The dream is a commentary on and an output from what is going on within us and does not contain information relevant to further guidance. It could also just be triggered by overwork and overactivity,[1] or there could be some sort of deception in it.

God may use dreams to speak to us, but He will do so in tandem with many other ways of communicating. As well as recording our dreams in order to reflect on them, we will also need to reflect on how events in our lives are unfolding and on how God is speaking to us when we prayerfully listen to Him, and we must ensure that we respond to any inner promptings that seem to come from Him to our heart or spirit. A dream from God may be just part of the picture that God is building up for us. Dreams bypass the mind, but inner promptings also tend to do this. Both types of experience may be offering guidance to us and presenting us with the next steps forward.

Dreams are also very often a commentary on recent life experiences; they are usually *not* disconnected and isolated events but are given in a timely way to inform us about our experiences in daily life or problems we are grappling with. Keeping close to God by practicing His presence and praying continually is the best way to receive ongoing guidance from Him. Learning to interpret dreams should be part of this. Interpretation should be a prayerful process. We are taking our dreams and offering them back to our Creator. We are asking Him to reveal the meaning, to make it clear to us. *What are You saying to me, God? What is my own heart saying to me?*

A great deal of caution needs to be applied when starting to interpret your own dreams, and in a sense, even more caution is needed when you have some limited experience. Some dreams are simple and their meanings relatively obvious. There is a danger that successful interpretation of them will lead us to misinterpret more complex dreams and then to take action we were never meant to take. As Herman Riffel emphasizes, proficiency in dream interpretation is developed over many years.

At the same time, though, we should not walk in a fearful way when it comes to the interpretation of dreams. Interpreting dreams is a learning process. If we get an interpretation wrong as we grapple with a strange, symbolic language, God is able to inform our understanding and lead us toward the correct meaning. We will not like the time delay, but God is able to get us there.

When we considered false and ungodly dreams, we looked at some examples from Scripture where interpreters of dreams advocated pursuit of "foreign gods," that is to say, the demonic. The warning in Scripture was to turn away from such people and to discard their message.[2] Sometimes when dreaming, it is at the very least possible desires normally hidden from the conscious mind will arise and then drive an ungodly dream. While it is good to know what is in your heart, it is also true that "The heart is deceitful above all things, and desperately wicked; who can know it?"[3]

If the dream contradicts God's guidance and revelation through Scripture, it is always the dream that is wrong, not the Word of God. It could even be that by reading the Word and letting it soak in, you have given the Holy Spirit greater access to you than before, and He is stirring up in you what still acts in opposition to Him. It then manifests its presence by way of a dream.

> For the word of God is quick, and powerful, and sharper than any two-edged sword, piercing even to the dividing asunder of soul and spirit, and of the joints and marrow, and is a discerner of the thoughts and intents of the heart. (Hebrews 4:12, KJV)

Finally, although I believe that far more dreams have meaning than many people think, I do not believe that all dreams necessarily are meaningful. If a dream is merely caused by overtiredness or even some medication we are taking because of an illness, it would be time-wasting to attempt to interpret it! Overtiredness can cause your mind to meander in a random way, and the dreams you experience at such a time, if they are truly dreams at all, can also tend to lack meaning.

At the same time, though, if you focus on dreams and use discernment when interpreting and acting on them, you will find that the majority of your dreams do have meaning and purpose to them. If you are walking with God to the best of your ability, you will also find that of these meaningful dreams, many may be from God, given that they contain a wisdom and intention that does not come from you.

In conclusion, I emphasize that all dreams need to be tested. This is because they can be from our own unconscious and hence are not divine; they can come from God; or they can come from the demonic. If a dream comes from the demonic, it should be banished in the night as firmly as in the following example taken from section 20 of Saint Patrick's *Confessio*, his account of his life:

> That same night while I was sleeping, Satan strongly put me to the test—I will remember it as long as I live! It was as if an enormous rock fell on me, and I lost all power in my limbs. Although I knew little about the life of the spirit at the time,

how was it that I knew to call upon Helias? While these things were happening, I saw the sun rise in the sky, and while I was calling "Helias! Helias!" with all my strength, the splendor of the sun fell on me; and immediately, all that weight was lifted from me. I believe that I was helped by Christ the Lord, and that his spirit cried out for me. I trust that it will be like this whenever I am under stress, as the gospel says: "In that day, the Lord testifies, it will not be you who will speak, but the Spirit of your Father who speaks in you."[4]

CHAPTER 14

Apocalyptic Dreams: Visions of the End Times

We now shift to an account of two dream-visions that God gave to Daniel. The text does not imply that Daniel was asleep and dreaming, but that he had visions during the night. He was so troubled by them that he asked angels to interpret them for him. For the first of these accounts by Daniel, now as the visionary, we also shift forward in time to about 550 BC and the first year of Belshazzar's reign as Babylonian co-regent.

The 550 BC is probably significant. Daniel had been at court throughout Nebuchadnezzar's long and successful reign of forty-three years. Yet after Nebuchadnezzar's death in 562 BC, Daniel observed that while the empire continued to be successful militarily, it had begun to deteriorate rapidly from within. At the time of this first vision, it had only about eleven years left. Nebuchadnezzar's son, Amel-Marduk, reigned only for about three years and was murdered by his brother-in-law, who in turn was deposed in 556 BC in a coup d'état by Nabonidus, the last Babylonian emperor per se.

Although successful militarily, Nabonidus actually had very little interest in ruling the empire and took himself off to an oasis just three years after becoming emperor to worship the god Sin for thirteen years, thereby incurring the displeasure of the Babylonian priesthood devoted to the god Marduk. Balshazzar, his son, was made co-regent with his father and second-in-command of the empire in 551 BC in an effort to hold things together. Balshazzar would meet his end in 539 BC when the Medo-Persians invaded to conquer the empire. The fate of Nabonidus is unknown. Some sources indicate that he was permitted to retire, others that he died in 538 BC as a prisoner of war.

Daniel thus began to have his visions in a time of rapid political change when different internal factions had been fighting for power.[1] The near future was one of invasion and the complete transfer of power to an invading army from the northeast. Daniel also had his first vision while arguably the worst of the Babylonian rulers was in charge. Unlike his ancestor Nebuchadnezzar,[2] Balshazzar seems only to have mocked the King of heaven, even as the invading army was at the gates of Babylon the night before his execution.[3] In response, God brought his reign and his empire to an end. Balshazzar had been weighed by God's scales and was found wanting.

Daniel's Apocalyptic Dream-Vision of Four Kingdoms and the Ancient of Days

In the midst of so much political turmoil, Daniel has a vision of four great beasts, unlike any beasts humanity is familiar with, arising from a chaotic sea, one after the other, as the four winds of heaven blow on it. Each beast is unique and unlike the others. The first to rise up is like a winged lion. Its wings are torn off, and it rises up to stand on two feet like a man. A man's heart is given to it. The second beast looks like a bear raised up on one of its sides. It has three ribs between its teeth and is told to eat its fill of flesh. The third beast is a four-winged leopard with four heads. It is given authority to rule. Finally, a terrifying fourth beast appears with iron teeth, ten horns, and power to crush and trample all its victims. Another horn, possessing eyes like a man and a boastful mouth, rises up among the other horns, uprooting three of them.

As he continues to recount the substance of this dream-vision, Daniel says:

> As I looked, thrones were set in place, and the Ancient of Days took his seat. His clothing was as white as snow; the hair of his head was white like wool. His throne was flaming with fire, and its wheels were all ablaze. A river of fire was flowing, coming out from before him. Thousands upon thousands attended him; ten thousand times ten thousand stood before him. The court was seated and the books were opened.

Then I continued to watch because of the boastful word the horn was speaking. I kept looking until the beast was slain and its body destroyed and thrown into the blazing fire. (The other beasts had been stripped of their authority, but were allowed to live for a period of time.)

In my vision at night I looked, and there before me was one like a son of man, coming with the clouds of heaven. He approached the Ancient of Days and was led into his presence. He was given authority, glory and sovereign power; all nations and peoples of every language worshiped him. His dominion is an everlasting dominion that will not pass away, and his kingdom is one that will never be destroyed. (Daniel 7:9–14)

Before we consider the angel's interpretation, we can consider the following points. The entire dream indicates that it is God who ultimately has control over these kingdoms. It is He who has control over the winds of heaven and He who ultimately gives them power to rule. But the sea out of which they arise is the sea of humanity, of nations often in conflict, throwing up different human powers, all eager to conquer and rule.[4]

The sea also symbolizes the supernatural evil that gives energy and substance to this human power. Although the kingdoms differ across time and geographical region, the same evil power throws them up. Yet it is God who exercises overall control, limiting their time spans to specific allocations of years. He also possesses complete and perfect knowledge of what every kingdom, and everyone who has served it, has done. All this is contained in books that are opened to ensure that perfect judgment is carried out. The books are their own perfect witness to events, and so no appeal can be of any avail.[5]

Many commentators view the first kingdom as symbolizing Babylon, the power Daniel knew well. A winged lion image could symbolize their principal deity, Marduk, and the dream image may also symbolize a power that is able to swoop down with speed on any military adversary,[6] taking its captives back to the capital. The wings torn off could symbolize the rapid decline of the empire and the powerlessness of Belshazzar;

the dream was given when its last ruler, someone who would not lead the army in battle against the Medo-Persians, had just taken power. The symbolism then would be similar to the head of gold in Nebuchadnezzar's dream many years earlier, but not identical. At the same time, however, there is no statement in Daniel to confirm that all this supposition is correct. The first beast is unnamed.

The bear as the second beast is simply told, presumably by God, to eat its fill of flesh, to indulge a ravenous appetite. It makes sense to most commentators to apply this symbolism to Medo-Persia and its rule over the region for the next two hundred years. The fact that it was raised up on one of its sides may then be of more interest than the fact that it had three ribs in its mouth. Medo-Persia only existed as a successful military power because the Persians had conquered the Medes in 549 BC. The Persians then continued to dominate the empire. Commentators disagree on what the three ribs may mean. Certainly God is in overall control of these events as well; one of the key reasons for Medo-Persia coming to power was the benign policy of the Medo-Persian emperors Cyrus and Cambyses II[7] toward the Jews returning to Jerusalem and rebuilding their temple. This policy served God's purposes regarding His people and was part of the more widely applied Medo-Persian policy of freedom of religion for conquered people groups.

The bear symbol *could* closely parallel the silver chest and arms that Nebuchadnezzar saw, representing an empire inferior in some way to his own. Yet again Daniel does not name this beast, and the assumption that it symbolizes Medo-Persia is retrospective. That is, the assumption is from our current viewpoint looking back at the sweep of history up to the present day. If we consider things from Daniel's perspective as he looked forward, there is nothing in his text to suggest this interpretation. The second beast is unnamed.

Could the leopard image symbolizing the third beast mean Greece? This power would not conquer the region for another two hundred years, and possibly the dual leopard and wings symbolism fits Alexander the Great's empire and the speed with which he conquered Medo-Persia and Egypt. Commentators tend to suggest that the dual symbolism of four wings and four heads symbolizes the ongoing rule of Greece through Alexander's four generals after Alexander died in Babylon. However, as Charles Ozanne[8] points out, the symbolism does not quite fit that history, of one all-conquering ruler being replaced by four lesser ones. When the third beast first appears, it already has four heads! If it symbolized Greece, should the symbolism not be more complex? And again, Daniel does not name this third beast anyway.

The last beast with ten horns, altogether more terrifying than the other beasts, is to a large extent really what this dream-vision is about. It is likely that it has already appeared in Nebuchadnezzar's first dream; its ten horns were probably symbolized on the statue as ten toes. Now the revelation in Daniel's dream-vision builds on the king's dream. It develops the destructive nature of the final Gentile kingdom that will suffer a sudden defeat by God's intervention.

This final kingdom does not just appear in the book of Daniel. It appears in Revelation 13 and again in Revelation 17 in a vision given to the apostle John, yet on that occasion it too resembles a leopard (generally), a bear (its feet), and a lion (its mouth). As in Daniel's vision, John's vision of it is of an utterly malevolent and generic horror.

Does the symbolism in Daniel fit the Roman Empire, an empire that lasted much longer and collapsed more slowly than any of the preceding powers? Rome was the power that crucified Christ, sacked Jerusalem in AD 70, persecuted Christians, and continued to rule in some measure until AD 1453 and the fall of Constantinople and the eastern Roman Empire. But Daniel's dream moves on well beyond this time to the end of this present age, to another stage of prophecy. The ten-horned kingdom has still to arise, only to be destroyed by the Ancient of Days, just as the feet of iron and clay are yet to be smashed by the God of heaven whose kingdom will never be destroyed.

If the symbolism speaks of Rome, the spirit and power of the Roman Empire will first need to be recreated and reenergized for a brief time. For Daniel, the beast is unnamed, but we know when it will rule. It will rule in our future, at the end of this age. We know that it will be the last Gentile power ruling in its final form, governed by the Antichrist.

An alternative viewpoint is that all four of these beast empires are still in our future and have not so far been fulfilled completely by any power in history. The narrative does suggest in places that they appear in quick succession, even at the same time. Commentator W.M. Henry[9] further suggests that because the beasts' symbolism appears together in the later vision given to the apostle John[10] of just *one* beast coming out of the sea, these four powers seen by Daniel arise at more or less the same time. They are in conflict with each other to a degree but are all energized by the same underlying demonic power. They also unify to a degree under that same power.

Then a new scene appears before Daniel—he is looking at the throne room of heaven. The Ancient of Days, the God of heaven who lives from everlasting to everlasting, executes judgment on the beast that appeared so powerful in the earlier scenes in the vision. Anyone allied to the God of heaven, all those who lose their lives for God and the sake of the gospel,[11] all those who long for God's kingdom to come on earth, will therefore also be victorious. Daniel says that he saw the court being seated and the books opened. He is one of several biblical authors who describe this event, the first being Moses in Exodus 32:32 and the last being the apostle John, the author of Revelation.

The fourth beast is destroyed suddenly and easily, and its body is thrown into the fire. And then a divine yet human person appears. As in a coronation, he is given all power, glory, and authority, he is worshipped as God, and it is *His* kingdom that will last forever. In his apocalyptic vision, Daniel sees this "Son of Man" coming with the clouds of heaven. He is given a vision of the distant future and sees the appearance of an ascended and glorified Jesus Christ. As the psalmist says,[12] Jesus "makes the clouds his chariot."

While on earth, Jesus used the title "Son of Man" of Himself sixty-nine times as recorded in the four gospels. He also referred to His glorious appearing at the end of days while before the Sanhedrin. He stated, "But I say to all of you: From now on you will see the Son of Man sitting at the right hand of the Mighty One and coming in the clouds of heaven" (Matthew 26:64). Daniel had seen this event ahead of time, seeing God the Father and God the Son in the same vision. Much later, the martyr Stephen cries out as he is given a vision of heaven and sees the Son of Man standing there;[13] while the apostle John, right at the start of his own apocalyptic vision, also sees the Son of Man when he turns around to see who it is who has a voice like that of a trumpet.[14]

The Interpretation of Daniel's First Dream-Vision

Daniel is greatly troubled by aspects of the vision and seeks an interpretation from one of the angels[15] who is also present. The angel confirms that the four beasts symbolize four kingdoms that will achieve power on earth for a time. Yet the "saints of the Most High" will inherit a different kingdom, one that will last forever. This angelic interpretation is taken up in the New Testament in letters that encourage Christian believers who face all kinds of trials in this present age.[16] In turn, Daniel's vision alludes to this future situation, the persecution of God's elect, both Christian and Messianic Jewish. In his expansion of the vision, he recounts to the angel that he saw the fourth beast's little horn waging war against the saints and defeating them until the Ancient of Days judged in their favor and enabled them to possess their everlasting kingdom (Daniel 7:21–22).

The fourth crushing and devouring beast, which is unlike the others, with its ten horns, little horn with pompous mouth, iron teeth, and bronze claws, especially unnerves Daniel. And so he asks the angel what the true meaning of it is. The meaning is that unlike the three previous kingdoms, this one will devour the whole earth. Ten kings will arise from this kingdom, and an eleventh king will arise thereafter, supplanting three of them.

> He will speak against the Most High and oppress his holy people and try to change the set times and the laws. The holy people will be delivered into his hands for a time, times and half a time. (Daniel 7:25)

The Aramaic term used and sometimes interpreted as "oppress" can, in the Hebrew equivalent, mean to wipe out or eradicate.[17] In all likelihood, the attempt to change set times and laws indicates that the ruler represented by the little horn will attempt to gather all earthly power to himself alone as dictator and deify himself as the Caesars went on to do. He will seek to banish all the Judeo-Christian past for humankind by rearranging all human affairs—all marking of time, all customs, and all laws. His reckless, futile attempt to blaspheme God and set himself above God is also prophesied by Paul as he describes the Antichrist in one of his letters.[18]

In possible localized precursors to this radical changing of set times, humanistic and communist revolutionaries in France and Russia in the late eighteenth and early twentieth centuries AD abolished the Judeo-Christian seven-day week with its day of rest on the seventh day and instituted ten-day and five-day weeks respectively. Both attempts failed within twelve years, with the collapse of the French First Republic and with Stalin facing a disastrous falling away of worker productivity.

The rule of the little horn ruler over the saints is limited to a "time, times and half a time." Many commentators assume this equates with a period of three and a half years, and although the angel does not say that, it could well be the correct interpretation. Significant emphasis is placed on the "half a time": the swift cutting off of the ruler's power, and presumably, his life. God will intervene, vanquish His enemy, and transfer all power to the Son of Man. Along with His saints, Christ will rule forever in His eternal kingdom.

In a similar vision in Revelation, the saints are shown to be priests of God and of Christ, reigning with Him in His millennial kingdom[19] after Satan has been thrown into the abyss but before the last judgment and the renewal of all things in a new heaven and new earth.

Daniel's Apocalyptic Dream-Vision of the Ram, the Goat, and the Little Horn

For Daniel's second dream-vision, we only move forward another two years, to about 548 BC and the third year of Belshazzar's reign as Babylonian co-regent. Although Daniel indicates that this dream-vision was the same type as the earlier one, it is different in the sense that he also sees himself in a particular location: the citadel of Susa in the Babylonian province of Elam. He is transported in the vision to a position beside the Ulai Canal. Unknown to Daniel at the time, this relatively obscure location was to be built up in the near future to become the main capital of the Medo-Persian empire, scheduled in God's timing to conquer Babylon about ten years after his vision occurred. Babylon and two other locations would become secondary capitals of the new empire. It is also noteworthy that just prior to Daniel's vision, in 550 BC, Cyrus[20] overcame Media at the battle of Pasargadae and established Medo-Persia as one empire. Daniel would have been well aware of this event.

The book of Esther, recording events in Medo-Persia around 483 BC, opens with the emperor Xerxes ruling from his palace complex in the citadel of Susa, the location of Daniel's vision, and holding a banquet there for the Medo-Persian officials and princes. Esther records that the banquet lasted six months. Intriguingly, historians believe that it was this grand event and its conference that planned the disastrous war against Greece. Medo-Persia and Greece are the focus of Daniel's second vision, and thus even the geographical location of Daniel's vision is symbolic and prophetic.

The future scope of his second vision focuses initially on a relatively limited timeline of about 350 years. It ignores the empire Daniel was living in and also ignores the establishing of God's eternal kingdom. Some of the events detailed, however, have a meaning that Christ Himself also prophesied about and are yet in the future, destined to occur at the very end of this age. In effect, Christ said to the Jews in His discourse on signs of the end that what Daniel described in this vision regarding their temple was still to happen in the future (see Matthew 24:15).

Daniel says:

> I looked up [from the Ulai Canal], and there before me was a ram with two horns, standing beside the canal, and the horns were long. One of the horns was longer than the other but grew up later. I watched the ram as it charged toward the west and the north and the south. No animal could stand against

it, and none could rescue from its power. It did as it pleased and became great.

As I was thinking about this, suddenly a goat with a prominent horn between its eyes came from the west, crossing the whole earth without touching the ground. It came toward the two-horned ram I had seen standing beside the canal and charged at it in great rage. I saw it attack the ram furiously, striking the ram and shattering its two horns. The ram was powerless to stand against it; the goat knocked it to the ground and trampled on it, and none could rescue the ram from its power. The goat became very great, but at the height of its power the large horn was broken off, and in its place four prominent horns grew up toward the four winds of heaven.

Out of one of them came another horn, which started small but grew in power to the south and to the east and toward the Beautiful Land. It grew until it reached the host of the heavens, and it threw some of the starry host down to the earth and trampled on them. It set itself up to be as great as the commander of the army of the LORD; it took away the daily sacrifice from the LORD, and his sanctuary was thrown down. Because of rebellion, the LORD's people and the daily sacrifice were given over to it. It prospered in everything it did, and truth was thrown to the ground. Then I heard a holy one speaking, and another holy one said to him, "How long will it take for the vision to be fulfilled—the vision concerning the daily sacrifice, the rebellion that causes desolation, the surrender of the sanctuary and the trampling underfoot of the LORD's people?" He said to me, "It will take 2,300 evenings and mornings; then the sanctuary will be reconsecrated." (Daniel 8:3–14)

We learn in the interpretation of the vision that the ram and the goat symbolize two great conquering empires, Medo-Persia and Greece, and that the goat's horn symbolizes the latter's first king. Although unnamed, the horn is clearly Alexander the Great, who at the height of his power died in Babylon in 323 BC, a mere thirteen years after succeeding to his father's throne. The clash between the animals symbolizes the empires' relatively brief three-year war. The Greek attacks are so swift that Daniel's vision depicts them as being like an aerial attack—the goat's feet do not touch the ground.

After Alexander's death, the empire was too large to be held together. Dying at the age of thirty-three, he also left no heir. A futile struggle for power arose between the generals, and after eight years of this, it was agreed that Alexander's top four generals would subdivide the empire among them. They were known as the *diadochoi,* which, in ancient Greek, means "the successors." Again as the interpretation later makes clear, they would "not have the same power" (Daniel 8:22). None of them had the same power as Alexander. Although two of them, Ptolemy Lagi and Seleucus Nicanor, forged important empires and dynasties controlled from Egypt and Babylonia respectively, they were still much smaller empires than the one created by Alexander, while the other two held even lesser territories further west. It was the Ptolemaic empire that controlled Jewish territory from 323 to 198 BC; but the Seleucids then held it, off and on, until the arrival of the Romans in 63 BC.

How different this little horn is from the one in Daniel's previous vision is debatable. Their characters and behavior are so similar that at one level, surely they are both prophecies concerning the end-of-days Antichrist. But many commentators are firmly of the opinion that the little horn in Daniel's second dream-vision symbolizes Antiochus IV Epiphanes, who ruled from 175 to 163 BC and single-handedly created a crisis for the Jewish people every bit as great as their former exile to Babylon.

Could Daniel's vision be about this man's geographical conquests, his character, and his behavior toward the Jewish people and their temple in Jerusalem? Antiochus did rule with legendary cruelty, gave himself divine status and therefore became an antichrist, murdered many Jews, stole the temple treasures, defiled the temple in different ways at different times,[21] and instituted a death penalty for anyone observing the Sabbath or any of the Jewish festivals. All Jews had to worship the Greek gods. He could even be said, in terms of the vision, to be attacking God by attacking His temple. Eventually, the Jews rebelled against him in the Maccabean revolt of 166 to 142 BC, a war lasting twenty-four years. To them, the blaspheming, arrogant Antiochus was known as *Epimanes* or the madman.

Yet for the present writer, something just does not ring true. What would Daniel's viewpoint be? He knew nothing of an Antiochus figure, but he did know, through the revelations we have considered, of an end-times empire with a despotic antichrist ruler. It is very likely that the little horns are the same man appearing twice, while Antiochus is merely an early forerunner of him.

Toward the end of Daniel's vision, he was privileged to hear a conversation in heaven between angels about what he had seen, specifically about the length of time the defilement of the Jewish temple would last before it was purified again for godly worship. He was informed that God was in control and had decreed the exact length of time. The 2,300 evenings and mornings probably means 2,300 twenty-four hour periods; that is to say, 2,300 days. This is surely about a desecration at the end of this age; historians have been unable to find any decrees, events, or circumstances in the reign of Antiochus that correspond to the period of 2,300 days. We should remember that the whole tenor of Daniel's revelation is about "the appointed time of the end" (Daniel 8:19).

Daniel's Second Dream-Vision Interpretation

The angel Gabriel appeared to Daniel as he was trying to understand the vision, and he heard a voice, presumably God's, say, "Gabriel, tell this man the meaning of the vision" (Daniel 8:16). (Gabriel later appears in Luke's gospel to the priest Zechariah and to Mary to announce the births of John the Baptist and Jesus,[22] saying to the former, "I am Gabriel. I stand in the presence of God.") The meaning of the vision causes Daniel acute distress; he is appalled by its meaning and lies ill for several days after the experience. In his encounter with the speaking angel, he also falls into a deep sleep until the angel lifts him back up from the ground;

Abraham possibly experienced something very similar in his dealings with God many hundreds of years earlier.[23]

Gabriel explains that the two-horned ram is Medo-Persia, the implication being that the longer, more recent horn is Persia. He then states that the goat is the king of Greece and its horn the first king. The four horns that replace the first horn "represent four kingdoms that will emerge from his nation but will not have the same power" (Daniel 8:22). Being split into four smaller empires ruled by the *diadochoi*, Greek history fulfilled this prophecy.

The little horn king coming from one of these four kingdoms, Gabriel says, "will become very strong, but not by his own power. He will cause astounding devastation and will succeed in whatever he does. He will destroy those who are mighty, the holy people" (Daniel 8:24). Two somewhat different ways to interpret this are to say that although his own power was limited, he used intrigue and deception to increase it, or that he was provided with demonic power. He would destroy his opponents in battle and persecute to death many faithful Jewish believers.

When the forerunner, Antiochus, was stopped eventually in his invasion of Ptolemaic territory in Egypt by Rome, he returned to Israel and took it out on the Jewish people and their temple. Yet the meaning of Daniel's vision is greater than just one man's behavior during this time. The dream-vision predicts and describes the final antichrist at an apocalyptic end of this present age. Believers living then will take comfort from Daniel and Revelation. Forerunners such as Antiochus and many of the Roman Caesars also fit well with the vision. Believers living in these times past also took comfort from the apocalyptic Scriptures.

In his interpretation, Gabriel adds that this ruler will "exalt himself in his heart" or "consider himself superior." Again, if we consider the forerunner, Antiochus, as a type of things yet to come, we see that he declared himself God in the name he assumed: *Epiphanes* means "God manifest." This was something no Hellenistic ruler had ever done before. Paul prophesied about a very similar ruler at the end of this age who will sit down as God in the temple of God.[24] But the angel says of him, "Yet he will be destroyed, but not by human power" (Daniel 8:25b).

Christ will directly intervene to slay the Antichrist with the breath of His mouth.[25] As for the early forerunner, Antiochus was not killed in battle or assassinated. He died suddenly from an unknown disease in 164 BC. He did not die by human power either!

Once Gabriel completed his interpretation, there was nothing Daniel could do but lie in bed until he had sufficiently recovered to go about the king's business as usual. He said the vision "was beyond understanding." Perhaps he would have liked a much more detailed explanation and timeline than Gabriel provided. But he had to be content with the revelation he had been given. He was commanded to "seal up the vision, for it concerns the distant future." That is, the vision had no application for the time being. No doubt Daniel's record of it encouraged the Jews who continued to live in exile and then in their homeland but under Hellenistic persecution.

In the future, when the prophecies start to be fulfilled by world events, the vision that was sealed will blaze out from the book of Daniel and illumine both the reader and the events he or she is witnessing. Even today it can encourage us with a revelation that no evil rule can prevail for long. It will be cut off by God at the appointed time.

Conclusions

Although there is much more in Daniel's book that merits in-depth study (chapters 9–12, for example), the eighth chapter completes the symbolic presentations through dreams and dream-visions of future events. There could be a close parallelism within and across the dreams that we can outline here. In short, both Nebuchadnezzar and Daniel may at least sometimes be dreaming of the same powers and events. They also certainly both dream of a historical process culminating in an apocalyptic ending of humanity's corrupted rule over the earth by God's sudden intervention at the end of days to establish His own kingdom.

Nebuchadnezzar's dream of a head of gold may be paralleled, just possibly, by Daniel's dream of a winged lion, and the meaning certainly of the head of gold is the Babylonian empire (Daniel 2:36–38). The statue's chest and arms made of silver may be paralleled by the ram, which appears in Daniel's second dream-vision. The ram is interpreted as the Medo-Persian empire (Daniel 8:20). Next we have the statue's bronze belly and thighs, paralleled perhaps by the goat with this animal interpreted as Greece (Daniel 8:21). Finally, in terms of humankind's rule over the earth, we have the statue's legs of iron and feet of iron and clay, paralleled in Daniel's visions of a terrifying beast in his first dream-vision. The ten toes correspond to the last beast's ten horns and symbolize ten kings. We can infer that this symbolism fits the last Gentile empire in its final state at the end of this present age. It is one global power but with ten subdivisions.

Occasionally, the dream symbolism is almost the same, but because of the symbols' contexts, the interpretation must differ. The little horn arising from the goat "which started small but grew in power" (Daniel 8:9) can be interpreted as the antichrist figure Antiochus IV Epiphanes as well as the final Antichrist; the little horn arising from among the terrifying beast's ten horns cannot. This latter horn exclusively symbolizes the more powerful, final Antichrist figure at the end of this present age. We see the recurring theme, though, of antichrist figures rising up against God and His people only to be crushed by a higher power. The first one, living even before Christ is born, is a type of the Antichrist yet to come.

Why are certain powers symbolized for Nebuchadnezzar and Daniel in their dreams—why not other powers? It is probably because each of the three powers mentioned explicitly (and we conjecture Rome could also be implied by the text) had taken or would take control of Jerusalem and reign over the Jewish people for a time. It is the conquest of the holy land and its capital city that makes these powers important to the biblical account. There is also a commonality regarding the city of Babylon and its importance to these four powers. Babylon was the capital of the first empire; it was an important provincial capital in Medo-Persia; Alexander the Great intended that it *would* be his capital had he not died there; and we know from Revelation that Babylon will regain substantial importance at the end of days.

The one remaining parallel across the dreams is the supernatural rock seen by Nebuchadnezzar as crashing into the statue. After the wind sweeps the statue's pieces away, this rock becomes a huge mountain that fills the earth. A parallel appears in the first of Daniel's dream-visions when the Ancient of Days takes his throne in the heavenly court. The last great beast is killed and thrown into the blazing fire. And "one like a son of man" comes into the Ancient of Days' presence and is given authority, glory, and power to rule an everlasting kingdom (Daniel 7:9–14).

The significance of these four dreams cannot be overemphasized. Through them, God reveals His purposes for the world, His people Israel, and the Gentile powers. He reveals something of the mystery of evil as it continues to conspire beneath humanity, empowering individuals and their bestial empires to rise up against both God's people and God Himself. As time goes by, humankind's rule will wax worse and worse. Like the changing metals of the statue, human civilization will deteriorate toward a worthless end while its rulers become harder and harder. Yet God further reveals that all such temporal powers only exercise authority within the confines, temporal and geographical, that He Himself sets around them.

Most of all, though, God reveals a message of His own sovereign rule and His own complete victory in the end of days. He reveals that He Himself will destroy all evil power and reign thereafter over a kingdom that will never end. Some of the messages of Daniel's vision are still sealed. It is possible that Daniel's dream of four kingdoms is about four contemporaneous kingdoms, as commentators such as Charles Ozanne[26] and Allan Harman[27] suggest, with the Antichrist ultimately ruling over them all as Revelation 13:2 would seem to indicate. If so, then such visions are for their own time, and believers living in that time will take comfort from these dreams and their interpretations. The meaning of the words that have been closed up and sealed will be clear, everyone written in the book of life will be delivered out of their distress, and the outcome of all things will be certain.

CHAPTER 15

Angelic Commands and Warnings

Matthew's gospel was written sometime between AD 40 and AD 100, with many commentators suggesting a midpoint in that range. Like the other three gospels, it is a distinctive selection and arrangement of material about Christ. The four gospels include significant overlaps in the events they describe and combine to form a complete witness to Christ, but each gospel is also unique in its own way. Matthew's inclusion early on in his narrative of five angelic dreams is one of the ways in which *his* gospel distinctively and uniquely portrays some of the events in Christ's life.

Who was Matthew? The evangelist was one of the twelve chosen by Jesus. He describes how this happened in Matthew 9:9, which the NIV subtitles "The Calling of Matthew." "As Jesus went on from there, he saw a man named Matthew sitting at the tax collector's booth. 'Follow me,' he told him, and Matthew got up and followed him." Jesus had just called a well-educated, literate scribe who was experienced in keeping meticulous written records in Greek, the language his gospel would be written in.

Matthew then tells us what happened soon after, when he invited Jesus into his home for dinner:

> While Jesus was having dinner at Matthew's house, many tax collectors and sinners came and ate with him and his disciples. When the Pharisees saw this, they asked his disciples, "Why does your teacher eat with tax collectors and sinners?" On hearing this, Jesus said, "It is not the healthy who need a doctor, but the sick." (Matthew 9:9–12)

Matthew wrote the most Jewish of the four gospels, and this may be one of the reasons the dreams appear. He sometimes included them to explain how and why the early events in Jesus' life occurred and how they fulfilled Old Testament Jewish prophecies about the Messiah. The dreams explain how supernatural events caused the fulfillment to happen. It is very probable then that Matthew was writing initially for a Jewish Christian audience, a group of early Jewish believers in Jesus Christ as the longed-for Messiah.

At the same time, Matthew focuses later on the wider community of believers. His gospel is the only one that mentions the concept of "church," as used by Christ. For example: "And I tell you that you are Peter, and on this rock I will build my church, and the gates of Hades will not overcome it" (Matthew 16:18). Also, like Daniel, Matthew firmly believed in the apocalyptic, that Christ had become incarnate in the end of days, and that soon this present age would end when Christ returned in glory. There would then be eternal reward for some but eternal punishment for others. He quotes Christ as saying that the former would need to enter their eternal life by the narrow gate, "For wide is the gate and broad is the road that leads to destruction, and many enter through it" (Matthew 7:13).

Matthew's main purpose then was to write as clearly as possible about Jesus—His origins, life, teaching, miracles, and divinity. Matthew states clearly in the first verse of his gospel that Jesus is the Christ (that is, the Messiah), and later in the chapter, he narrates how the angel states in a dream that He is to be named Jesus or "the Lord saves" because "he will save his people from their sins" (Matthew 1:21). Later on, it is Matthew alone who captures Christ's words about His death, that His purpose is to forgive sins: "This is my blood of the covenant, which is poured out for many for the forgiveness of sins" (Matthew 26:28). Matthew wanted his readers to trust in Christ as God for their salvation, the One who after His resurrection from the dead had been given "All authority in heaven and on earth" and who is "with you always, to the very end of the age" (Matthew 28:18, 20).

Joseph's Dream about Jesus and His Birth

Matthew's account of the birth of Jesus Christ begins with Mary, who is pregnant and betrothed to Joseph. Since Joseph realizes he is not the father of her child, he quietly decides not to go through with the marriage. However, Joseph's train of thought is interrupted in the following way:

> But after he had considered this, an angel of the Lord appeared to him in a dream and said, "Joseph son of David, do not be afraid to take Mary home as your wife, because what is conceived in her is from the Holy Spirit. She will give birth to a son, and you are to give him the name Jesus, because he will save his people from their sins." All this took place to fulfill what the Lord had said through the prophet: "The virgin will conceive and give birth to a son, and they will call him Immanuel"[1] (which means "God with us"). When Joseph woke up, he did what the angel of the Lord had commanded him and took Mary home as his wife. But he did not consummate their marriage until she gave birth to a son. And he gave him the name Jesus. (Matthew 1:20–25)

Through this dream, the angel explains the child's divine origin to Joseph and gives him commands as to how to proceed. The effect is that Joseph obeys and chooses to become the father of Jesus Christ in a legal sense, giving Him his family line as well as his protection during the events that lay immediately ahead. The fact that such a divine messenger appears in the dream emphasizes God's precise direction of the events of Christ incarnate's earliest days to conform them to the prophecies about Him. It also indicates the importance of the divinely revealed name *Jesus*, that it signified both who He was and what His purpose would be.

We do not know the angel's name, nor does the account focus on his appearance. Matthew's account only focuses on what the angel actually said. By contrast, in Luke's account, it is to Mary that an angel appears, presumably in a waking vision, and he is named as Gabriel, the same being who caused Daniel to fall terrified to the ground.[2] But in both scenarios, it is the angel's discourse that really is extraordinary. The angel states that the father of the child is Almighty God, and to Joseph the angel adds a prophecy about His destiny—the child will save His people.

The dream also relieved Joseph of the fears the angel acknowledged; he must surely have awakened at peace and with newfound courage. Joseph changed his mind at once and decided to marry Mary. Together they made their way to Bethlehem because of the Roman census decree, described in Luke's gospel,[3] which required everyone living in the Roman world to register at their town of origin. The angel must have considered this and seen how this God-fearing man obeyed gladly and at once. It is interesting that in the events to come, the angels were never that far away. An angel would appear to Joseph in his dreams at night on at least two further occasions.

The Dream of the Magi

After Jesus was born in Bethlehem, wise men from an eastern country arrived in Jerusalem seeking where "the one who has been born king of the Jews" had been born. They had seen His star and had come to worship Him. King Herod was disturbed by this news and sought out the Jewish chief priest and teachers of the law. The original Greek language of the gospel conveys a sense of terror both on the part of Herod and in Jerusalem at this news.[4] Herod asked them where this birth would occur. The Jewish priests were happy to quote the prophet Micah, who foretold that the Christ would be born in Bethlehem, although the teachers of the law made no effort to believe the prophecy and visit Bethlehem themselves! Herod then passed Micah's insight on to the Magi and said to them, "Go and search carefully for the child. As soon as you find him, report to me, so that I too may go and worship him" (Matthew 2:8).

The wise men proceeded on their journey again and found that the star they had been following went ahead of them once more until it stopped in the sky above the place in Bethlehem where Christ was.

When they saw the star, they were overjoyed. On coming to the house, they saw the child with his mother Mary, and they bowed down and worshiped him. Then they opened their treasures and presented him with gifts of gold, frankincense and myrrh. And having been warned in a dream not to go back to Herod, they returned to their country by another route. (Matthew 2:11–12)

This dream is presented by Matthew explicitly as a warning dream, and it falls easily within the range of warning dreams described by Job:

For God does speak—now one way, now another—though no one perceives it. In a dream, in a vision of the night, when deep sleep falls on people as they slumber in their beds, he may speak in their ears and terrify them with warnings, to turn them from wrongdoing and keep them from pride, to preserve their lives from the pit, their lives from perishing by the sword. (Job 33:14–18)

The Magi were to avoid Herod, and therefore, they needed to take a different route to return home. It is likely that the dream was warning them to avoid Herod because he would kill them, as their actions had shown the king that they perceived this child to have far greater authority and status than Herod. And there was, of course, truth in that—the child had His own star! As for Herod, he was only half-Jewish anyway, and he was Rome appointed. What if the child was from a true Jewish kingship line? In point of fact, this was indeed the case, as Matthew points out in his introductory genealogy.

If the child was in Bethlehem, He was located well within Herod's territory. He could therefore be killed once Herod knew precisely where He was. He was a threat to Herod's kingdom, and we know that Herod was absolutely committed to wiping out "by the sword" all possible threats to his rule. Although we are not given the details contained in the dream, we can assume that the warning was twofold: it related to the lives of the Magi and to the life of Christ. At the same time, as Russ Parker points out,[5] the dream is a dream of discernment. Within it, the Magi see uncovered the true intentions of the king who had sought to dupe them.

Joseph's Three Dreams of Warning and Command

In the next verse, Matthew 2:13, Matthew brings the action back to Joseph and says the following:

> When they had gone, an angel of the Lord appeared to Joseph in a dream. "Get up," he said, "take the child and his mother and escape to Egypt. Stay there until I tell you, for Herod is going to search for the child to kill him." So he got up, took the child and his mother during the night and left for Egypt, where he stayed until the death of Herod. And so was fulfilled what the Lord had said through the prophet: "Out of Egypt I called my son." (Matthew 2:14–15)

Matthew then recounts Herod's fury at being outwitted by the Magi and his orders to execute all boys in Bethlehem and the surrounding area who were two years old and younger. The events the angel had warned Joseph about were now unleashed, but Jesus and His parents had escaped. Matthew states that these events, the flight into Egypt followed by the massacre, fulfilled prophecies given by Hosea (11:1) and Jeremiah (31:15) respectively, with the journey out of Egypt recapitulating Israel's exile into and exodus from that country.

There has been some doubt over exactly when Herod the Great reigned, with some scholars disputing the conventional 37 BC–4 BC dates. For instance, Andrew Steinmann[6] extends the king's reign from 39 BC to 1 BC in order to include all the datable evidence and many historical references to the events of Herod's reign. What has never been in doubt, though, is his legendary cruelty and his determination to hold on to power and increase his grip on it by any means. He imprisoned and executed several of his ten wives, at least three of his own sons, and many other relatives at different times as it suited his purposes or his disposition at the time. Some of his actions were clearly triggered by genuine conspiracies against him, but many of his executions seem to have been caused merely by his own paranoia. There is also something of a grand and sweeping scope to Herod's reign of homicidal terror. In fact, it was the greatness of his acts of cruelty that caused him to be accorded the title "the Great," not his religious and secular construction works.

Herod was responsible for a number of mass executions, including the slaughter of forty-five of Israel's top landowners in order to seize their estates, using their resources to pay additional tribute to Rome while simultaneously scaring other landowners into submission. He had some teachers and pupils burned alive after they removed a Roman eagle sculpture from the entrance of Jerusalem's temple. There is also strong evidence that when he was close to death, fearing that his country would not exactly mourn his passing, he gave orders that much of the country's remaining nobility were to be rounded up and executed in Jericho on his death, thereby ensuring that some genuine mourning did, in fact, occur. Fortunately, that particular order was ignored.

Herod's last few years in power were his most deranged. It is probable that he had the monastery at Qumran burned to the ground around 8 BC. He murdered two of his sons around 7 BC and 4 BC. Matthew's account of the mass killing of male infants on Herod's express orders is therefore in keeping with the secular accounts of the king's reign, which largely come down to us from the books written by Flavius Josephus.[7] There are also one or two other accounts, such as that by the fourth-century writer Macrobius, who also asserts that Herod ordered the killing of infants aged two and under in Syria. It is possible that Macrobius refers to the same event as Matthew, since at the time Judea was considered part of Syria.

In what could have been up to four years later, we learn that the angel was true to his word and appeared again to Joseph in another dream.

> After Herod died, an angel of the Lord appeared in a dream to Joseph in Egypt and said, "Get up, take the child and his mother and go to the land of Israel, for those who were trying to take the child's life are dead."

So he got up, took the child and his mother and went to the land of Israel. But when he heard that Archelaus was reigning in Judea in place of his father Herod, he was afraid to go there. *Having been warned in a dream,* he withdrew to the district of Galilee, and he went and lived in a town called Nazareth. So was fulfilled what was said through the prophets that he would be called a Nazarene. (Matthew 2:19–23, emphasis mine)

This last dream warning is as understandable as the two dreams regarding Herod the Great. Even before he set out for Rome to submit his claim to Caesar Augustus over the southern part of his father's territory, Herod Archelaus had executed about three thousand Pharisees in a single massacre during a Passover celebration. He is reckoned to be the worst of Herod's various sons. Although Caesar accepted his claims, Archelaus only lasted nine years in power. The Romans had to remove him, banishing him to Gaul because of his cruelty and the complaints made against him. They then instituted direct Roman rule, a situation that was to result in Pontius Pilate ruling the territory as governor.

When Joseph opted for Galilee, he chose to live in territory ruled by Archelaus's half-brother Herod Antipas, who seems to have been less dangerous at this time. But he would later become infamous in his own right as the minor ruler who slew John the Baptist and who would question Jesus mockingly in Jerusalem shortly before His crucifixion.[8] Jesus had earlier referred to him as "that fox."[9] Herod Antipas remained in power much longer than his half-brother to the south, but he too was deposed in AD 39, this time by the new emperor Caligula. And like his half-brother, he was to die in exile in Gaul. Caligula may have had him executed within a year of his exile, but historians are undecided about this.

We see throughout this account that God warned and directed the family at every stage whenever there was imminent danger and that Joseph always acted at once, doing exactly what was commanded. Christ's life was thereby saved, and He was able to go on to fulfill His destiny, even accomplishing the salvation of His people.

The Dream of Pontius Pilate's Wife

One last warning dream occurs much further on in Matthew's gospel in the penultimate chapter. It is given to someone whose name is unrecorded, but we know she was married to Pontius Pilate, the governor of Judea from AD 26 to AD 36. Various Christian traditions, such as the Greek Orthodox, name her as Claudia Procula. Pilate presided at the trial of Jesus and found Him not guilty of the charges made against Him regarding sedition against Rome. During the proceedings, Pilate was also aware of the custom during Passover for the governor to release one prisoner chosen by the crowd. Matthew's gospel records Pilate putting a choice before the crowd: should he release a notorious criminal called Barabbas to them, or should he release Jesus? And we read that before the crowd formulated a response, Pilate received a message.

> While Pilate was sitting on the judge's seat, his wife sent him this message: "Don't have anything to do with that innocent man, for I have suffered a great deal today in a dream because of him." But the chief priests and the elders persuaded the crowd to ask for Barabbas and to have Jesus executed. "Which of the two do you want me to release to you?" asked the governor. "Barabbas," they answered. "What shall I do, then, with Jesus who is called the Messiah?" Pilate asked. They all answered, "Crucify him!" "Why? What crime has he committed?" asked Pilate. But they shouted all the louder, "Crucify him!" When Pilate saw that he was getting nowhere, but that instead an uproar was starting, he took water and washed his hands in front of the crowd. "I am innocent of this man's blood," he said. "It is your responsibility!" (Matthew 27:19–24)

As mentioned previously, this dream is a good example of the type of warning dreams mentioned in Job 33:14–18. Most of what Job says applies directly to Pilate's wife's dream. It warned Pilate just ahead of time, and it certainly terrified his wife. There was something in the dream that caused her to be very uneasy about her husband's dealings with Christ, and it caused her to suffer "a great deal," not just a little. The purpose of the dream was to give Pilate the opportunity to turn away from condemning Jesus and thereby *not* make a decision that would condemn Pilate's soul to hell. The dream compounded his unease over and above the unease he already felt at having an innocent man tried before him—its message of Jesus's innocence confirmed what Pilate had already realized.

But despite that, Pilate did not turn away from the decision. His concern for his own position and possible harm to himself[10] became greater than his fears about condemning an innocent man. He attempted to place the burden of guilt onto the crowd, and they willingly take the burden. The handwashing was a desperate and futile attempt to absolve himself of responsibility, since he was still exercising his power unjustly, and the outcome was unchanged by the theatrics. It was Pilate alone who condemned Christ to death, because he alone had the authority to do that. Almost certainly, Pilate's eternal destiny was sealed at that moment. To put it in Job's terminology, he had *not* preserved his soul from the pit.

What of Pilate's wife? She comes across as a sympathetic Gentile woman who is open to the voice of God in a dream. The dream's message was not about her or for her. But she was meant to pass it on to her husband, and this she did. She was faithful to what the dream required her to do. Pilate would have realized that his wife wanted the man released. It is likely that Pilate's dispute with the crowd was triggered by his wife's dream; his understanding of it compelled him to seek the life of Jesus until the clamor and threats weakened his resolve. Perhaps Pilate's wife believed that Jesus was who He said He was. She would certainly have heard about Him.

Conclusions

All six dreams described and discussed in this chapter fall within Job's description of God-given dreams and their purposes. Five of the six dreams gave clear warnings about impending disaster, and in four instances, whenever the recipient was God-fearing, he took action at once to avoid the disaster. In Pilate's case, however, he pushed the dream aside and did not heed its message.

In all five cases, though, the warning was saying to the dreamer: don't do what you are going to do. Or don't stay here; you must go now. Or do not journey to meet that king; avoid him and take a different route to your destination. If you obey, either by doing something or not doing something as the case may be, you will avoid the disaster.

In addition to this, the first of the dreams in Matthew's gospel is one where Joseph is given guidance and direction. Joseph was living in a unique, divinely created set of circumstances, and it took divine revelation for him to understand what the situation meant and what he was to do next. The child's name was communicated in the dream, as was something of His purpose and destiny. It was a dream, along with Mary's own angelic vision and their experience with the Magi visiting their new-born child, that caused this young couple to continue to obey at once the warnings they were subsequently given through Joseph's dreams. The clarity of the angel's commands would also have given Joseph and the Magi the courage they needed to carry them out. For both Joseph and the Magi, to obey always entailed a sudden and unexpected journey. The dreams, therefore, helped to establish peace, courage, and determination within for the journey ahead.

Through these dreams, God was guiding His people, saving their lives and outworking His purposes of salvation. The Bible asserts that from the time of these events in Matthew's gospel onward, God will continue to work through dreams and visions, giving guidance, salvation, and revelation. For instance, after His resurrection from the dead and His ascension into heaven, Christ Himself became the object of the vision that He gave to Saul as he made his way along the road to Damascus:

> As he neared Damascus on his journey, suddenly a light from heaven flashed around him. He fell to the ground and heard a voice say to him, "Saul, Saul, why do you persecute me?" "Who are you, Lord?" Saul asked. "I am Jesus, whom you are persecuting," he replied. "Now get up and go into the city, and you will be told what you must do." (Acts 9:3–6).

When the Holy Spirit was poured out by Christ during Pentecost, causing the many gathered to praise God in languages they could not have learned, Peter quoted from the prophet Joel: "In the last days, God says, I will pour out my Spirit on all people. Your sons and daughters will prophesy, your young men will see visions, your old men will dream dreams" (Acts 2:17).

When Are These Last Days?

When are these "last days" of which Acts speaks? They are now. Matthew and Peter were living when this era began, and we are living in these last days now. These are the days of prophecies, visions, and dreams given by God. Discernment is needed, but God-given revelation is here to be discerned.

Through the prophet Malachi, God says something important about His nature: "I the LORD do not change" (Malachi 3:6). He also made it very explicit earlier on that He intended to communicate in dreams. The book of Numbers records an event in which God confirms this to Israel while they are still in the wilderness after departing from Egypt.

> At once the LORD said to Moses, Aaron and Miriam, "Come out to the tent of meeting, all three of you." So the three of them went out. Then the LORD came down in a pillar of cloud; he stood at the entrance to the tent and summoned Aaron and Miriam. When the two of them stepped forward, he said, "Listen to my words: 'When there is a prophet among you, I, the LORD, reveal myself to them in visions, I speak to them in dreams.'" (Numbers 12:4–6).

God then goes on to tell them that in the case of Moses, His faithful servant, He speaks to him clearly, face to face, rather than in riddles.

Just as He spoke to believers and unbelievers alike in the Old Testament through a dream, so He continues to do in the New Testament. He has spoken to humankind for thousands of years in this way, and it is a reasonable assumption that He will continue to do this according to His purposes. He does not alter or change. And humankind continues to dream. We were made that way.

PART III

MODERN CASE STUDIES
AND TESTIMONIES

CHAPTER 16

Five Dreamers and Visionaries

History testifies that God has continued to speak to His people in dreams. In many of the following examples, supernaturally inspired dreams were inspirational for the dreamers and gave them direction, sometimes literally and geographically, but primarily regarding calling and ministry. The dreams detailed in this chapter also changed the dreamers; the dreams were usually revelatory and caused profound shifts and changes in those who experienced them. Together these five case studies give some clear indicators of the differences between dreams that are from God and dreams that come purely from the unconscious.

John Newton, 1725–1807

Preacher and hymn writer John Newton was born in London in 1725 and is best remembered today for his hymn "Amazing Grace." He was an evangelical minister of the gospel and toward the end of his life exercised considerable influence. He worked closely with William Wilberforce to end the slave trade, a trade he himself had been closely involved in as a younger man.

Newton's godly mother was intent on bringing him up in the Christian faith and taught John to memorize Scriptures and to pray to God. But she died when he was seven years of age. His father and stepmother had no such interest in faith. Leaving school at the age of eleven, he traveled with his father, a sea captain, on long voyages, and when he was home, he would run free and frequently get into trouble. Periodically, John would try to shake himself down and return to the prayer and reading of Scripture that his mother had emphasized. He even fasted and for three months became a vegetarian.[1] Yet the ascetic behaviors did not bring him closer to God. He would eventually rebel against these pursuits, travel by sea for months at a time, and go along with whatever his friends on board were doing.

When John was seventeen, his father stated that his goal for him was to get involved in the slave trade between Africa and Jamaica, become a slave overseer, and in due course, become wealthy and enter the House of Lords. Yet because John had fallen in love with a girl he would marry some years later, he allowed the ship to sail without him. His father was furious and commanded his son to sail as a common sailor on a month's long voyage. By the time he reached Venice, he had thrown his mother's religion and scruples overboard. John and the crew spent their shore leave in Venice doing what sailors have done for thousands of years.

After the leave ended, they boarded the ship and sailed out of the harbor. John fell asleep, and he soon had a remarkable dream. In it, he was pacing across the deck of a ship in Venice harbor at night, keeping watch. A mysterious man suddenly approached him and gave him a ring of exceptional beauty and value, instructing him to look after it well—it was the key to all true joy. If he kept it, all would be well, and he would have both happiness and success. But if he should lose this ring, all would be misery for him. John put on the ring, but as he gazed at it, he wondered if he would manage to keep it.

Then in the dream, another stranger approached him out of the surrounding gloom of night and scornfully derided the ring and his newfound faith in it. This was just a superstition, the stranger said. John repeated to him what the first man had said about joy if he kept it and misery and ruin if he did not. But the second man embarrassed him—how could he put such faith in a mere trinket like that? Throw it away! The second stranger kept at it, and slowly, he prevailed over John, who considered the ring on his finger with increasing disdain. Finally, the young sailor took off the ring and cast it overboard.

At once, as John Dunn says in his biography of Newton, all hell broke loose in the dream.[2] The man hissed at him: *You have just thrown God's mercy away from you. It is the pit and fires of hell for you now!* At the same time, a volcano behind Venice exploded and set fire to the entire hillside behind the city. Fire ascended high into the night sky. John was terrified and in terrible distress, saying aloud that he must now go to be consumed by those flames, which burned so fiercely behind the city.

Then in the dream another stranger appeared to him; Newton wondered on reflection if it was, in fact, the first man now returned. He asked Newton why he was so troubled, and so he told him everything, expecting that he too would offer no solace after such a foolish decision. The man confirmed that yes, he had indeed been foolish, but he asked him a question: would he be more careful of such a precious gift if he was given another opportunity? John could hardly believe that this was possible. At once, the man dived overboard, retrieved the ring, and climbed back onto the deck. As soon as the stranger was aboard, the flames behind the city died down, and everything on land became much calmer.

Newton's fears had now subsided, so in the dream he reached toward the man's outstretched hand to take back the ring. But the man said that, unfortunately, Newton could not be trusted with it. Because he might just throw it away again, the stranger would keep it for him in trust and produce it whenever it was needed.

Looking back, Newton recounts that it was just as if he had been like prey, a captive, but then taken from the hands of a mighty enemy and delivered. He also commented many years later, "O what an unspeakable comfort is this, that I am not in my own keeping!"[3]

When Newton awoke, he could neither eat nor sleep for days, and he was so shaken up that for weeks he avoided the roughness and folly of his fellow crew. He tried to get back to religious pursuits. Yet by the time they reached their destination, he had once more neglected the gift that the dream had been symbolizing. Indeed, he forgot the dream completely, and it was not until many years later that an event triggered a memory of it and it all came back to him.

For now, the dream and its meaning were lost, and Newton's life soon became one of impetuous folly, periods spent in jail, terrible privations aboard ship, and such abandonment of God that it caused him to lead other semi-pious sailors astray as well. At times, he thought of casting himself overboard and drowning to end it all, but what restrained him, at least in his conscious thoughts, was the love he had for the girl he had met as a teenager in England.

A rebellious enemy of ship captains, Newton was jettisoned in Sierra Leone and lived in such penury that many of the black slaves pitied him, even sharing their meager rations with him! Yet while still a young man of twenty-two, many of the Bible verses he had memorized as a child started to come back to him, and before he married, he began his journey to faith. At times the verses would return when he thought he was going to die.

On one pivotal occasion, on a voyage from Brazil to Newfoundland, the storm was sweeping sailors overboard, the ship was splitting apart, and Newton could only bail the water out by being tied fast to the ship. As the storm fought to destroy the vessel, he increasingly clung to the Scriptures his mother had taught him and the hope that he could still be reached with the mercy and forgiveness of God. When the ship finally landed in Ireland, the verses had made a tremendous impact on him. Later, as he survived slave uprisings, fever, storms, and starvation, he became more and more aware of God's grace.

Newton was married in 1750 to his childhood love Mary Catlett, and the marriage was a success. At the same time, he began to captain slaving vessels as they plied their gruesome trade between Africa and the Caribbean. His faith continued to gain hold in him, but progress in some areas was as slow as the ships he captained. He would pray for the slaves he carried down below.[4] In time, a mere distaste for what he was trading in would develop into something much stronger.

Because Newton was so often at sea, it was very difficult for him to find Christian company; but when he did find it, he greatly appreciated it and learned through it. In time, an opportunity in the civil service opened up, which he accepted. He also decided to spend his free time attending the meetings of all the main evangelical preachers of the time, including John Wesley. Eventually, he became a preacher himself, first in rural Olney and then in London.

As a minister, John Newton became well-known for his emotional, fervent preaching and his true pastor's care and concern. His services were always packed, even in his declining years when he was blind and deaf. He was also well-known then, as he is now, for his hymn writing, and he would often focus almost entirely on the hymn he was working on for about a week. At the end, he said to a friend of his, "My memory is nearly gone; but I remember two things: that I am a great sinner, and that Christ is a great Savior."

In 1788, John Newton appeared as a "star witness" before Prime Minister William Pitt's committee. The purpose of the committee was to investigate the trade in African slaves. John eloquently told the harrowing story as seen from the inside of the trade. He was the only man in England prepared to witness to its grim and sordid nature.

The following is a portion of the lyrics of John Newton's famous and inspirational hymn:

> Amazing grace! How sweet the sound
> That saved a wretch like me!
> I once was lost, but now am found;
> Was blind, but now I see.
> 'Twas grace that taught my heart to fear,
> And grace my fears relieved;
> How precious did that grace appear
> The hour I first believed.[5]

William Booth, 1829–1912

The founder of the Salvation Army, William Booth was born in Nottingham, England, in 1829. He was the son of an illiterate builder who had once made a relative fortune but lost it through unwise speculation. When the family's resources finally collapsed completely, William was forced by his father to leave school at age thirteen to work as a pawnbroker's assistant. Through this job, which he hated, William came up against poverty and degradation far worse than his own family's. About a year after he started working, his father died.

As the pawnbroker's assistant, William lived above the shop for five years, and at this time he started attending a Methodist chapel. He enjoyed the outstanding singing and preaching, but during a Bible class, he was struck by the question of what would happen to him if he died. He mulled the matter over and after a time responded, "God shall have all there is of William Booth."[6] His conversion occurred when he was fifteen. Two years later he joined some of the other Bible class members and went into the slums of Nottingham, preaching salvation.

Booth's success in evangelism and the genuine repentance in many of those he preached to created a problem. The slum dwellers were unwelcome in the now "respectable" Methodist church. So he continued to preach to them in gatherings in the slums. Then, on moving to London, he did the same there. The slums were larger, and the needs were even greater. At the age of twenty-two, he made a breakthrough when, after preaching at a local Methodist chapel, he was offered the funding to go into full-time ministry. From then on he rapidly gained a reputation as a preacher in London and across England. He initiated a support system for new converts by pairing each one up with a church member who would ensure they received a Bible and attended church regularly.

After an engagement of three years, William married Catherine, a woman he had met through Methodist circles, in 1855. The couple, intent on preaching together, split from the Methodists because the denomination was unhappy at having a woman preach. Barred from many churches, they hired a circus tent and ran revival meetings throughout England and Wales, encouraging former drunks and criminals to testify to the crowds about how God had saved and changed them. Catherine became known as "the amazing female preacher." At the same time, they became increasingly concerned about people's squalid living conditions in London, the child alcoholics, and the dirty, starving beggars. Already with a population of several million, London was more than a lifetime's work. Again William based himself in a tent, pitched this time in the East End. In due time, he was given a building.

Revival meetings gave rise to many other ventures, such as soup kitchens, rallies, reading classes, and discussion groups, all intent on pulling up the people and their aspirations. The mission work and the charitable work alike grew rapidly and spread out geographically. All this came with persecutions, sporadic violence, and turmoil, some of which reached the national press. Given that they could be pelted with anything from rocks to dead cats, it was like being in a war.

The American Civil War had ended some years earlier, but it had been such a momentous event that it was still talked about in 1878 in England. A number of trains of thought came together for William and his collaborators. They renamed their mission the Salvation Army. This precipitated many other unusual changes within an evangelical church: the culture changed, and ranks, citadels, forts, and uniforms all were introduced. The effect was electric. Huge crowds flocked to the Army's meetings from that point on to hear the gospel. At the same time, the Salvation Army launched many more social services and programs in response to the chronic needs of the homeless and unemployed.

In one particular campaign, William Booth succeeded in overturning and transforming an entire industry. In London, the trade of making matches employed four thousand people, mainly widows and their children, who made matchboxes and the matches to go in them. Because it was cheaper in production costs, they were forced to use yellow phosphorous rather than red phosphorous and were compelled to work ninety-six hours a week. Excluded from any learning and exhausted by the work, the children even struggled to summon the energy to eat anything. In addition, yellow phosphorous was poisonous. In due time, a worker's jaw would turn green and then black, rotting from inside. An agonizing death from starvation followed, since the person could not eat. Booth soon created a very successful match factory, exemplary for the times, where no yellow phosphorous was allowed, and he sowed the legislative seeds that would lead to new labor laws for factory work.

William Booth wrote extensively, and much of his work has been reprinted recently.[7] Many of his other sermons and speeches have also survived intact, sometimes as audio recordings made toward the end of his life. A number of commentators and pastors, such as David Buffaloe,[8] have alluded to the vivid waking vision that William Booth describes in one of these recordings. In it, William begins by describing where he was when the vision occurred: in a train gazing out the window, contemplating the careless lives of the many beyond, millions disregarding their eternal destiny, absorbed instead with the cares and pleasures of this life. As he thought of this, he experienced the following vision.

Above a stormy sea containing countless human beings struggling, screaming, and drowning in the tempestuous waves, thunderclouds rolled and lightning flashed. Then a mighty rock rose up through the ocean to ascend so high that its peak was above the clouds. At its base was a wide, flat ledge, and this allowed some of the people to climb out of the waves. William was delighted when he saw that some of them would then reach down to rescue others as well, helping them climb up. Some used ladders or ropes; others used boats; and a few would jump back in themselves, risking their own lives to save lost souls. But as he continued to look on, he observed that the majority safe on the ledge did none of these things. They had seemingly forgotten how dangerous it was in the ocean, even for their own relatives who were still struggling there. Instead, they were engrossed in business and making money, in eating and drinking, in music and even in growing flowers on the side of the rock! So all around them, the majority kept on struggling and drowning.

The vision continued.

A mighty being had entered the stormy sea and was trying to rescue those who were in it still. He implored the people on the rock to lend assistance, yet, instead, these people were mainly looking elsewhere and calling out to him, praying that he would take them to the mainland now or praying that he would see to it that they were as secure on the rock as possible. After all, they did not want to slip off and back into the ocean.

William understood his vision in the following way. The ocean was real human life in a perishing world, all the lost human souls facing a lost eternity, while the lightning was the flashes of truth coming from God Himself. The thunder was God's wrath. The rock represented Christ's sacrifice on the cross, the only means of salvation, and the people on it were those who had already been rescued by their faith in what Christ had done for them. Those who were trying to rescue others, however, were the relative few among the saved who struggled as "true soldiers of the cross of Jesus." And God's voice in the vision represented Christ's own continuing struggle to save the lost, imploring the saved to work with Him in the salvation of the world.

As he turned his attention away from the vision and toward his audience, Booth said, "Don't be deceived by appearances—man and things are not what they seem. All who are not on the rock are in the sea!"

William Booth had to endure much opposition and hostility because of this vision. But it captured his attention as well as all his energies. At the same time, some influential men rallied to the vision and to the work of the Army. While Thomas Huxley fired off anti-Army letters to the *London Times* like a machine gun, men like Winston Churchill and Charles Spurgeon rallied to William's defense. Yet to Booth, neither ridicule nor approval mattered very much. He knew and said aloud that in fifty years' time, none of it would count. What would matter was how he had dealt with the work that God had called him to do.

When he died in 1912, Booth's body lay in state for several days. During that time, over one hundred and fifty thousand people walked slowly by to pay their respects. His funeral took place in Olympia Hall, London. Only the first forty thousand people were able to get in.

Derek Prince, 1915–2003

International Bible teacher Derek Prince was born in Bangalore, India, in 1915 but was educated in England, first at Eton and then at Cambridge University, where he specialized in philosophy, training under the philosopher Ludwig Wittgenstein. During World War II, Prince joined the Royal Army Medical Corps. While in his barracks in 1941, he decided to read the Bible as a philosophical exercise. At a certain point during this time he had a "supernatural experience" where he met with Christ. From this encounter, he concluded two things: that Christ was God and that the Bible was true and as relevant today as it had been when it was written. This, he said, dramatically changed the course of his life.

While in the British Army, Prince was posted to various locations in North Africa and the Middle East and eventually arrived with a unit in Palestine. While there, he met and married Lydia, a Danish woman, who was running an orphanage in Ramallah. The Princes stayed on in

Palestine and supported the foundation of the State of Israel, but in 1949 they moved to the United Kingdom and set up a Pentecostal church in Notting Hill, London. In subsequent years, they moved to and worked in Kenya, where Derek ran a school; Canada; and the United States. Lydia, who was twenty-five years older than Derek, died in 1975.

Derek took the death of his wife very hard and felt an acute sense of loneliness. Then in 1977, he and some close friends decided to go on a pilgrimage from the USA, where they all lived, to the Holy Land. The pilgrimage went well, and Derek decided to stay on in Israel for a while longer. One of his reasons for staying was that he wanted to thank ministry staff there for all the work they had done in translating and distributing the many books he had written. But when he inquired, he learned that one of them, Ruth Baker, was off sick with a serious back injury. He decided to drop by the lady's house and pray with her for her recovery. She was lying out on a couch when he arrived, and he prayed for a few minutes with her. He then left to return to the main reason why he had stayed on in Jerusalem. He needed to pray for God's guidance as to whether he should recommence a ministry in that city. He felt there was still a purpose for him there, but he was not sure, and he had no understanding of exactly what it would be.

The time drew closer to leave. Derek had nearly run out of time. He had not heard from God, and lying in bed late at night, he was all too aware that his flight out of Ben Gurion Airport was early the next morning. Then in the early hours of his last night in the city, a vision of the night suddenly appeared before him.

In it, Derek saw a detailed, vivid image of a steep hill very much like Mount Zion, seen from a specific vantage point in Jerusalem's Old City, sloping upward with a path laid out on it. The path sharply changed course as it wound its way upward. He says:

> Instinctively I knew that this represented the path back to Jerusalem for me. The most striking feature in the picture I saw before me was the figure of a woman seated on the ground just at the point where the path started up the hill. Her features

were European, her coloring blonde. But she was wearing what looked to be an Oriental-style dress, in a color hard to define but predominantly green. What particularly struck me was her unusual posture. Her back was bent forward in a strained, unnatural position, suggesting pain. Suddenly I recognized her. It was Ruth Baker.[9]

He adds that, in a moment, before he even put a question before God, he understood that it was God's intention that he was to marry this woman. In fact, this was the critical first step in his journey back to Jerusalem.

Derek said nothing to anyone about this. He knew next to nothing about the woman and had met her very briefly only once. Yet as he returned home and the months went by, the vision became clearer and clearer. Having said that, no further guidance came either. The striking vision was all there was.

Eventually, Derek wrote to Ruth. He received a positive reply, and they were able to meet up in the USA. But when they met in Kansas, she explained that her back pain required her to sit on the floor rather than on a chair. When she did so, she assumed exactly the posture he had seen in his vision. She was also wearing exactly what he had seen her wear in the vision, in both style of dress and color! She had bought an Arab-style dress in Jerusalem. At that point, he says, he was flooded with an incredible love for this woman. He also learned that in a few months' time, their itineraries required them to be in Jerusalem at the same time. He turned up with an engagement ring.

Derek and Ruth were married in 1978, and from then on he lived in Jerusalem for about six months of the year. Together they developed a range of ministries, including a healing ministry and a worldwide outreach program making Bible teaching materials freely available to church leaders around the world. Derek said often that Ruth's love, support, and partnership enabled him to gain the confidence to successfully take on a whole variety of challenges that he otherwise would have put to the side. In her practical help, she enabled him to adapt quickly to the many changes of temperature and diet an international traveling ministry required.

I was fortunate enough to hear Derek Prince preach over a number of evenings in the summer of 1999 at the Towards End Times conference held at Wadebridge Agricultural Showground in Cornwall, England. Although by then he was in his mideighties, he was still a powerful preacher and eagerly anticipating the soon return of Christ. He was trying to come to terms with Ruth's death the previous year, and from time to time, had to stop preaching as emotions almost overwhelmed him. Derek Prince died in Jerusalem in 2003.

Leanne Payne, 1932–2015

Healer and writer Leanne Payne was born in Omaha, Nebraska, in 1932 but grew up in Little Rock, Arkansas, where her family was from originally. Her father died of encephalitis when he was only twenty-nine and Leanne was three years of age. She grew up in difficult economic times but in a Christian home; her mother had a deep faith in Christ that developed out of her grief at having lost her husband so early on.

In her autobiography,[10] Payne describes herself as an impulsive and impatient child, determined and hopeful, but at the same time grief-stricken and fearful of further loss connected with her father's death. Throughout her childhood, her mother taught Leanne and her sister from the Bible daily. Her mother was also something of a prayer warrior, often closeting herself away to pray and make intercession for the church and the nation. The lack of a father, however, meant that there was a lack of the affirmation and direction in Leanne's life that a good father would have provided.

The surrounding time and culture expected girls to marry in their late teenage years and certainly by twenty-one. Leanne did not wait that long. Her impulsiveness, she says, caused her to marry a high school dropout aged seventeen, before she finished high school, and a difficult ten years or so ensued. A daughter was born, but the marriage failed very early on. Leanne did clerical work to make ends meet. In her midtwenties, she married again, and this marriage, failing too, brought her to the end of herself. She repented and was converted in the sense that she gave her complete will over to God, stepping onto a path of obedience to Him, the path of true life lived in and with Christ.

Through the early part of the1960s, Payne became involved in healing ministry and also became aware of the errors, quite common even then in Christian healing circles, which were later described as the "gnosticisms of the left and right." On the left were Jungian speculations, myths, and false wisdom, sometimes referred to loosely as and usually to be incorporated within the New Age Movement. On the right were the extravagant, overactive, and overimaginative ministers of the "prophetic," that is to say the *falsely* prophetic, who often traversed across the United States and who acted in a lone ranger capacity without oversight and without responsibility. Both types of practice and approach would inevitably involve some measure at least of divination and the occult.

Within it all, Payne sought to understand the true gifts of the Holy Spirit as they were meant to operate, and in particular, to understand spiritual and emotional healing. She also came across and was impacted by the genuinely prophetic ministry of others while she still lived in Arkansas. In addition, she was actively writing a prayer journal where she sought to write out insights gained through listening prayer.

Payne then accepted a job as a house parent at Wheaton Academy near Chicago, so she and her daughter traveled north to Illinois. She worked in the job for two years. There was never a dull moment. One of the girls she looked after was Edie. This girl caused her a lot of distress, as she did all those who sought to help her, since an overwhelming compulsion in Edie caused her to have one-night stands with men time and time again. After each occurrence, she would repent wholeheartedly, and each time, when Payne prayed with Edie to seek understanding into the roots of this conduct, the girl would be greatly troubled by a distressing memory—one of her earliest memories. She would sob and sob as she recounted it. As the memory came up again to the surface, she remembered the police entering their home, dragging her drunken parents away, and removing her two little brothers, who were filthy, deprived of all care. She had been so attached to them both, yet she was never to see them again. She would also never see her parents again.

Although the memory seemed connected to Edie's behavior, there was an impasse in Payne's understanding of it all, and during a camping trip, she prayed for the answer—what was going on? There in the wilds of Oklahoma, she was going about cleaning the campsite and walked over to a large boulder. As she turned around, something akin to a vision suddenly came to pass. She stepped through time and back to an earlier era. Same location, different time. Two Native American braves stood in front of her, staring at her, looking bewildered. She saw them, and they saw her. Behind the braves, the Oklahoma landscape was as it had been hundreds of years ago before European settlement. It all happened in an instant.

Astonished and scared, she turned and ran back to the camper van and prayed hard. What had just happened? The answer came quickly: all times are held by God. He is aware of them all; they are all His. He had allowed the natives to look forward in time and see her, and He had allowed her to simultaneously look back and behold them as they had once been.

Given this, there was an answer for people such as Edie. In her case, the memory and experience of traumatic separation was both the root cause and the overriding driver of her compulsive sexual behavior. Christ could forgive and heal these root causes if they were given over to Him by a minister collaborating with Him in the healing gifts of the Spirit. The past, present, and future were all present to Him anyway. Therefore, time was no barrier to healing—if He was invited into the traumatic memory to heal it, comfort Edie, and restore her soul. God could even heal early events that went so far back in someone's childhood that they were beyond memory. Absent from the consciousness of the person in distress, they were still present to Him.

Leanne developed her practice of listening prayer and a healing prayer ministry arising largely from it, with the ministry impacting many thousands over the past forty years or so. She was often used in one-to-one ministry where even the earliest traumas, such as separation from the mother at birth by being placed for a time in an incubator, were healed as the separation anxiety was given over to God. She also ministered to hundreds of people at once, typically during Pastoral Care Ministry Schools held at Wheaton College and other locations in the United States and Europe.

The present author experienced these schools a number of times, and the presence of God during them was sometimes palpable. On one occasion, it was like being closer to the sun than usual, near to a fierce presence akin to heat that emanated in waves from the front of the chapel in Chicago where the healing meeting was held. The presence could be coped with. It was wonderful. But if it had been turned up any more, would it still have been bearable? At the same time, it was as if God was singing lullabies to the infant or the young child within as Leanne prayed and sang from the front.

The time-related vision given to Leanne was one of the key events that enabled such a ministry to develop. In it and subsequent to it, God raised her awareness regarding the nature of time and reality and what He can do. He exists out of and beyond time, just as He is beyond His creation. All that ever was and ever will be is present to Him. What God wants and longs to do is to save and heal people in distress.

Moving from Wheaton Academy to Wheaton College, a Christian liberal arts college, Payne studied for a number of degrees and worked there as well. On the outside, much of this all came together in her first book about God's incarnational presence in our world as understood by C.S. Lewis and originally published in 1979 as *Real Presence*.[11] However, she describes how this book and subsequent books actually came to her in dreams. She refers to the first of these dreams as occurring around 1973 and as being something more than a dream—as being an impartation to her from beyond herself of a fully formed book. She knew what she was meant to write, but she would also need to do the groundwork—the research. In her dream, the book was symbolized as a baby boy handed over to her by a nurse in a hospital.[12] But the birth of the book itself into reality was much more difficult.

Payne discovered she had a writer's block that only manifested when she desired to write a book for publication. Unlike her previous writing of college papers, this writing was to be for public consumption. She was unable to write the book.

Referring to this struggle in some detail, she tracks right back to the time when the source of the block first came to light. She was in a prayer group led by a number of people including Herman and Lillie Riffel and Barbara Schlemon. Schlemon had been leading the group in a healing-of-memories prayer. When the group was remembering their early childhoods, a voice from Payne's "deep heart" said, *Forgive your father for dying!* At the time, not really understanding how a small child experiences the death of a parent as rejection, and thinking it strange, she did it all the same.

This did not resolve the writer's block, but it did trigger a series of six vivid dreams she believes on reflection were God-given. In these dreams, the female figure of the writer she was to be rose up. She was standing by the side of a swollen river wanting to cross it, but the bridge that had once been there had been washed away a long time ago. She jumped anyway and was badly injured. The same dream came again, but this time she stood there too afraid to cross and be exposed to the danger. Other similar dreams came where, although the symbolism differed, the message was repeated. It was a struggle to interpret all this, but in another book[13] she outlines her dream interpretation approach, while in her autobiography she acknowledges the help that Herman and Lillie Riffel were able to provide.

Leanne's fear of exposure was rooted in the loss of her father, the bridge that had been swept away. His loss had exposed the family to economic difficulty and a lack of protection. It had caused her to feel inadequate and exposed, and now these inner effects were connected to the part of her that felt called to a huge, creative undertaking. She realized she needed to shift away from her stoicism and seek forgiveness for not confessing all these fears to God. She did this and opened herself up to His healing power at the primal, deep heart levels where she needed it. She recalls that she was soon able to complete the first book. In the years since, she wrote seven more, and collectively, the eight titles have sold around a quarter of a million copies.

Leanne Payne passed away in 2015 at age eighty-two. Her memorial service was held at Wheaton College, Illinois, and she was buried in Little Rock, Arkansas, near where she grew up. She never liked to be called a healer. I believe that many were healed through her ministry, but she always said that it was the LORD who healed.

Jackie Pullinger (1944–Present)

Missionary to China Jackie Pullinger was born in London in 1944 and attended a conservatoire, the Royal College of Music, whose alumni include Lord Andrew Lloyd Weber, Gustav Holst, and Ralph Vaughn Williams. She became a Christian while she studied there. Even earlier, while Jackie was still in school, a visiting missionary had planted the idea of working, like her, in the harvest field.

After Pullinger graduated from college, she taught music, but fairly soon the idea of becoming a missionary resurfaced. She was intent initially on traveling to Africa to work there, but contacting many organizations, she found that none of them wanted her skills. Yes, they were looking for teachers—of English or math, not music.

However, when she was twenty-two years of age, she had a series of experiences that caused her to change her plans and travel to Hong Kong instead. In a dream, she was with her entire family pouring over a map of the world. She spied a pink-colored territory labeled "Hong Kong" and discussed it with her aunt in the dream. After this, she sought a teaching job in the territory but again was turned down.

Because of the impasse, Jackie went to a quiet village church and prayed for a time. While sitting there, a vision suddenly appeared before her of a despairing young woman with her arms held out toward her. She then saw the words, "What can you give us?"[14] *What indeed,* she thought. *Music lessons?* She realized that what the woman needed was Jesus' love. She could give the woman that.

Jackie felt clearly that God was telling her to go, but she did not know where. When she sought a pastor's advice, he told her that she had better go anyway. If she did not know where, she should buy a ticket for a boat going the longest journey and then pray as to when to disembark. Looking back, she feels that this could have been irresponsible advice had it been given by someone else to a young graduate, but in her situation, it was the Holy Spirit who gave the pastor the words. Sometime later, she arrived in Hong Kong by boat with no return ticket and the equivalent of £6 (about $8). When the immigration official discovered this, along with the fact that she knew no one in the territory, he refused her permission to disembark—until she remembered that she did actually know someone there after all, her mother's godson, who was a member of the police. She was waved through.

So began Pullinger's career of helping and witnessing to the inhabitants of the Walled City, *Hak Nam* in Chinese, which translates as "Darkness"—a series of ruined skyscrapers and alleyways built in and falling apart in an administrative no-man's-land between British-ruled Hong Kong and mainland China. A lawless place of vice, corruption, disease, drug dens, Triad gangs, and unremitting squalor, the Walled City was formidable. No one could tell how many people lived there, whether thirty or sixty thousand. There were only two stinking cesspool toilets. She started off by teaching English and music three times a week and helping out in a small church.

Later, Jackie started a youth club. She describes how God gave her a special love for many of the teenagers who attended it, as well as for their families. Her testimony describes the remarkable conversions in those attending and in gang members. Although God always protected her from being beaten up, the youth club was trashed late at night some four years after opening. Thereafter, the top Triad boss of the Walled City had the club protected, even though Jackie insisted that Jesus was protecting her. After some days of guard duty, the Triad member protecting them from outside the door entered the club and praised God, praying continuously first in Cantonese and then in another language, a tongue, and was instantly set free from his drug addiction.

Shortly after this, Jackie took a group of boys, many drug addicted, out of the Walled City and across the bay to Lamma Island, and they camped on a mountain there. One of the boys, Ah Ming, ran out of drugs. When he started to go through withdrawal, he was intent on escaping to get more, but he was prevented from leaving the tent by the monsoon pouring down. He reluctantly agreed to pray to Jesus to remove his pain—if Jesus was God.

Going to bed that night, Ah Ming felt confused. He fell asleep and had a dream. He was lying in bed in a wooden hut. The rain was pouring down outside. There was a knock on the door, and he refused to answer since he was going through terrible withdrawal. The knock occurred again, and this time he looked out through the window to try to see who was there. He saw a man holding a candle. Feeling angry as well as ill, he returned to his bed. The man then knocked a third time, and given what the weather was like outside, Ah Ming got up and opened the door, letting him in. This is what he said happened next:[15]

> The man, who seemed oddly familiar, came into the hut and over to the bunk bed where he put down the candlestick. He asked Ah Ming to sit up and then gently put His hands on his head. The withdrawal pains disappeared: he never had any pain again. "I knew He was a healer," said Ah Ming reveling in his release from drugs.

The following morning Ah Ming was looking around his bunk. When another boy asked him what he was doing, he replied that he was looking for candle wax. The dream was so vivid to him, he was sure that Jesus must have dropped some. Later, when he had already and instinctively waded into an inter-Triad gang fight, he remembered his salvation and suddenly dropped to his knees, praying hard. He was surrounded by his astonished enemies, who stared down at him, asking him what on earth he was doing. He told them all about what had happened to him. They were impressed, and many started attending the youth group.

Hong Kong has moved on. The Walled City is no more; it was pulled down years ago. Yet Jackie Pullinger has remained in the city, and her story with its charismatic healing ministry of innovative drug rehabilitation houses continues to this day, containing much more than dreams. But dreams, these and others, have been part of her story from the beginning. As she says, it was a dream and a vision that caused her to travel east.

CHAPTER 17

Conclusion

When we interpret our dreams correctly, as I believe we can sometimes do, we can implement changes to our approach to life and many of life's situations to our great benefit. There are wisdom, insight, and revelation in dreams which we can capitalize on.

The revelations from our own hearts are, in and of themselves, well worth paying attention to. Added to this, though, is the reality of a God who wishes to communicate by means of dreams. He never changes. He is the same yesterday, today, and forever, and we have considered the very substantial extent of His communication in dreams throughout the biblical record written over many hundreds of years.

At the same time, though, there is such a complexity and depth to dreaming that some dreams can be rendered unfathomable. Unless we seek and find God's direct revelation of their meaning, as for instance Joseph did, the meaning will be lost to us.

If we are progressing with our own inner healing, we will be in a better position to understand our dreams. A thinking process cannot interpret the language of the heart if the intellect is cut off from the emotional and largely unconscious ways of perceiving; the typical mistake will be to come up with superficial interpretations that are too literal.

As you focus more on your dreams now and record them, remember the importance of timeline. Most dreams pertain to the immediate past, present, and future of the dreamer, the situations of life and those involved. Yet sometimes the heart is focused on the dreamer's childhood or teenage years and on matters which have still to be resolved or healed. Occasionally, a prophetic dream will, through sweeping imagery, reveal events to occur well into the future or will focus on the immediate future, taking a concern of the present as its starting point.

In all these things, we can endeavor to seek out the meaning and take the right action. We will be all the more successful with this if we allow ourselves to partner with the God of dreams. It is He whom we must seek out, getting to know Him better until the day comes when we meet Him face to face.

If you have not already done so, please receive Jesus Christ, who is the God of Dreams who wants to communicate with you. He wants you to come into the salvation and blessing He offers. To do this you need to turn from your sin, repent of it, confess Him as your Savior and Lord who died for you and rose from the dead, and believe in Him in your heart. As you follow Him up the narrow, often winding road of life that leads to the heavenly city, He will bring you into all truth.

ENDNOTES

Chapter 1

1. Fausset's Bible Dictionary, www.bible-history.com/faussets

2. See Genesis 20:12.

3. An interesting precursor to the much more well-known series of plagues unleashed on Pharaoh and his kingdom by God in the future time of Moses.

4. See Genesis 20:17–18.

5. This can be calculated from Bruce K. Waltke's research into wage rates in antiquity. He has discovered, for instance, that a Babylonian laborer was usually paid six shekels a year. See Bruce K. Waltke's *Genesis* (Grand Rapids, MI: Zondervan, 2001).

Chapter 2

1. Eugene Aserinsky and Nathaniel Kleitman, "Regularly occurring periods of eye motility and concommitant phenomena during sleep," *Science* 118 (1953), 273–274.

2. J.F. Pagel, *The Limits of Dream: A Scientific Exploration of the Mind/ Brain Interface* (Oxford, UK: Academic Press, 2008), Preface.

3. Denise J. Cai, Sarnoff A. Mednick, Elizabeth M. Harrison, Jennifer C. Kanady, and Sara C. Mednick, "REM, not incubation, improves creativity by priming associative networks," *Proceedings of the National Academy of Sciences of the United States of America* 106 (25), 10130–10134, June 8, 2009.

4. http://biblios.com, Greek OT (Transliterated): Septuagint.

5. Russ Parker, *Healing Dreams: Their Power and Purpose in Your Spiritual Life* (London: SPCK, 1993), 8.

6. Herman Riffel, *Dreams: Giants and Geniuses in the Making* (Shippensburg, PA: Destiny Image, 1996), 13.

7. Chuck D. Pierce and Rebecca Wagner Sytsema, *When God Speaks: How to Interpret Dreams, Visions, Signs and Wonders* (Ventura, CA: Regal Books, 2005).

8. Jane Hamon, *Dreams and Visions* (Santa Rosa Beach, CA: Christian International Ministries Network, 1997), 35.

Chapter 3

1. Commentators such as Joyce Baldwin infer from various sources that when it came to a large number of sons, this birthright was a double portion compared to any other sibling's portion. See Joyce G. Baldwin, *The Message of Genesis 12–50* (Nottingham, UK: IVP, 1986). Yet if there were just two sons, the firstborn would inherit everything and become head of the family.

2. See Genesis 12:8.

3. Bruce K. Waltke, *Genesis: A Commentary*, 390.

4. Genesis 32:28.

5. Hebrews 1:14.

6. Matthew 26:53–54.

7. Lance Lambert, *Jacob I Have Loved* (Lancaster, UK: Sovereign World, 2007), 93.

8. This was because each wife, at the time she stopped conceiving children, instructed her maid to go in to Jacob to conceive on her behalf. According to the laws and social conventions of the time and place, the wife's maid would have children on behalf of her mistress; see Genesis 30:3–13. Regarding Leah and Rachel, the marrying of two sisters by the same man while they both lived was later banned in law (see Leviticus 18:18).

9. See Genesis 31:3.

10. Household gods or *teraphim*, possession of which may have entitled her to an inheritance.

Chapter 4

1. Sigmund Freud, *The Interpretation of Dreams* (London: Macmillan, 1913).

2. See Jeremiah 17:9.

3. Walter Brueggemann, "The Power of Dreams in the Bible," *The Christian Century*, June 28, 2005, 28–31.

4. C.G. Jung, *Modern Man in Search of a Soul* (London: Ark, 1990), 5.

5. Jerome D. Levin, *Introduction to Alcoholism Counseling* (Philadelphia, PA: Taylor & Francis, 1995).

6. See John 14:23.

7. C.G. Jung, *Memories, Dreams, and Reflections* (London: Fontana Press, 1995).

8. James Martin, *Suffering Man, Loving God* (Edinburgh, UK: The Saint Andrew Press, 1969).

9. See Leanne Payne's section entitled "Gnosticism: its syncretism, dualism, and capacity for false revelation," in *The Healing Presence: Curing the Soul through Union with Christ* (Grand Rapids, MI: Baker Books, 2003).

10. Douglas Groothuis, "The Hidden Dangers of Carl Jung," *Christian Counseling Today* 5(1), 1997), 44–47.

11. C.G. Jung, *Memories, Dreams, and Reflections,* 1995.

12. See, for instance, the chapter by Claire Douglas, *The Historical Context of Analytical Psychology,* in *The Cambridge Companion to Jung* (Cambridge, UK: Cambridge University Press, 2008) on page 24.

13. See Matthew 5:29–30.

14. See 1 John 1:5.

15. Habakkuk 1:13 as amplified by Robert L. Reymond in *What Is God? An Investigation of the Perfections of God's Nature* (Fearn, UK: Mentor, 2007).

16. Ernest Hartmann, *The Nature and Functions of Dreaming* (New York: Oxford University Press, 2010).

17. See, for instance, Clara E. Hill, "The 2002 Leona Tyler Award Address: Working with dreams: a road to self-discovery," *The Counselling Psychologist* 31(3), May 2003, 362–372.

Chapter 5

1. This date is taken from Larry and Marion Pierce's chronology, *The Annals of the World* (Green Forest, AR: Master Books, 2003). However, other biblical chronologies such as Jewish and Septuagint vary; see Henry M. Morris, *The Genesis Record* (Grand Rapids, MI: Baker Books, 1976), 45, 676. Time elapsed between events detailed in Genesis 30 onward is clear enough from the biblical narrative.

2. See Genesis 35:22 and 1 Chronicles 5:1–2.

3. See Genesis 37:2.

4. This is not quite the same dream as before—it is even more encompassing in terms of those who are bowing down low before Joseph.

5. Henry M. Morris, *The Genesis Record* (Grand Rapids, MI: Baker Books, 1976), 620.

6. John Paul Jackson, *Basics of Dreams, Visions, and Strange Events*. Talk given at the 33rd Annual Lutheran Conference on the Holy Spirit, North Heights Lutheran Church, Arden Mills, MN, USA, August 4–7, 2004.

7. James Poole, *Joseph* (Norwich, UK: The Open Bible Trust, 1991).

8. See Genesis 37:8.

9. See 1 Chronicles 5:1–2.

10. See Hosea 11.

11. The Revelation 21 reference does not name the twelve; earlier reference occasionally substitutes Joseph for Ephraim. For example, see Revelation 7:5–8.

12. See John 6:48.

13. God places all things in Christ's hands: Matthew 28:18; John 3:35.

14. Joseph exemplifies the same total forgiveness of his brothers that Christ did with His disciples after His resurrection and, indeed, as

God does with us; for instance, by not revealing to others what his brothers had done to him and by reassuring them. For an in-depth discussion of this, see R.T. Kendall's *Total Forgiveness: Achieving God's Greatest Challenge* (London: Hodder & Stoughton, 2001).

15. To lift up his head is a literal interpretation of the Hebrew expression meaning to release in the context of freeing the prisoner, the same meaning as in 2 Kings 25:27.

16. Clay and Mary McLean, *Dreams: Pictures from the Heart* (Boone, NC: McLean Ministries, 1996).

17. See 1 Corinthians 2:15.

18. For a number of case study examples of these with interpretations, see Greg Cynaumon's *God Still Speaks through Dreams: Are You Missing His Messages?* (Nashville, TN: Thomas Nelson, 2002).

19. John Calvin put it like this: "true and lawful prophets of God do not barely predict what will happen in future; but propose remedies for impending evils"; as quoted by Pete Wilcox in *Living the Dream: Joseph for Today* (Bletchley, UK: Paternoster, 2007), 45.

20. Commentators agree that Joseph's elevation was most likely made by a Hyksos (Asiatic) Pharaoh, but it has so far been impossible to determine which one. See, for instance, Joyce Baldwin's *The Message of Genesis 12–50* (Nottingham, UK: IVP, 2007) and Derek Kidner's *Genesis* (Nottingham, UK: IVP, 1967).

21. Liam Goligher, *Joseph: The Hidden Hand of God* (Fearn, UK: Christian Focus, 2008), 173.

22. Herman Riffel, *Dream Interpretation: A Biblical Understanding* (Shippensburg, PA: Destiny Image, 1993).

23. James 1:2–4.

Chapter 6

1. Commentators such as John Paul Jackson and John Sandford sometimes refer to this approach as the use of dark speech. See, for instance, John and Paula Sandford's *The Elijah Task* (Lake Mary, FL: Charisma House, 2006).

2. See Mark 4:1–20.

3. See Acts 10:3–8.

4. George H. Martin, "The God who reveals mysteries: dreams and world evangelization," *Southern Baptist Journal of Theology*, 8(1), 2004, 60–72.

5. Malachi 3:6.

6. Hebrews 13:8.

7. George H. Martin, *Southern Baptist Journal of Theology*, 8(1), 60–72.

8. John Woolner, *Encounters: Authentic Experiences of God* (Oxford, UK: Monarch Books, 2007).

9. Paula A. Price, *The Prophet's Dictionary* (New Kensington, PA: Whitaker House, 2006), 181–182.

10. Leanne Payne, *Listening Prayer* (Grand Rapids, MI: Baker Books, 1994).

11. Benny Thomas, *Exploring the World of Dreams* (New Kensington, PA: Whitaker House, 1990), 54.

Chapter 7

1. As in "one who cuts down."

2. See, for instance, *Who is the Angel of the Lord?* www.preceptaustin.org/angel_of_the_lord.htm.

3. A clan belonging to the tribe of Manasseh.

4. Judges 8:10.

5. Jeff Lucas, *Gideon: Power from Weakness* (Milton Keynes, UK: Spring Harvest Publishing Division, 2004).

6. Although God accedes to Gideon's requests, "putting out a fleece" or laying down a condition before God is, generally speaking, not a biblical method for obtaining guidance and making decisions. In particular, his second request to God for the reversal of the sign is a request for a miracle.

7. See Judges 7:12.

Chapter 8

1. See, for instance, Russell Chandler's *Understanding the New Age* (Milton Keynes, UK: Word Music & Publishing, 1988).

2. Joe Ibojie, *Dreams and Visions* (Pescara, Italy: Destiny Image Europe, 2005).

3. For a discussion of Jesus' half-brothers, see Dick Lucas and Christopher Green's *The Message of 2 Peter and Jude* (Nottingham, UK: Inter-Varsity Press, 1995).

4. Stephanie Meyer on Oprah Part 1, November 13, 2009; https://www.youtube.com/watch?v=DC80zKBi2JE

5. For an exposition of this doctrine, see John Blanchard's *Whatever Happened to Hell?* (Darlington, UK: Evangelical Press, 1993).

6. For example, see Derek Kidner's *The Message of Ecclesiastes: A Time to Mourn and a Time to Dance* (Nottingham, UK: Inter-Varsity Press, 2007).

7. J. Alec Motyer, *Isaiah* (Nottingham, UK: Inter-Varsity Press, 2009), 214.

8. Barry Webb, *The Message of Isaiah* (Nottingham, UK: Inter-Varsity Press, 2007), 126.

9. Brian D. Papworth, "What in the world is happening?" *Prophetic Witness* 14 (163), December, 2009, page 20.

10. See 1 Corinthians 3:10–15.

Chapter 9

1. See Proverbs 3:5–6.

2. Jim Driscoll and Zach Mapes, *Dreams: A Biblical Model of Interpretation* (Charlotte, NC: Orbital Book Group, 2010).

3. Daniel 4:22.

4. Chuck D. Pierce and Rebecca Wagner Sytsema, *When God Speaks: How to Interpret Dreams, Visions, Signs and Wonders* (Ventura, CA: Regal Books, 2005), 92.

5. Ira Milligan, *Understanding the Dreams You Dream, Volume 2* (Shippensburg, PA: Treasure House, 2000).

6. Benny Thomas, *Exploring the World of Dreams* (New Kensington, PA: Whitaker House, 1990), 112–115.

7. See, for instance, the critique of such practices by Ray Yungen in *A Time of Departing* (Silverton, OR: Lighthouse Trails, 2008).

8. See, for instance, Leanne Payne, *Listening Prayer: Learning to Hear God's Voice and Keep a Prayer Journal* (Grand Rapids, MI: Baker Books, 1994).

9. Revelation 1:10.

10. Daniel 4:19, KJV.

Chapter 10

1. See Matthew 6:28–29; Luke 12:27.

2. See 1 Kings 11:9–13.

3. See, for example, 1 Kings 7:7–8.

4. It is worth saying that God's favorable response is given despite Solomon's recent marriage to a pagan princess and his sacrifice at a high place with pagan sacrificial significance. It seems that God chooses not to focus on these activities but on Solomon's love for Him. See, for instance, 1 Kings 3:3.

5. See Genesis 13:14–17.

6. James 1:5.

7. John 14:2, KJV.

8. Russ Parker, *Dream Stories* (Oxford, UK: The Bible Reading Fellowship, 2002), 67.

9. See Joshua 3:14–16.

10. See Joshua 6:4–20.

11. For example, see Stephanie E. Keer and Richard W. Naimark, "Arbitrators do not 'split-the-baby': empirical evidence from international business arbitrations," *Journal of International Arbitration* 18(5), 2001, pages 573–578.

12. Dale Ralph Davis, *1 Kings: The Wisdom and the Folly* (Fearn, UK: Christian Focus Publications, 2008).

13. See 1 Kings 11:5.

14. Jane Hamon, *Dreams and Visions* (Santa Rosa Beach, CA: Christian International Ministries Network, 1997), 77.

15. The ark of the covenant remained lost throughout the time of the rebuilt Herodian temple in Jerusalem, which was destroyed by the Romans in AD 70. There are those who say that the ark of the covenant will be recovered and installed in the last-days temple at Jerusalem. See, for instance, Randall Price's *The Lost Ark and the Last Days: In Search of Temple Treasures* (Eugene, OR: Harvest House, 1994).

Chapter 11

1. See Psalm 8:5.

2. See Genesis 40:16.

3. Ira Milligan, *Understanding the Dreams You Dream* (Shippensburg, PA: Treasure House, 1997).

4. John Paul Jackson, *Understanding Dreams and Visions* (Dallas, TX: Streams Ministries International, 2012).

5. Herman Riffel, *Dreams: Wisdom Within* (Shippensburg, PA: Destiny Image, 1994), 56.

6. Jane Hamon, *Dreams and Visions* (Santa Rosa Beach, CA: Christian International Ministries Network, 1997), 133.

7. Steve Berger and Sarah Berger, *Have Heart: Bridging the Gulf Between Heaven and Earth* (Franklin, TN: Grace Chapel, 2010).

8. See Revelation 6:2–8.

9. Revelation 5:5.

10. 1 Peter 5:8.

11. Russ Parker, *Healing Dreams: Their Power and Purpose in Your Spiritual Life* (London: SPCK, 1998).

12. Greg Cynaumon, *God Still Speaks Through Dreams: Are You Missing His Messages?* (Nashville, TN: Thomas Nelson, 2008).

13. J.F. Pagel, *The Limits of Dream: A Scientific Exploration of the Mind/ Brain Interface* (Oxford, UK: Academic Press, 2008).

14. Paula A. Price, *The Prophet's Dictionary* (New Kensington, PA: Whitaker House, 2006), 418–419.

15. Russ Parker, *Healing Dreams: Their Power and Purpose in Your Spiritual Life.*

16. James 4:2.

17. Matthew 7:7.

18. Herman Riffel, *Dreams: Wisdom Within*, 117.

19. Daniel 2:5, KJV.

20. John Paul Jackson, *Understanding Dreams and Visions* (Dallas, TX: Streams Ministries International, 2012).

Chapter 12

1. His name means "(the god) Nabu protect my son."

2. Nabopolassar.

3. Allan M. Harman, *Daniel* (New York: Evangelical Press, 2007).

4. See Daniel 5:12.

5. Gordon McConville, *Exploring The Old Testament Volume 4: The Prophets* (London: SPCK, 2002).

6. See 1 Peter 2:6–8.

7. Sir Robert Anderson, *The Coming Prince* (Grand Rapids, MI: Kregel, 1957), 31.

8. Bob Fyall cites extrabiblical sources to argue that the dream occurred in the same year as the final fall of Jerusalem to Nebuchadnezzar's

army. The king may have felt contented that the troublesome Jewish nation had been conquered at last. His dream and its prophesied events completely overturn his self-satisfaction. See Bob Fyall's *Daniel: A Tale of Two Cities* (Fearn: UK, Christian Focus Publications, 2006), 60–61.

9. The Aramaic word also appears in the Qumran *Genesis Apocryphon,* referring to an angel.

10. Charles Ozanne, *Empires of the End-Time through Daniel's Telescopic Lens* (Reading, UK: Open Bible Trust, 2007), 47.

11. Job 42:10–12.

12. See Psalm 111:7; Psalm 145:13; Isaiah 14:27; Job 9:12.

13. Matthew 5:3–5.

14. Mark 8:36.

15. Joyce G. Baldwin, *Daniel* (Leicester, UK: IVP, 1978), 107.

Chapter 13

1. Ecclesiastes 5:3.

2. Deuteronomy 13:1–3.

3. Jeremiah 17:9, KJV.

4. It is likely that "Helias" refers directly to Christ. The Greek word for the sun is *helios,* and later in the *Confessio,* section 60, Saint Patrick refers to Christ as the Sun that does not perish. Saint Patrick's *Confessio* can be accessed online through the Royal Irish Academy's Hypertext Stack Project; http://www.confessio.ie/etexts/confessio_english#01; accessed October 15, 2015.

Chapter 14

1. Babylonian history is reasonably well-documented. The works of Dutch historian Jona Lendering expand on this turbulent period. Visit his website: www.livius.org.

2. Possibly his grandfather.

3. Daniel 5:22–30.

4. See, for instance, Isaiah 17:12 and Revelation 17:15.

5. See also Revelation 20:12–15.

6. Babylon is symbolized earlier by Jeremiah as both a lion and an eagle in several of his prophecies (see Jeremiah 4:7 and combined in 49:19–22).

7. More than one hundred years earlier, the prophet Isaiah correctly predicted that an emperor named Cyrus would allow the Jews to rebuild Jerusalem and its temple (Isaiah 44:28). Later, Cyrus's son Cambyses II is referred to as Artaxerxes by Ezra.

8. Charles Ozanne, *Empires of the End-Time through Daniel's Telescopic Lens,* 72–73.

9. W.M. Henry, "Kings and Kingdoms"; *In Search* magazine No. 142, October/November 2007, 20–21.

10. Revelation 13:1–9.

11. Mark 8:35.

12. Psalm 104:3.

13. Acts 7:55–56.

14. Revelation 1:12–13.

15. Possibly Gabriel; see Daniel 9:21.

16. 1 Corinthians 6:2–3.

17. Allan M. Harman, *Daniel* (New York: Evangelical Press, 2007), 183.

18. 2 Thessalonians 2:4.

19. Revelation 20:6.

20. Cyrus the Great, a worshipper of Marduk, is the subject of Isaiah's prophecy in Isaiah 45:1–6: "I will strengthen you, though you have not acknowledged me." Dying in battle about twenty years after this victory at Pasargadae, Cyrus was buried close by the battle site. According to Strabo, his tomb contained the following inscription: "Passer-by, I am Cyrus, who gave the Persians an empire, and was

king of Asia. Grudge me not therefore this monument." The inscription does not survive.

21. He erected an idol to Zeus in the Jewish temple and sacrificed pigs on their altar. The idol prefigures a still future "abomination that causes desolation" located in the rebuilt Jewish temple and prophesied by Christ in Mark 13:14.

22. Luke 1:5–20, 26–38.

23. See the account of God's covenant with Abraham in Genesis 15:12.

24. 2 Thessalonians 2:4.

25. 2 Thessalonians 2:8.

26. Charles Ozanne, *The Fourth Gentile Kingdom in Daniel and Revelation* (Worthing, UK: Henry E. Walter, 1982); see also *Empires of the End-Time through Daniel's Telescopic Lens.*

27. Allan M. Harman, *Daniel* (New York: Evangelical Press, 2007).

Chapter 15

1. Isaiah 7:14; Isaiah was prophesying about seven hundred years earlier about "God with us."

2. Daniel 8:15–17.

3. Luke 2:1–3.

4. J.C. Fenton, *The Gospel of Saint Matthew* (London: Pelican Books, 1987), 46.

5. Russ Parker, *Dream Stories* (Oxford, UK: The Bible Reading Fellowship, 2002).

6. Andrew E. Steinmann, "When Did Herod the Great Reign?"; *Novum Testamentum*, 51(1), 2009), 1–29.

7. Books by Josephus such as *The Jewish Antiquities* were based on a personal account written by Nicolaus of Damascus, a close personal friend of King Herod.

8. Luke 23:7–12.

9. Luke 13:32.

10. See, for instance, John 19:12–13.

Chapter 16

1. Geoff Thomas, "John Newton (1725–1807)," *Banner of Truth Magazine*, January 17, 2007.

2. John Dunn, *A Biography of John Newton* (Coromandel East, Australia: New Creation, 1994).

3. As cited by James W. Goll and Michal Ann Goll in *Dream Language* (Shippensburg, PA: Destiny Image, 2006), 59.

4. Chris Armstrong, "The amazing graced life of John Newton," *Christian History and Biography*, Issue 81, 2004.

5. John Newton's hymn "Amazing Grace" was published in 1779, about twenty-four years after he left the slave trade.

6. Janet Benge and Geoff Benge, *William Booth: Soup, Soap, and Salvation* (Seattle, WA: YWAM, 2002).

7. William Booth, *In Darkest England and the Way Out* (Champaign, IL: Book Jungle, 2008).

8. Pastor D.E. Buffaloe, "Be not weary"; sermon preached at the Mercer Baptist Association, Brooks County, Georgia, on October, 10, 2000.

9. Derek Prince and Ruth Prince, *God Is a Matchmaker* (Old Tappan, NJ: Chosen Books, 1986).

10. Leanne Payne, *Heaven's Calling* (Grand Rapids, MI: Baker Books, 2008).

11. Leanne Payne, *Real Presence: The Christian Worldview of C.S. Lewis as Incarnational Reality* (Grand Rapids: Baker Books, 2002).

12. Payne, *Heaven's Calling*, 212–213.

13. Leanne Payne, *The Broken Image: Restoring Personal Wholeness Through Healing Prayer* (Grand Rapids, MI: Baker Books, 2004).

14. Jackie Pullinger with Andrew Quicke, *Chasing the Dragon* (London: Hodder, 2010), 19.

15. Ibid., 100–101.

BIBLIOGRAPHY

Anderson, Robert. *The Coming Prince*. Grand Rapids, MI: Kregel, 1957.

Armstrong, Chris. "The amazing graced life of John Newton." *Christian History and Biography*, Issue 81, 2004.

Aserinsky, E. and W. Kleitman. "Regularly occurring periods of eye motility and concomitant phenomena during sleep." *Science 118*, 1953, 273-274.

Baldwin, Joyce G. *Daniel*. Leicester, UK: Inter-Varsity Press, 1978.

Baldwin, Joyce G. *The Message of Genesis 12-50*. Nottingham, UK: Inter-Varsity Press, 1986.

Benge, Janet and Geoff Benge. *William Booth: Soup, Soap, and Salvation*. Seattle, WA: YWAM, 2002.

Berger, Steve and Sarah Berger. *Have Heart*. Franklin, TN: Grace Chapel, 2010.

Blanchard, John. *Whatever Happened to Hell?* Darlington, UK: Evangelical Press, 1993.

Booth, William. *In Darkest England and The Way Out*. Champaign, IL: Book Jungle, 2008.

Brueggemann, Walter (2005). The power of dreams in the bible. *The Christian Century*, June 28, 2005, 28-31.

Buffaloe, D. E. *Be Not Weary*. Sermon preached at the Mercer Baptist Association, Brooks County, GA, October 10, 2000.

Cai, Denise J., Sarnoff A. Mednick, Elizabeth M. Harrison, Jennifer C. Kanady, and Sara C. Mednick. "REM, not incubation, improves creativity by priming associative networks." *Proceedings of the*

National Academy of Sciences of the United States of America, 106 (25), June 8, 2009, 10130-10134.

Chandler, Russell. *Understanding the New Age*. Milton Keynes, UK: Word, 1988.

Cynaumon, Greg. *God Still Speaks Through Dreams: Are You Missing His Messages?* Nashville, TN: Thomas Nelson, 2002.

Davis, Dale Ralph. *1 Kings: The Wisdom and The Folly*. Fearn, UK: Christian Focus Publications, 2008.

Douglas, Claire. The historical context of analytical psychology, in *The Cambridge Companion to Jung*. Cambridge, UK: Cambridge University Press, 2008.

Driscoll, Jim and Zach Mapes. *Dreams: A Biblical Model of Interpretation*. Charlotte, NC: Orbital Book Group, 2010.

Dunn, John. *A Biography of John Newton*. Coromandel East, Australia: New Creation, 1994.

Fenton, J. C. *The Gospel of Saint Matthew*. London: Pelican Books, 1987.

Freud, Sigmund. *The Interpretation of Dreams*. London: Macmillan, 1913.

Fyall, Bob. *Daniel: A Tale of Two Cities*. Fearn, UK: Christian Focus Publications, 2006.

Goligher, Liam. *Joseph: The Hidden Hand of God*. Fearn, UK: Christian Focus, 2008.

Goll, James W. and Michal Ann Goll. *Dream Language*. Shippensburg, PA: Destiny Image, 2006.

Groothuis, Douglas. "The Hidden Dangers of Carl Jung." *Christian Counseling Today*, 5(1), 1997, 44-47.

Hamon, Jane. *Dreams and Visions*. Santa Rosa Beach, CA: Christian International Ministries Network, 1997.

Harman, Allan M. *Daniel*. New York: Evangelical Press, 2007.

Hartmann, Ernest. *The Nature and Functions of Dreaming*. New York: Oxford University Press, 2010.

Henry, W. M. "Kings and Kingdoms." *Search Magazine*, 142, October/ November, 2007, 20-21.

Hill, Clara E. "The 2002 Leona Tyler Award Address: Working with dreams: a road to self-discovery." *The Counselling Psychologist*, 31(3), May 2003, 362-372.

Ibojie, Joe. *Dreams and Visions*. Pescara, Italy: Destiny Image Europe, 2005.

Jackson, John Paul. *Basics of Dreams, Visions, and Strange Events*. Talk given at the 33rd Annual Lutheran Conference on the Holy Spirit, North Heights Lutheran Church, Arden Mills, MN, USA, August 4-7, 2004.

Jackson, John Paul. *Understanding Dreams and Visions*, Course 201. Dallas, TX: Streams Ministries International, 2012.

Jung, C. G. *Modern Man in Search of a Soul*. London: Ark, 1990.

Jung, C. G. *Memories, Dreams, and Reflections*. London: Fontana Press, 1995.

Keer, Stephanie E. and Richard W. Naimark. "Arbitrators do not 'split-the-baby': empirical evidence from international business arbitrations." *Journal of International Arbitration*, 18(5), 2001, 573-578.

Kendall, R. T. *Total Forgiveness: Achieving God's Greatest Challenge*. London: Hodder & Stoughton, 2001.

Kidner, Derek. *Genesis*. Nottingham, UK: Inter-Varsity Press, 1967.

Kidner, Derek. *The Message of Ecclesiastes: A Time to Mourn and a Time to Dance*. Nottingham, UK: Inter-Varsity Press, 2007.

Lambert, Lance. *Jacob I Have Loved*. Lancaster, PA: Sovereign World, 2007.

Levin, Jerome D. *Introduction to Alcoholism Counseling.* Philadelphia, PA: Taylor & Francis, 1995.

Lucas, Dick and Christopher Green. *The Message of 2 Peter and Jude.* Nottingham, UK: Inter-Varsity Press, 1995.

Lucas, Jeff. *Gideon: Power from Weakness.* Milton Keynes, UK: Spring Harvest Publishing Division, 2004.

Martin, George H. "The God who reveals mysteries: dreams and world evangelization." *Southern Baptist Journal of Theology,* 8(1), 2004, 60-72.

Martin, James. *Suffering Man, Loving God.* Edinburgh, UK: The Saint Andrew Press, 1969.

McConville, Gordon. *Exploring the Old Testament Volume 4: The Prophets.* London: SPCK, 2002.

McLean, Clay and Mary McLean. *Dreams: Pictures from the Heart.* Boone, NC: McLean Ministries, 1996.

Milligan, Ira. *Understanding the Dreams You Dream.* Shippensburg, PA: Treasure House, 1997.

Milligan, Ira. *Understanding the Dreams You Dream, Volume 2,* Shippensburg, PA: Treasure House, 2000.

Morris, Henry M. *The Genesis Record.* Grand Rapids, MI: Baker Book House, 1976.

Motyer, J. Alec. *Isaiah.* Nottingham, UK: Inter-Varsity Press, 2009.

Ozanne, Charles. *The Fourth Gentile Kingdom in Daniel and Revelation.* Worthing, UK: Henry E. Walter, 1982.

Ozanne, Charles. *Empires of the End-Time through Daniel's Telescopic Lens.* Reading, UK: Open Bible Trust, 2007.

Pagel, J. F. *The Limits of Dream: A Scientific Exploration of the Mind/Brain Interface.* Oxford, UK: Academic Press, 2008.

Papworth, Brian D. "What in the world is happening?" *Prophetic Witness*, 14(163). December, 2009, 20.

Parker, Russ. *Healing Dreams: Their Power and Purpose in Your Spiritual Life*. London: SPCK. 1993.

Parker, Russ. *Dream Stories*. Oxford, UK: The Bible Reading Fellowship, 2002.

Payne, Leanne. *Listening Prayer: Learning to Hear God's Voice and Keep a Prayer Journal*. Grand Rapids, MI: Baker Books, 1994.

Payne, Leanne. *Real Presence: The Christian Worldview of C. S. Lewis as Incarnational Reality*. Grand Rapids, MI: Baker Books, 2002.

Payne, Leanne. *The Healing Presence: Curing the Soul through Union with Christ*. Grand Rapids, MI: Baker Books, 2003.

Payne, Leanne. *The Broken Image: Restoring Personal Wholeness through Healing Prayer*. Grand Rapids, MI: Baker Books, 2004.

Payne, Leanne. *Heaven's Calling*. Grand Rapids, MI: Baker Books, 2008.

Pierce, Chuck D. and Rebecca Wagner Sytsema. *When God Speaks: How to Interpret Dreams, Visions, Signs, and Wonders*. Ventura, CA: Regal Books, 2005.

Pierce, Larry and Marion Pierce. *The Annals of the World*. Green Forest, AR: Master Books, 2003.

Poole, James. *Joseph*. Norwich, UK: The Open Bible Trust, 1991.

Price, Paula A. *The Prophet's Dictionary*. New Kensington, PA: Whitaker House, 2006.

Price, Randall. *The Lost Ark and the Last Days: In Search of Temple Treasures*. Eugene, OR: Harvest House, 1994.

Prince, Derek and Ruth Prince. *God is a Matchmaker*. Old Tappan, NJ: Chosen Books, 1986.

Pullinger, Jackie with Andrew Quicke. *Chasing the Dragon*. London: Hodder, 2010.

Reymond, Robert L. *What is God? An Investigation of the Perfections of God's Nature*. Fearn, UK: Mentor, 2007.

Riffel, Herman. *Dream Interpretation: A Biblical Understanding*. Shippensburg, PA: Destiny Image, 1993.

Riffel, Herman. *Dreams: Wisdom Within*. Shippensburg, PA: Destiny Image, 1994.

Riffel, Herman. *Dreams: Giants and Geniuses in the Making*. Shippensburg, PA: Destiny Image, 1996.

Sandford, John and Paula Sandford. *The Elijah Task*. Lake Mary, FL: Charisma House, 2006.

Schaeffer, Francis A. *Escape from Reason*, in Francis A. Schaeffer Trilogy. Wheaton, IL: Crossway, 1990.

Schaeffer, Francis A. *He is There and He is not Silent*, in Francis A. Schaeffer Trilogy. Wheaton, IL: Crossway, 1990.

Schaeffer, Francis A. *The God Who is There*, in Francis A. Schaeffer Trilogy. Wheaton, IL: Crossway, 1990.

Steinmann, Andrew E. "When did Herod the Great reign?" *Novum Testamentum*, 51(1), 2009, 1-29.

Stone, Perry. *How to Interpret Dreams and Visions*. Lake Mary, FL: Charisma House, 2011.

Stone, Sharon. *Dreams and Dream Interpretation*. Boston-on-Trent, UK: Christian International Europe, 2010.

Thomas, Benny. *Exploring the World of Dreams*. New Kensington, PA: Whitaker House, 1990.

Thomas, Geoff. "John Newton (1725-1807)," *Banner of Truth Magazine*, January 17, 2007.

Thompson, Adam F. and Adrian Beale. *The Divinity Code to Understanding Your Dreams and Visions.* Shippensburg, PA: Destiny Image, 2011.

Waltke, Bruce K. *Genesis.* Grand Rapids, MI: Zondervan, 2001.

Webb, Barry. *The Message of Isaiah.* Nottingham. UK: Inter-Varsity Press, 2007.

Wilcox, Pete. *Living the Dream: Joseph for Today.* Bletchley, UK: Paternoster, 2007.

Woolner, John. *Encounters: Authentic Experiences of God.* Oxford, UK: Monarch Books, 2007.

Yungen, Ray. *A Time of Departing.* Silverton, OR: Lighthouse Trails, 2008.

ABOUT THE AUTHOR

Dr. Archie Roy earned a Bachelor of Science degree from the Evangelical Bible College and Seminary in Greenacres, Florida, and a License in Theology from Victory Bible College in Scotland. He holds a PhD in Developmental Psychology from the University of Strathclyde and has worked in disability support and social inclusion. Currently, and for the past thirteen years, he has worked as a careers advisor at the University of Glasgow. He has had a lifelong interest in dreams and lives in Glasgow, Scotland, with his wife, Margaret, and their Burmese cat, Salome.

Connect with the Author at:
archie.roy@btinternet.com